James Meredith and the Ole Miss Riot

JAMES MEREDITH
AND THE
OLE MISS RIOT

A Soldier's Story

HENRY T. GALLAGHER

University Press of Mississippi / *Jackson*

www.upress.state.ms.us

The University Press of Mississippi is a member
of the Association of American University Presses.

First printing 2012
❧   ∞
Library of Congress Cataloging-in-Publication Data

Gallagher, Henry T.
James Meredith and the Ole Miss riot : a soldier's story / Henry T. Gallagher.
p. cm.
Includes bibliographical references and index.
ISBN 978-1-61703-653-8 (cloth : alk. paper) — ISBN 978-1-61703-654-5 (ebook)
1. University of Mississippi—History. 2. College integration—Mississippi—
Oxford—History. 3. Meredith, James, 1933– 4. African Americans—Civil rights.
5. Civil rights—Mississippi—Oxford—History. 6. Gallagher, Henry T. I. Title.
LD3413.G35 2012
378.76283—dc23   2012009069

British Library Cataloging-in-Publication Data available

To the men of the
716th Military Police Battalion
who served their country
in the Ole Miss crisis,
Oxford, Mississippi,
1962–1963

We Mississippians are cursed and blessed with the burden of history.

—BILL DUNLAP, a Mississippi painter

Contents

Foreword by Gene Roberts   ix

Preface   xiii

Acknowledgments   xv

Introduction: A Sense of Place   xxiii

1. The North   3

2. The Upper South   20

3. The Deep South   49

4. The Arrival   67

5. The Town   77

6. The Assignment   85

7. The Student   97

8. The Army   116

9. The Campus   136

10. The Return—1963   170

11. The Graduation   187

Epilogue   189

Afterword   201

Notes   207

Glossary   215

Index   225

Foreword

In an era in which the United States has elected an African American as its president, it seems almost unbelievable that, in the lifetimes of some of us, units of the U.S. Army had to be deployed twice to ensure racial integration that was token at best. President Dwight D. Eisenhower sent troops into Little Rock in 1957 to enforce court decrees that ordered the admission of nine Negro students to Central High School. Five years later, President John F. Kennedy dispatched paratroopers, military policemen, and National Guardsmen to Oxford, Mississippi, after mobs laid siege to federal marshals in an effort to keep a lone black man, James Meredith, a veteran of the U.S. Air Force, from attending classes at the University of Mississippi. Much has been written about the crises at Ole Miss and Little Rock by students, teachers, officials, historians, and journalists, but little has been heard from the troops who served at these trouble spots.

Now, a half century later, this book by Henry Gallagher fills that void in history. No one is better qualified to tell the story of the soldiers at riot-torn Ole Miss. As a young second lieutenant, he commanded the jeep that led a convoy of his military police battalion into Oxford, past rock-throwing rioters and onto a campus that still reeked of tear gas shortly after a mob had been pushed off the campus by another MP unit and the Mississippi National Guard. Members of his battalion then joined soldiers to rid the downtown Oxford area of rioters. After the violence was quelled, he stayed on for a total of five months in 1962 and 1963 as commander of the MP detachment that protected Meredith as he moved across the campus to his classes.

The very notion of having to move onto an American college campus to enforce racial desegregation boggled the minds of Gallagher and many of his fellow soldiers. Much of what was racially taboo in the American South was accepted practice in the military and had been since 1951 when the U.S. Armed Forces began implementing the desegregation order issued by President Harry S. Truman, the commander in chief. Soldiers, sailors, marines, airmen, and coast guardsmen marched together, ate at the same tables, slept in beds side by side, and, if they had children, often enrolled them in desegregated schools on military bases. Life on a military base in 1962 was, in reality, something more than equality among races. If a sergeant was black and a private was white, the sergeant was superior and his orders were obeyed. When a white private encountered a black officer, he saluted and addressed him as "sir," never as "boy," as was the custom of some white men when dealing with blacks in the Deep South outside the military bases.

One of the most poignant episodes in Gallagher's absorbing and eye-opening narrative occurs near Memphis at the staging area for troops bound for Ole Miss. An order is passed down that blacks are to step out of the ranks and remain behind. This stuns black soldiers, and whites as well. They were trained to think of themselves as soldiers, not as whites or blacks. One black sergeant refuses to step aside and obeys only after a quiet talk with a black captain. Someone high in the chain of command had decided black faces among the troops would further inflame the frenzied mobs on the campus. Thus, whites-only troops would initially enforce racial desegregation at the University of Mississippi.

What Gallagher has to say about this is riveting. It takes only a few hours of military police protection before Meredith notices that he, a black man, is being guarded exclusively by white soldiers. "Lieutenant," he asks, "where are the Negro soldiers? There must be some in your ranks." Gallagher tries to explain the military position, that black troops might be targets of gunfire on the campus. He knows, though, that Meredith has a point, one that resonated with the Department of Justice, which had authority during the crisis to give the military its marching orders. Soon, the military force at Ole Miss is desegregated along with the student body.

During an incident in downtown Oxford shortly after the military arrives, segregationists tell white troops that they have no quarrel with them, that all whites should be united in ousting Meredith from the campus. Some rioters, though, have already hurled rocks at the troops, and among the soldiers the military's buddy system takes over: fight my buddy, then you have to fight me. When one local, white die-hard gets too close, a white soldier decks him with the butt of his rifle.

The publication of a book such as Gallagher's, that significantly increases our understanding of the crisis at Ole Miss and how the defiance was overcome, is a welcome event to students of civil rights history. The crisis was one of those pivotal events that galvanized public opinion against segregation and made it easier for Martin Luther King and other civil rights leaders to focus attention on their drives for the Civil Rights Act of 1964 and the Voting Rights Act of 1965. As early as 1944, Gunnar Myrdal, in his deeply penetrating book *An American Dilemma*, prophetically wrote that "publicity" was of the "highest strategic importance" to American blacks. He said that most Americans believed in fair play and equal opportunity and that if the press were to cover white supremacy and segregation in indisputable detail, Americans—especially those in the North—would be "shocked and shaken" and would demand racial change.

"The Northerner does not have his social conscience and all his political thinking permeated with the Negro problem as the Southerner does," Myrdal wrote in the second chapter of *An American Dilemma*. "Rather, he succeeds in forgetting about it most of the time. The Northern newspapers help him by minimizing all Negro news, except crime news. The Northerners want to hear as little as possible about the Negroes, in the South and in the North; and they have, of course, good reason for that.

"The result," Myrdal added, "is an astonishing ignorance about the Negro on the part of the white public in the North. White Southerners, too, are ignorant of many phases of the Negro's life, but their ignorance has not such a simple and unemotional character as that in the North. There are many educated Northerners who are well informed about foreign problems but almost absolutely ignorant about Negro conditions both in their own city and in the nation as a whole."

Except for the black press, which few whites saw, newspapers and television did not view segregation as a story until after the Supreme Court's 1954 school desegregation decision. After that, their interest in racial news grew steadily and by 1962 few journalists doubted that race was a major American story. Their interest in the Ole Miss crisis was whetted by the defiance of Governor Ross Barnett and by the state's protracted legal battle to block Meredith from the campus. It was, ironically, as if Barnett and angry segregationists were determined to give segregated American blacks exactly what Myrdal said they needed most—maximum publicity.

On September 30, 1962, the day Meredith was enrolled at the university, reporters and photographers were in Oxford in droves. President Kennedy went on the air at 8 p.m. Mississippi time to urge respect for the law and to remind Mississippians that "the eyes of the Nation and the world are upon you and upon all of us."

Even as the president spoke, students and violent segregationists were attacking federal marshals with bottles, bricks, rocks, and steel pipes. To say that northerners were shocked and shaken by the racial hatred displayed on TV and reported from Oxford in their papers may well be an understatement. To many northerners, it was like watching warfare in a foreign land. Within an hour battered marshals were running out of tear gas and state highway patrolmen were leaving the scene. Within an hour and a half there was gunfire, and as it accelerated the night became a nightmare. President Kennedy decided to go with his fallback plan, deploying the military. "People are dying in Oxford," the president said in an urgent message to the military. "This is the worst thing I have seen in forty-five years. I want the military police battalion to enter the action. . . ."

Kennedy's order sent them, including Henry Gallagher and his men, into Oxford and led, ultimately, to this book.

—GENE ROBERTS

Pulitzer Prize–winning coauthor of *The Race Beat: The Press, the Civil Rights Struggle, and the Awakening of a Nation*

Preface

In September 1962, James Meredith became the first African American to be admitted to the University of Mississippi, a historic, civil rights, path-opening moment. It triggered a riot brought on by a mob of three thousand whites from across the South who had moved into the small college town of Oxford and onto the university campus during the afternoon and evening of September 30. Historians have called the events that led up to the mob violence nothing less than an insurrection and the worst constitutional crisis since the Civil War, prompting President Kennedy to send twenty thousand regular army in addition to federalized National Guard soldiers into the area to confront the rioters and respond to a breakdown of law and order. This is the recollection of one of the participants in the crisis, a young army second lieutenant, born and raised in Minnesota, whose military police battalion from New Jersey was sent into the riots, and who was thereafter assigned as the officer-in-charge of Mr. Meredith's security detail. This is the story of how that military unit adapted to a unique mission.

It's also the story of a black Mississippian who wanted an education at his state's brand-name university and who, in order to get it, challenged the status quo that had been in place for so many years in the deepest of the Deep South states. This then is the story of what I, as a young military policeman, saw in 1962 of James Meredith's attempt to claim the birthright that all white Mississippians took for granted.

Acknowledgments

I walked around with this story in my head for many years. Friends, family, and law school professors nudged me to put my thoughts into words.

I did have notes. If given the assignment as the officer-in-charge of the security patrol for the first African American student to attend a previously all-white university under considerable protest, violent and otherwise, any army officer would take notes. The jottings might be boring, dull, and insignificant, covering mundane scenes and events of a given day in the life of a university—descriptions of people and cars, license plate numbers, students' behavior and their comments, and campus events. The notes would become relevant if they were needed for an investigation, should the "day in the life" turn ugly or tragic. I'm thankful that my notes were never used for such a purpose. But the handwritings in two Woolworth's pocket notebooks ("Nifty Notes, 10 cents") did serve me years later. If one stares at them long enough, images reappear, scenes are replayed, and the pieces of a story start to come together.

Shortly after I left Mississippi following our first deployment in late fall 1962, I visited the library at Princeton University and went through its periodicals stacks. I made copies of articles written by reporters who were on the campus that night of violence and who, in some cases, stayed well into October. The articles came from the now-defunct *Life* and the *Saturday Evening Post*, as well as from *Newsweek* and *U.S. News & World Report*. My mother in Minnesota—once she calmed down from her anxious "mommy moment"—started to save copies of one of the hometown newspapers, the *Minneapolis Tribune*, which carried accounts of the Ole Miss events.

After I left the army, Ole Miss political science professor Russell Barrett interviewed me in 1964 in Washington, D.C., for his book *Integration at Ole Miss.* Not until years later did I start to pull together my own notes. I would stare at a photo or read hastily scribbled notes and the memories would start to kick in. I began to connect the dots that ultimately led to this account.

In 2000 I visited the army's Office of the Chief of Military History at Fort McNair in Washington, D.C., not only for some textual background for my story, but also for confirmation that my first-person account was close to what others had written about the 716th. I found the "After Action Report" (AAR) of the battalion. An AAR is a document prepared by a unit (usually battalion and above) after participation in a major event (training, exercise, combat), recording the highlights of what took place, often including "lessons learned." I wondered out loud which officer in a particular unit is usually assigned to write the report. With a half-smile, the head of the office said, "The colonel usually looks out from his office window and gives the task to the slowest-walking second lieutenant." This 716th lieutenant—slow walker or not—did a good job, and my memoir has benefited from his report.

Robert Wright, chief, Historical Records Branch at Fort McNair, and one of his archivists, Mary Haynes, directed me to the work of historian Paul Scheips. As a staff member of the Histories Division in the Historical Records Branch, Scheips had written a 1965 monograph on the army's role in the integration of the University of Mississippi. In 1962, he had been assigned to the Pentagon's Army Operation Center at the beginning of the army's participation in the officially named "Operation Rapid Road." (For the 716th, it was anything but that.) Frank Shirer, the current chief of the branch (at the now-renamed U.S. Army Center of Military History), said that, in such a capacity, Scheips should be considered a "chronicler" of the 1962–63 events.

For my account I was looking for a timeline (as well as context) and Scheips's work provided it. But I also wanted to create an "internal" timeline which I provide. It was the one followed by those of us in the 716th (though not its senior officers) who had, for the most part, initially thought that we were on a training exercise on our post. Once airborne we still had no knowledge as to our eventual deployment and mission. Only when the battalion landed at Memphis did the two parallel lines converge and we catch up with history. At the start of my narrative, I try to convey the sense of curiosity and confusion that existed in my mind (and the minds of the members of my unit) as a result of this dual timeline, in which we essentially operated "blind" at first, without knowledge of our ultimate mission or the events that were occurring in Mississippi that last week in September 1962.

Robert Wright also introduced me to Richard Boylan at the National Archives and Records Administration (NARA) in College Park, Maryland, who led me to the army's records of the Ole Miss operation. He had directed a staffer to bring out a four-wheeled cart laden with thirty-six library boxes of records. After a quick thirty-minute review through two of the cartons of documents I realized that the army throws away nothing. I even came across a page torn from one of those small "While You Were Out" message pads. On this one, marked "urgent" by the NCO (noncommissioned officer) handling what I can only think was a heavy stream of telephone messages on that riot night, was the scribbled question, "Where's the Army?" I looked up at all the unopened cartons, left them so, and glanced around the room of scholars and researchers working away. Minutes later, I left the building convinced that I would stay with my "smaller" story within Operation Rapid Road.

After my visit to Fort McNair and NARA, I started to write with some discipline.

My New York brother, John, a writer, was a source of ongoing support and early narrative direction. Armin Merkel, a retired high school history teacher in New York State, and, before that, a grunt in Vietnam, gave me his sought-for vote. I valued his approval of the way I described the life of the draftee in the citizen-soldier army that he knew in the early 1960s. The award for "best supporting author" goes to Nadine Cohodas (*The Band Played Dixie*). In 2001, she reintroduced me to Ole Miss by connecting me with two members of its journalism department, Associate Professor Burnis

Morris and Professor Stuart Bullion, the late chair, who together generously gave of their time to help me revisit the campus. Thereafter Nadine was a constant supporter and manuscript reader (with comments). In baseball we used to shout out to our teammates at bat, "Good eye, good eye." Nadine had that for my manuscript.

On my return trip to the campus, both Burnis and Stuart provided me with a clear picture of the strides the school had made in race relations since my first "visit," thanks in no small part to the efforts of former Mississippi governor William Winter and Susan Glisson at the Institute for Racial Reconciliation and the stewardship of the university by then-chancellor Robert Khayat.

Stuart helped me retrace the path of our convoy into the town thirty-nine years earlier. We got halfway. Despite our best efforts, we could not find the house with the side driveway down which the 716th passed as it moved toward the campus, thus bypassing the mob that had been pushed downtown. Shortly after that visit and a talk that I gave to one of Burnis's journalism classes, David Sansing, professor emeritus of history at the University of Mississippi, sent me an encouraging e-mail saying, "You should write about it."

Former U.S. congressman Jim Symington, an administrative assistant to Attorney General Robert Kennedy at the time, had traveled (with his guitar) to the campus during the first week of the riots. He provided me with a handful of anecdotes, some of which I have used. U.S. District Court Judge Louis Oberdorfer, a Department of Justice (DOJ) attorney who spent the riot night in the Federal Building not far off the square in Oxford, read the manuscript and gave me one piece of advice. "Whatever you do, don't take out the part about the phone call to your mother from the pay phone that first morning." Years later, to remind me that it is a small world, friend and neighbor Charlie McBride was in a position to confirm that the 716th soldiers had had C-ration breakfasts on the Lyceum curb that first morning. They shared their meal with him and fellow Louisiana State University classmates after they made an all-night drive over from Baton Rouge. I thank Mark Toy and Teresa

Zellefrow for confirming what Ron Barrett had told me about his home town of Kittanning, Pennsylvania.

Sidna (Brower) Mitchell, a voice of reason who spoke out that first week as editor of the campus newspaper, *The Mississippian*, was a source of support and anecdotes. Without the recall of Jan (Humber) Robertson, then the paper's managing editor, I would not know of the chartered bus from Alabama whose driver needed directions to the campus. Childhood friends Bud Black, Chuck Neerland, Jane Hagen Hess, and Bill Dye helped me by recalling stories about the small black population in our Minneapolis neighborhood years ago.

To others who supported, helped, and confirmed story facts, I thank northerners Sandy Horwitt, Cecelia Wirtz, Betsy Graves, Noel Kane, Amy Biederman, Caroline Kenney, Chris Thorne, Mark Perry, and Amy Schapiro. To those who gave me insight into their South, I thank former Mississippi governor William Winter, former University of Mississippi chancellor Robert Khayat, and his vice chancellor Gloria Kellum. Also on the list of those who provided support and insight and whom I'd like to thank are Ralph Eubanks (*Ever Is a Long Time*), Mac Hansbrough, Lou Ivy, Curtis Wilkie (*Dixie*), Bill Dunlap, Brent Gilroy, Susan Glisson, Will Lewis, Carey Rivers, and Maralyn and Hanh Bullion.

Another southerner, James Meredith, sent me a note saying, "It's about time you wrote your book."

A special thanks to Gene Roberts, Pulitzer Prize–winning newspaper editor (*Philadelphia Inquirer*) and coauthor (*The Race Beat*), for his quiet counsel and his introduction to Leila Salisbury at the University Press of Mississippi. I also want to thank author Bill Doyle (*An American Insurrection*) for his perspective.

To my former colleagues in the battalion, thank you. As I write this paragraph, I am standing at attention and saluting the six of you: Peter Frechette, Guay Wilson, Carl Hirsch, Rich Mitchell, David Steinberg, and the memory of the late Ronald Barrett (my first Ole Miss driver). You provided (or corrected) details in the text, contributed photos, and gave me "humor in uniform" pieces to add a human touch to the narrative, all in an effort to give a balanced account of this unusual mission that the U.S. Army (and the 716th) undertook fifty years ago. And thank you, Dave Epstein, a former major in a later 716th MP battalion (Vietnam), who encouraged me to tell the story and then helped refine and correct many of the terms I use about the U.S. Army's military police of the 1960s. I am grateful to Colonel Lewis "Bob" Sorley USA (Ret.), not only for frequent support, advice, and encouragement, but for editing the terms in the glossary. To Bill Rataczak and Colonel Vic Tambone USAF (Ret.) in that other service, thank you for advising me of the characteristics and operations of the C-130.

My consulting editor, Carren Kaston, reviewed several early drafts of this book, providing not only editorial corrections but invaluable developmental advice as to shape, tone, and content. In doing so, she helped me become a writer (and not just a lawyer who writes). After her hand, Leila Salisbury at the University Press of Mississippi (UPM) helped me become an author. I also wish to thank my copy editor, Carol Cox, who skillfully polished the final manuscript for publication.

My retired librarian wife, Le-Chi, was a great help when I came to the notes section of the memoir. She brought to the task a sense of patience and diligence that I did not have. I was pulled back to my first-year law school legal research class and she came out of retirement to get me through the madness that often forces nonfiction writers to turn to fiction.

I should say something about the before-and-after riot photos from the *Memphis Press-Scimitar* that I was able to find, courtesy of Special Collections, University of Memphis. Ed Frank, a preservation and special collections librarian at the university, passed on an anecdote that's worth repeating. It reveals the passion and the vision which librarians, curators, archivists, and others in the "helping profession" (his words) have for the preservation of the historical record. Frank remembered that, at the time of the closing of the newspaper in 1983:

The "morgue" files (clippings, photos, and ephemera) of the [*Press-Scimitar*] were staged on their loading dock, awaiting transfer to the dump, when someone in [the paper's] hierarchy began to think they might be a valuable historical resource. A call was made to the (then) Memphis State University library, and the curator of special collections immediately [jumped into her station wagon and] started hauling the files and the all-important index cards to [our] campus.

I also wish to thank these others in that "helping profession": Jennifer Ford, head of special collections at the J. D. Williams Library, University of Mississippi, and her staff, with particular appreciation to Pamela Williamson; and Roslyn Pachoca, reference specialist at the Library of Congress, who was helpful in providing me with additional archival material.

Finally, although he didn't encourage me to write a story, nor check a footnote, nor read a draft of the manuscript, I want to thank a navy shore patrolman I'll call Seaman "Jarrell," whom we kidnapped to help guide us from Tennessee and into Mississippi for a bit. Without him, the battalion might not have gotten to Oxford that dawn morning when it did. So, wherever you are, Seaman Jarrell, you were and are an integral part of my account. I just hope you got back to your base safely that night and that your superior officer believed your AWOL defense, implausible though it may have sounded. I offer myself as a corroborating witness, should your grandchildren not believe you when you tell them of the time Yankee soldiers kidnapped you off your duty post fifty years ago.

INTRODUCTION
A Sense of Place

Where Y'all From?

They call it "sense of place," a phrase overused by travel writers and essayists who get paid to craft messages about idyllic venues. College marketing consultants and small town chambers of commerce too are paid to craft such messages about "place." Not all such venues evoke a "sense of place." But the campus of Ole Miss is one place that does—maybe the town as well, even parts of the state.

I remember a coed in the fall of 1962 at the fraternity party at the University of Mississippi that Lieutenant Peter Frechette and I crashed. She turned to me and asked (translated into my Minnesota-speak) where I was from. I assumed that few, if any, of her fellow students were "townies," from Oxford itself, so I thought it a natural question. I was to learn later that it was asked then (and continued to be asked on the campus) with a bit more study and purpose than the same question would have been asked at a college party up North. At an Ole Miss party, if a "hit" was registered after the first question, then the follow-up would have been, and perhaps still is, "Oh, then you must know so-and-so." The dynamic would move on, in an almost tribal way, with the inevitable "Well, then your people must know my people." The result is a constantly expanding network of people that covers the state. All this follows from the first question that starts with geography, with land. That's not to say college parties up north don't feature the same kind of

conversation starters, but somehow the answers down south seem
to entail a bit more consequence.

Mississippi is not Michigan, nor Montana. The question "Where
y'all from?" was a natural and even expected inquiry in the state
because home and place were and are of paramount importance.
Most of the Ole Miss students would answer that they were from
"over in," "up in," or "down in" some place in Mississippi, always
Mississippi. Not even New Orleans or Memphis. Outsiders were
hoping to become accepted "inside" if they were new to Ole Miss.

Northerners too value "place," but not to the same extent. In
the South, the word implies permanence, or at least a "stay a while"
invitation. I later found out that Ole Miss students may travel away
from their place—to nearby Memphis and New Orleans on breaks
and maybe for jobs—but the straying across the state line didn't
change their sense of home or their affection for place.

Place fuels story. Southerners have story. To be sure, northerners have it too. But someone from the North somehow doesn't have
story the same way a southerner has it. It's no accident that the
home of the National Storytelling Festival is in Jonesborough, Tennessee. Moreover, even song is story and no one ever sang North
Dakota or Illinois, "you're on my mind." And James Taylor was
"going to Carolina in my mind," not to Pennsylvania.

You can't have story unless you stay in one place for a while, not
"sneak out the back door" on the day after graduation. You stay a
while. Northerners don't stay. We go. People in the South stay and
listen to their mothers, their grandfathers, uncles, and other older
people tell stories. And that story is so often about the past, about
roots. People from the region don't seem to stray as far from their
roots as we northerners might from ours. Or we pull ours up and
try to replant them elsewhere. And they often don't survive such
a replanting. Not that we're unmindful of our roots, but those of
southerners seem to go deeper. A Mississippi story starts shallow
and just keeps going down. And that going down is often a linkage
to a past that was not always happy.

Moreover, story often dwells on the "southern way of life" that everyone seems to be talking about down around here—everything that is home, family, loyalty, and land. Montana and Wisconsin have land, but they don't have a "way," maybe because they haven't lost a war. In any event, I've never heard of a "northern" way of life. Maybe we northerners have some sort of "way," but it is a lukewarm version, not a heated one as in the South. Maybe the southern way and awareness of place have to do with the Civil War and its wrenching aftermath. Perhaps the war's outcome was an enduring sense of loss and yearning that, like a kind of *Last Picture Show*, now screens subliminally over and over again at the back of southern consciousness.

When I was growing up in Minnesota and overheard an older person speak of "the war," I assumed the reference was to World War II. That's not what a reference to "the war" meant in the South fifty years ago, maybe not even today. And for the hold-onto-history people, the "southern way of life" naturally included race separation.

Then along came James Meredith, himself a Mississippian, with his own deep roots, his own place. He no longer wanted to sit up in the balcony, to step aside on the narrow sidewalk to allow the white person coming towards him to pass. He wanted to stay on the sidewalk, to keep walking, to be part of the Mississippi way and the larger southern way. Place and story. He simply wanted to enlarge them to include his home and his family, his loyalty, and his land. He wanted to be counted.

James Meredith and the Ole Miss Riot

1

THE NORTH

In the last week of September 1962, Mississippi was headed toward racial convulsion. The federal government was making plans to safeguard public order and enforce constitutional law. But in keeping with U.S. government policy, the army kept some units, including mine, in the dark about these plans and the role we were to play in them. My mind was still on summer softball games at Camp Drum, in upstate New York. Reality was proceeding on two tracks. It was not until we were in Memphis that the two tracks converged and we caught up with history.

"Lieutenant, it's just an exercise."

Fort Dix, New Jersey, September 28, 1962
I'm in a dream and a telephone is ringing in it. Suddenly, the dream is gone and the ringing keeps on. I reach down onto the floor of the room at the BOQ (Bachelor Officers' Quarters), pick the receiver up, hold it for a second, and place it back in its cradle. I'm not ready to be back here. Probably a call from some lieutenant who wants to party.

It rings again. I pick the receiver up again. This time I whisper into it.

"Hello, this better be serious."

One of my eyes works and it looks down over the edge of the mattress and sees slants of light on the floor coming down through the window blinds. I guess late afternoon. Still Friday.

"It is, sir. We're on alert. The whole battalion, Lieutenant. I'll send a jeep over once you let me know you're packed and ready."

I recognize the voice, a reluctant one. Hey! It's Private Steinberg. He ought to know that C Company just came back to New Jersey last night. He was with us on the return to Fort Dix after five months at Camp Drum. We started out in upstate New York at dawn, all day and into the night, in a long convoy of jeeps, trucks, and trailers, three hundred miles that seemed like six hundred.

"Look, Steinberg, why can't they just leave us out of this? They have to know we just came down from Drum."

"Lieutenant, it's just an exercise. But they want all of us."

I wonder who the *they* is that the army always talks about. Are there no names?

"All right, I'll call you back."

I can't believe this. I roll over and squint at the calendar on the wall. Now both eyes are working. It's still May in my room because I have yet to tear off the pages of the months that I've been gone. Outside on the rest of Dix it's September 28.

"The army might become involved. . . ."

Camp Drum, New York, Summer 1962
I'm a twenty-three-year-old U.S. Army second lieutenant stationed with a military police (MP) company at an outpost in upstate New York. We're winding down an assignment providing security for the summer residents—army reservists from the New England area undergoing their annual two-week training obligations. We've been up here since early May, oblivious to events in the civilian world.

> *New Orleans, Washington, D.C., Jackson, Miss., June–September 1962.* A three-judge panel of the U.S. Fifth Circuit Court of Appeals, hearing the [Meredith case] found by a two-to-one decision that [he had] been denied admission to the University of Mississippi because he was a Negro. It . . . ordered the

district court to enjoin the University and other officials from refusing to admit Meredith. . . . [After repeated delays] on 13 September 1962 District Court Judge Sidney C. Mize [Jackson, Mississippi] issued a sweeping injunction to guarantee Meredith's admission to the University and his attendance there without discrimination.[1]

I'm midway through a two-year active-duty tour as a platoon leader in C Company. The company is about to return to its home base at Fort Dix, New Jersey, to rejoin its parent unit, the 716th Military Police Battalion.

I enjoy this temporary duty in upstate New York. It's far enough away from our gung-ho battalion commander down in New Jersey. I last saw the major at dawn that morning five months ago when we departed from Dix. There he was, standing curbside on a New Jersey traffic circle outside the post, decked out in heavily starched battle-ready fatigues. He was cheering on our convoy as it moved through the main post gate toward the New Jersey Turnpike and on its way up to Camp Drum.

For the major, it was a send-off befitting a combat operation, and he had been in many as a sergeant in World War II. It's no wonder that our battalion was constantly sent on training exercises out in the vast expanses of those New Jersey woods. We were MPs. Silly us, we thought that the hills were surely to be reserved for the hundreds of infantry trainees who pass through Dix. But the major missed his years in the infantry. He chafed at being in charge of an MP battalion when he came back into the service after a few boring civilian years in Superior, Wisconsin. He probably resented the fact that his men would have to share the roads up to Drum with civilian traffic.

The major loved the STRAC (Strategic Army Command) designation that the 716th had been given and with it the battalion's attachment to the XVIII Airborne Corps down at Fort Bragg in North Carolina. We were to provide combat military police support in the event of a major crisis. When the "balloon" went up, STRAC units could be deployed worldwide on short notice.

Meanwhile:

The Pentagon, Arlington, Va., September 8. Maj. General
Creighton W. Abrams, Jr. [Assistant Deputy Chief of Staff for
Military Operations in Civil Affairs] . . . conferred with Secretary of the Army Cyrus R. Vance and came away with the
knowledge that the Army might become involved in the Meredith case.[2]

September 14. [A senior Abrams staff officer] obtained infor-
mation on the Naval Air Station at Millington, Tennessee
(MNAS), about seventeen miles northeast of Memphis, which
then entered into the military planning as a staging area for the
Oxford operation. . . . [I]t had the virtues of being both close to
Oxford and outside of Mississippi.[3]

The Army's planning for possible intervention was to be
guarded so closely . . . that the matter was not to be discussed
openly and military personnel (with limited exceptions) were
not to go to Mississippi while planning was underway. . . .Gen-
eral Abrams . . . urged "that every precaution must be taken to
conceal the Army's interest in" the [Meredith] matter.[4]

In addition to its distance from Dix, I also find the small army
outpost of Camp Drum, not too far from the Canadian border, a
good personal fit. With its pine trees and cool weather, it reminds
me of my home state of Minnesota, where I would be now had
the "Wall" not gone up last year. The "Berlin Wall crisis" suddenly
threw many of us newly minted 1961 ROTC (Reserve Officer Training Corps) second lieutenants into two-year assignments—cancel-
ing out the coveted six-month options we had chosen that would
have left but a slight imprint of the military life on us.

Washington, D.C., September 25. [In a telephone conversation
with Attorney General Robert Kennedy, Mississippi's Governor

Barnett] declared he was going to Oxford to take charge of the state police personally "and that he would go to jail and spend the rest of his life in jail before he would see the university integrated."[5]

But the summer's over and it's time to leave Drum this last week in September. I'm ready to go back to Dix. I am coach of C Company's softball team, and we've just notched our twentieth loss against four wins playing the visiting New England reservists. I don't know why junior officers pull this kind of coaching duty when NCOs (noncommissioned officers) can take on the task. And they can double as player-coaches while I, an officer, am not allowed to be on the field, even though I played small-college baseball. In any case, without any good fast-pitch throwers now—before the advent of the more popular slow-pitch game—we were doomed on these late summer afternoons.

> *Shreveport, La., September 26.* [Former army general Edwin A. Walker] made a statement on radio station KWLH at Shreveport, Louisiana, urging people to "[r]ise to stand beside Governor Ross Barnett. . . ." He contended that the people had "talked, listened and been pushed around far too much. . . ."[6]

In 1961 General Walker was relieved of a division command in Germany after complaints that he tried to influence the voting of his troops. He is an avowed member of the John Birch Society, a "right wing" group.[7]

Company grade officers (lieutenants or captains) also lead convoys and that's my assignment for the return to our home post in New Jersey, scheduled for tomorrow. I entrust my '54 Pontiac to Private David Steinberg to drive back. Then I call my parents in Minneapolis to give them one of my infrequent "check-ins" as to where I am and where I'll be going . . . down to New Jersey.

On Thursday, September 27, C Company sets off before dawn. Any military convoy of jeeps and trucks moving over our nation's highways can be a challenge. But I think it will be no problem this morning, since another lieutenant brought the company up from Dix in the spring with minimal breakdowns and stragglers.

On a far right lane of one of President Eisenhower's new interstates, we move down through the middle of New York, cross into Pennsylvania, and then over to the Delaware Water Gap. Tracking the Delaware River along the New Jersey side we end up at the sprawling military post outside of Trenton hours later than we had planned. Convoy discipline is nonexistent, despite the shepherding by company NCOs. Dozens of jeeps and deuce-and-a-halfs, drivers, and soldiers are strewn across the Pocono Mountains and parts of northern New Jersey. The last of the vehicles limps into Dix early Friday morning. It's a convoy of which no military unit can be proud.

As much as Drum was a good place to be for a summer in the army—unless I was career-bound—I look forward to getting out of the woods and back to the life of the big post. The officers' club is just across the street from my BOQ building and the restaurants and bars in the nearby towns will still be crowded, as will the gyms and clubs on McGuire Air Force Base, adjacent to Dix.

Dallas, Tex., September 27. [Walker] said that if federal troops moved into Mississippi, "I will be there." He called for "10,000 strong, from every state in the union" to "rally to the cause of freedom."[8]

Best of all, I hear that the overzealous major has moved on to another command after a promotion. His replacement is a laid-back lieutenant colonel from Oklahoma on his retirement tour. Emmett T. Brice is hardly STRAC. His previous career assignments were in the CID (Criminal Investigation Division). Good. No more combat training in the woods. One more year at Dix on the back side of my two-year tour and then home to civilian life in Minnesota.

The army has been good enough to leave my room vacant over the months I've been gone. I move back into it early Friday morning and sleep well into the afternoon.

The Pentagon, Arlington, Va., September 28. The possibility that Governor Barnett might become liable to arrest . . . which would broaden the Army's mission, indicated the desirability of identifying the additional troops that might be needed. . . . [A third task force would be created.] Built around the 716th Military Police Battalion at Fort Dix, New Jersey, and commanded by Lt. Col. Brice Emmet [*sic*], it had the 5th and 17th Field Hospitals and an information section (from Fort Dix) attached to it, together with a composite military intelligence detachment.[9]

And then the dream-interrupting phone call comes into my room. And the calendar is wrong. It truly is September 28. I tell Private Steinberg that I'll call him back once I pack what little I had unpacked.

I knock on the door of the adjoining room of the BOQ duplex. A second lieutenant from one of the advanced infantry training units on the post opens it.

"Jack, we're on alert again and I have to write my will. You're getting the Pontiac again. It's in the lot out back." I think, it's got to be there because Steinberg's back. "Here's the keys. Title's in the glove compartment, somewhere."

"But, Hank, it's such a dog. It'll be condemned in a week and I'll have to—"

"Don't worry. I'll be back tomorrow night and rip up the will."

We all know the drill. In the past we'd go on alert, pack our gear, and report to a staging area. Then, after an endless wait for one of the exercise umpires to come along with his clipboard and whistle, we'd stand down. This is all done to meet our STRAC preparedness requirements. Yes! Combat-ready MPs. This time I guess they were just waiting for us to return from Drum in order to pull the alert for the whole battalion.

That's it! To test the new colonel.

With nothing really to unpack, I rezip the duffel bag, dirty clothes and all, and call the battalion clerk. Minutes later I go down the back stairs and outside to an idling jeep and a waiting driver. I glance over at the officers' club across the street. Junior officers are already pulling into the parking lot for their Friday night ration of drinks and relaxed lieutenant-to-lieutenant talk. I should be over there with them.

We drive four short blocks. The three companies and the head-quarters detachment of the 716th Military Police Battalion are housed in two long concrete-block buildings, three stories high. The architectural style is the kind more likely seen on a military post in East Germany in these Cold War years. At full strength the battalion numbers well more than six hundred officers and men.

I go upstairs to check on my platoon. The enlisted men's quarters are in long bays at both ends of the floors, with bunk beds lined up against windows along each side. The company commander, his staff, and the company first sergeant are in offices midway down a central hallway. As is customary, there are no desks for second lieutenants.

Voices come at me.

"Sir, what's this all about?"

"C'mon, Lieutenant, we just got back."

The phrase, "C'mon, Lieutenant" is sometimes heard in direct address from the big-city draftees who think they're still back in the "hood." They would never say "C'mon, *Captain*" or "*Major.*"

I shrug. *As if I would know.* Don't these guys remember me? I'm still a second lieutenant and I'm still the one they were with last week at Drum. Lieutenants often get their information on upcoming exercises and the army world in general from veteran sergeants. Nothing yet from them for this lieutenant.

Everyone moves around with the bored efficiency of soldiers who've been through these alerts before—just going through the motions. Bulging duffel bags start piling up in the hallway. "Been there done that" has yet to become a popular phrase, but it would have worked here. I recognize a corporal from B Company who's come up onto our floor to visit a buddy. He welcomes me back and then chides me about C Company's softball record up at Drum. "Four and twenty, huh, Lieutenant?"

I look out a bay window and see the married officers and NCOs in the 716th pulling into the parking lot below, called in from their homes on post or in nearby Mount Holly and Pemberton. One of them is Second Lieutenant Peter Frechette, University of Wisconsin ROTC, my classmate at the MP officer orientation course at Fort Gordon, Georgia, exactly one year ago. Their families expect them back, at the latest, for Sunday morning breakfast. That's the normal length of the exercises . . . if we stay on post.

The weekend-pass rush of the soldiers stationed at Dix is well under way. The outgoing cars are backed up at the main gate, meeting a trickle of incoming ones, many of which are driven by our battalion members. They received the "alert-return-to-post" phone calls while out on pass.

For me, it's a reunion of sorts, not having seen many of the unit officers for more than five months. I avoid any talk about our four-and-twenty softball record.

Citizen Soldiers

The U.S. Army in these days looks like a cross-section of American society more than it will a few years later. Then it'll be reconfigured by the student deferrals of the Vietnam era and the later all-volunteer army of the '70s. Now the ranks of the 716th are filled with draftees just out of high school or college, sprinkled with a few soldiers who have volunteered for the army. The enlisted men. Pity these Regular Army (RA) three-year enlistees in the battalion. There's no end to the harassment they get from the two-year draftees on this floor. "Hey, lifer, they gonna teach you a trade, huh?" Finally, there are some in the battalion who had been discharged and gotten on with their lives, only to be called back into the army because of the Berlin Wall crisis. But be they draftees, enlistees, or returnees, most of the 716th are from well-known cities and not-so-known small towns in the Northeast, and they bring their accents and street-corner ways into the barracks with them.

> The unit was made up of a diverse group of individuals, both black and white, from different parts of our country. A large percentage came from the northeast. There were high school dropouts, high school graduates as well as college graduates. . . . The company was made up of a large percentage of draftees.[10]

The ranks of our battalion are led by career sergeants, a few of them veterans of World War II, others veterans of the Korean War. The company grade officers are college ROTC graduates, with a few OCS (Officer Candidate School) graduates, most of them "in-and-out" lieutenants on two-year assignments as platoon leaders. Above them, as company commanders, are career-bound captains, topped off by a major and a lieutenant colonel. There's not a West Point, VMI (Virginia Military Institute), or Citadel (The Military College of South Carolina) man in sight. Those graduates prefer active-duty assignments in the combat arms branches of the army, which are filled mainly by RA enlistees and career NCOs. If there are citizen-soldiers these days, the 716th is full of them.

The barracks activity slows down. A rush and then everything and everyone remains in place. We stand down. The wait continues into the night. The men sleep in the barracks while the married personnel return to their homes and the single (and unaccompanied officers) return to their BOQ rooms, all with instructions to report back at dawn.

We all hold on to the unshakable expectation that this is an exercise; none of us really discusses the option that we might be going real-world operational. Yet, exercise or not, we still haven't received any briefing from battalion headquarters.

Jackson, Miss., September 29. Walker arrived in Jackson, Mississippi, and held another press and television conference in which he called for "violent vocal protest."[11]

On Saturday morning, the operational "readiness" condition remains in place. Stuck.

In the afternoon Post Finance calls over to inform the battalion duty officer that I'm the designated payroll officer for C company. I'm to report to draw down the payroll for C Company.

Payday has been advanced from Monday to today, Saturday. (This should be a signal to me that this isn't going to be an exercise.) I drive over to the finance office on the post where a senior warrant officer hands me the payroll, a payout for more than two hundred men, all of it in tens, fives, and ones. In an imperious tone, he tells me that I am responsible to "Uncle Sam for every last penny," as he taps his ballpoint on the counter, looks at me . . . and smiles.

I sign for it. He asks me if I have any protection. Every pay officer has to be armed. I remind him that I'm an MP officer and point to the .45 on my right hip. I then say that I can't disburse because of the alert situation over at the battalion. He responds that he's heard about it and throws an official U.S. Army money belt down onto the counter. I sign for this as well and he wishes me good luck. I secure the canvas belt around my waist and, after an exchange of salutes, leave the building, for the moment a very wealthy second lieutenant. Back at the battalion, word's gotten out that I'm the payroll officer. But, with no time for me to sit at a desk and disburse, they watch my every move.

The packing is complete. Everything is loaded into the mess and supply trucks and trailers as well as the steel conex containers. They'll carry whatever battalion supplies and equipment can't be stuffed into duffel bags or lashed onto vehicles. I hand over my signed "Last Will and Testament" to the company clerk, one more of the "things-to-do" to get a good grade on the STRAC exercise.

"Sir, are you white?"

We load up and the 716th trucks itself out the back gates of Dix and over the few blocks to McGuire Air Force Base. Still an exercise? Why not? STRAC-designated readiness has as much to do with unit preparedness in-place as with coordination with other services—this time the U.S. Air Force. It makes sense to show how quickly an army battalion can move to an air force facility. Yeah, an exercise . . . a joint army–air force one to show the Pentagon that indeed we're ready for Berlin, Cuba, or wherever. There's always going to be a *wherever*.

> There really were thousands of Americans preparing to march on Oxford, from coast to coast, both on their own initiative and in response to the general's [Walker's] call, though it was impossible to verify what was real and what was bluster.[12]

My driver, Spec-4 John Adams, follows the jeeps ahead of us through a base gate. He turns to me and asks me what I think is going on. I tell him that I have no idea. Again, *as if we second lieutenants have a clue.*

All I can do is stare at the long line of vehicles ahead of us in this convoy, the second one I've been in within the past twenty-four hours, though this one is the whole battalion, not just one company. We stop alongside a fenced area just inside the base perimeter. We've come a short distance from the dark of a sleeping Fort Dix into the light of this huge airbase. McGuire is a busy transit center, with MATS (Military Air Transport Service) planes ferrying army personnel and dependents to bases in Europe. It's always awake.

It reminds me of those new all-night gas stations on Lake Street back in Minneapolis, with the fake sunlight of bright neons overhead, only here magnified hundreds of times. No press around. No cameras. Just us warriors of the Cold War. *On the Ground and in the Air While America Sleeps*! And there's that familiar noise—the roars from the arriving and departing aircraft that we often hear from our beds over at Dix.

The scuttlebutt continues down the line that we're simply on an exercise, to be over soon. Yet still no sign of that umpire with the clipboard and whistle. And no NCOs to say, "Lieutenant, it's just a drill." But we're performing according to the book—the army one. Adams turns to me and says that we're doing pretty well and that means three-day passes into New York.

> The troops affected and inquiring reporters alike would be told that the alert was in keeping with the units' STRAC status, despite the fact that the newspapers were full of news about the Mississippi situation.[13]

I glance at my watch: 2300 hours.

A few unfamiliar officer faces begin to appear in the formation that's parked along the fence. Since I've been gone for the summer, I haven't met any of the newly assigned lieutenants. I'll go over and introduce myself. But I hang back a bit when I see different branch insignia on their collars. Not the crossed pistols of the MP Corps, but Signal and Medical Service Corps, even an Infantry collar. I look down the line and see an ambulance with a huge red cross on its side panel, pulling into the rear of the convoy.

Years later I will hear from an infantry lieutenant stationed at Dix:

> I was asleep in my room [Friday night] in Battleship BOQ . . . when the telephone out in the hallway began ringing incessantly. After a while, I finally got up and . . . answered it. [After a few questions about my name and rank] the voice at the other end asked, "*Sir, are you white?*" "Yes sir!" "Get your field gear and wait outside the front entrance. A jeep will be by to pick you up."[14]

So . . . OK, this must be a mixed-branch experiment. Augmented personnel from non-MP units. Well! Some kind of exercise this is becoming.

Regardless of the differences in branch insignia, the clusters of conversation down the line of jeeps conform to the dictates of army tradition—officer-to-officer and enlisted-to-enlisted. We also find ourselves acting out another army tradition: "Hurry up and wait."

Still no briefing. Why all the hush-hush? Either *they*—the all-knowing superior officers—know and won't tell us or, worse yet, won't tell us because they haven't the foggiest. Which one is it? What is this?

Then, it all changes.

One of the sergeants comes over, screaming to be heard above the noise of the base.

"Lieutenant, I don't think we're on an exercise."

"What do you mean?"

He points to the planes landing on a far runway and taxiing over toward us.

"Look at those tail markings on the C-130s, sir. Those aren't MATS planes, you know, the ones stationed here at McGuire. The ones that go back and forth to Europe. Sir, those are TAC. We're a designated STRAC unit, right? Part of the XVIII Airborne Corps out of Bragg? I bet these planes are up from Pope, across from Bragg. I was stationed there two years ago."

I try to connect his words to what I see going on in front of me. "TAC"—Tactical Air Command, "Pope"—air base, "Bragg"—North Carolina. *OK, what the hell is going on here tonight?*

Langley Air Force Base, Va., September 29. The Tactical Air Force [TAC] ordered execution of its operational plans to provide airlift for Task Forces Alfa and Charlie [716th MP Battalion]. . . . Alfa and Charlie would move to the Memphis staging area by air. . . . Apparently the President wanted a force of 500 military policemen at the Memphis staging area, in addition to those already scheduled for arrival there, as soon as possible.[15]

Two, then three, of the big planes are quickly on top of us. They're huge, loud, and a bit frightening with their size. I take a few steps back from one approaching monster. A voice pipes up in the dark. "Hey, we're army. We don't do things this big." Thank God for army humor.

Then there's Quinlan, the irrepressible New Yorker. "Lieutenant, we're going on a field trip, just like fourth grade. It's a slumber party, this time in tents, out under the stars. OK? We're gonna get some hot chocolate, sing some silly songs, and be back home after breakfast tomorrow morning."

Soon, more of the giant four-engine flying machines begin crowding each other on the tarmac, as if they were vying for passengers. They close in on their assigned positions opposite our parked battalion.

I recognize the new colonel as he comes by with the battalion sergeant major. He motions to our company commander to start loading his platoons onto the assigned planes. The same order goes out to the other battalion companies down the line.

By now I stop looking for the exercise umpire with his clipboard. Adams does not; he still views this as an exercise. He looks over at me and, over the noise, shouts, "Sir, all we're going to do is load up the planes and taxi down the runway. Then, we'll all pull up, get off and go home. Drill's over."

Snaps his fingers.

"That's it, I know. You're new to this, sir. But I've been here before."

Air force personnel are all over us on the ground now, yelling instructions to the jeep drivers above the noise of it all. The cargo ramp at the rear of the huge aircraft in front of us slowly comes yawning down. An air force enlisted comes running down, yelling, "OK, driver, line your wheels up at that ramp. Go! Yes, you! You! Slow, slow . . . OK, track it up the ramp! OK, next! You! Move! Move!"

No one at this moment has any doubt that this enlisted man is in charge. Not the colonel, not any major, not even the pilot of this plane, wherever he might be. It's this air force sergeant and we all better do what he says. The first driver moves his jeep over and edges its front wheels onto the beveled lip of the ramp. He strains its engine up the tracks and into the huge electric lightbulb–filled bay of the plane. It's an airborne parking garage! Yes, we don't do things this big. The engines of the planes remain running, props turning. The air force calls it "engines running on load." I guess somebody's in a hurry. The earsplitting noise is so loud you can't think about anything but the power of these planes.

All we can do is stare at the jeeps. Yes, our jeeps—the ones the 716th MPs drive around every day on the post. Where is the U.S. Air Force taking them? And we're going with them. I look around and check with the NCOs to make sure that the platoon's ready.

I also press my hand over the bulge of the money belt around my waist. I'm probably carrying around three times the amount of money that my dad had the day he paid for our first house in Minneapolis.

It all goes so fast. Air force people are running all over now. The jeeps are strapped down in the middle track of the C- 130, three per plane. They're lined up tight, bumper to bumper, as in a parking lot, only now in a plane. Then we—as if the passengers are after-thoughts—are ordered up the gang plank into the belly of the flying ark. "Noah," the pilot, is still nowhere to be seen. It's like entering an acoustical-effects test auditorium. Noise and vibration surround us.

We stumble as we edge up along the sides of the tied-down jeeps. Slide and trip-step into canvas-webbed seats rigged against the wall of the cargo bay. Of course, no passenger windows . . . air force economy class, steerage, as if it were the U.S. Navy and we walked up a ramp into a boat. We just sit there, docile guests of the U.S. Air Force.

Moments later, the huge rear door bangs shut, metal on metal. The plane jumps into a move. It turns sharply, like the sudden jerk of a car driven by a high school show-off. Jeeps jiggle around in their tie-downs. Penned-in sheep. I sense that we're out on a run-way now, pushing up the speed. The movement is not smooth as it might be in a civilian airliner. But I doubt that many of the troops in this flying barn tonight have ever been on a commercial flight, maybe any kind of a plane, for that matter.

The aircraft shakes. The jeeps shake. We all shake. I hope the pilot's not shaking. It's like sitting in the open bed of a fast-moving truck, except that we can't see out. I recall a plane from my teenage years that was called a "Flying Boxcar." Suddenly, the bumping stops and the vibration lightens up a bit. We're airborne.

So much for all that STRAC exercise talk. Where the hell's my driver, Adams? Seated far down on the right from where I am. Turns away from my stare.

The White House, September 29, midnight. Meanwhile, at one minute past midnight . . . President John F. Kennedy put his name to [a proclamation]. Declaring that the Governor of Mississippi and other officers and persons in that state were "willfully opposing and obstructing the enforcement" of Federal court orders, that . . . the President commanded "all persons engaged in such obstruction of justice to cease and desist therefrom and to disperse and retire peaceably forthwith." He stated his authority as "the Constitution and the laws of the United States. . . ."[16]

[Followed by] Executive Order No. 11053: "Assistance for Removal of Unlawful Obstructions of Justice in the State of Mississippi" . . . declared that . . . "The Secretary of Defense is authorized to and directed to take all appropriate steps to enforce all [Federal court orders] . . . [and] to use such of the armed forces of the United States as he may deem necessary . . . and to call into active military service of the United States as he may deem necessary."[17]

2

THE UPPER SOUTH

"A Negro is trying to break the color line."

Aboard a C-130 somewhere over the mid-Atlantic states, early morning, September 30. Now the questions, shouted above the noise, are more somber and tension filled.

"Sir, where're we going? Cuba? Berlin?"

"Lieutenant, where're you taking us?"

Fair questions. They weren't asked of the pilot of this flying garage. Sure, he's up front. And all he and his air force buddies do is pick us up and drop us off somewhere with not so much as a "Have a nice day." He gets the hell out of the way while we stay . . . wherever that might be. Nor are these questions asked of our battalion commander, nor of any of his immediate subordinate officers. Not one of them is in sight. And I don't see any stewardess struggling up alongside the jeeps and the troops, asking if anyone wants a pillow. The question "Where are you taking us?" was asked of me, a second lieutenant, sitting a few seats down from the private who asked it. In the army, sergeants and lieutenants (to a lesser extent) do the "taking" of men off on assignments. Officers more senior than I am—and that's all the rest of them—*order* the taking. That's the way it should be. But normally the takers have been briefed about it by those officers, so we can answer the "Where're you taking us?" questions. But I wonder tonight if even the captains know. Just what the fuck is going on?

Once we level off after a climb that seems to last half an hour, the same air force enlisted guy comes back, the loadmaster. Above the clatter, he shout-asks for the officer-in-charge, eyes sweeping over the cramped bay of curious soldiers looking back at him. He's looking for the collar insignia of an officer and sees mine at the same time I raise my hand. The sergeant stumbles along the cargo and the seats to get over to us, pins himself against a tied-down jeep, and looks down at me. He yells over the noise and the vibration, "Lieutenant . . . ETA, Millington Naval Air Station . . . 0645 hours."

"Millington"? That sounds like England. Yeah! Cold War. They're still on our side, right? OK, so that's five, six hours across the Atlantic from New Jersey, right? No . . . that takes a lot longer. I'd better check.

The loadmaster guy turns to go back to his comfortable surroundings up in the front of the plane, but I wave him back.

"Hello! Sergeant! Wait! Where is this Millington?" (waving him back over the noise).

"Sir? Tennessee, sir!"

I think, Tennessee! *You gotta be kidding!*

As best he can in the noise, my platoon sergeant passes the identity of our destination along to the men, many of whom have taken more comfortable seats in the strapped-down jeeps in the center track. They stretch out and try to sleep. Tennessee? And here I think the "balloon" has gone up and we've moving from a cold to a hot war. We're on our way out over the New Jersey coast and across the Atlantic on our way to some flash point in Europe. Or, just as likely these days, making a right turn and going down the coast to Guantánamo, with the rest of Cuba across the fence lines.

OK, so why land in Tennessee? A sudden movement for our STRAC battalion means rapid deployment into a Cold War incident or into a hot one overseas, not something domestic. And in such a mission, the troops are told at least something. We have nothing. Only the name of some navy base in the South.

Hey! Maybe it's an exercise after all. Rapid mobility. An army post to an air force base to a naval station. We still have no idea.

Then again, the army isn't the best at telling its ranks what's going on in the civilian world outside the Dix gates. So, nobody has a clue as to why Tennessee.

"Sir, we're the first to go and the last to know."

Fine . . . snappy jingle, Bradley. Maybe I'll write about this someday.

Then, another shout-out to me: "Sir, I read somewhere that a Negro is trying to break the color line at some college down in the South and there may be trouble. With the state too, I think."

No State shall make or enforce any law which shall abridge the privileges or immunities of citizens of the United States; nor shall any State deprive any person of life, liberty, or property, without due process of law; nor deny to any person within its jurisdiction the equal protection of the laws. (U.S. Const, Amend. XIV, §1.)

I lean back.

Maybe it's news that hasn't been on the front pages. Even if it were there, soldiers usually turn to the sports or the comics pages of the papers that come into the unit dayrooms. There're no twenty-four-hour newscasts on TV, as there'll be years later.

But there's also something to the insular life that one leads in the military, enlisted and officers alike.

The ranks might feel that current news events are for civilians. Do your shift and go back to the barracks to play cards or sleep. Or, go into town or to the various on-post NCO and EM (enlisted men) clubs. Maybe the men will get interested in civilian news once their tours are over and they get back to the nonsoldiering life, where news is important. For now, though, their real lives are on hold. No need to worry about what's going on outside the post gates. Maybe they, and I, missed this news about the "Negro" student. (We find out later that the country at large was caught up short on this story, not by chance, but by plan. Civilian and military planners for the operation said little in advance to the press. And little to some of the MP units involved, except to the 503rd MP Battalion at Fort Bragg.)

Now in the plane we find out that somebody wants us to go someplace. And so we go.

§ 502. (a) Enlistment Oath. . . .—Each person enlisting in an armed force shall take the following oath:
I, [name], do solemnly swear (or affirm) that I will support and defend the Constitution of the United States against all enemies, foreign and domestic . . . and that I will obey the orders of the President of the United States and the orders of the officers appointed over me. . . . So help me God.
  Armed Forces 10 U.S.C., Sec 502

Riot control. We're trained in it, aren't we? That's it! The STRAC major didn't have us out in the woods in foxholes all the time. We still had to train for civil disturbances in riot control formations back on the Dix parade field. "High port! Forward, march! On guard!" The men moved in lockstep, like an eighteenth-century closed skirmish line, but now in the shape of a "V" or a wedge. Tear gas ready, bayonets up, NCO in the middle voicing out the movement commands, officer to the rear. So, there you are.

"How do we get to Cuba from here?"

Millington Naval Air Station, Tenn., September 30. The plane lands at 0615 hours and, after a few stops and starts, comes to a halt again. Is this airport that busy that we have to wait in line? Moves again. The back door (I'm sure the air force has a technical name for it . . . to us army guys it's a back door) swings down to sunlight. I'm the first down the ramp. I squint. A navy guy standing at the bottom sees my rank.
    "Sir, welcome to Millington Naval Air Station."
    "In what state?"
    "Sir? Tennessee, sir."
    Well, that confirms what that air force guy told us maybe five or six hours ago. No, we're not in England. OK, good, no World War III.

We disembark from the plane and the NCOs form the ranks up on the tarmac. Once again, I pat the bulge on the money belt. That's all I really care about right now.

A voice shouts out, "Hey, Lieutenant, how do we get to Cuba from here?"

He was new to the platoon and somehow was not aware that my rank didn't start out with the word "hey," but it was too noisy on the tarmac for his sergeant to correct him. Probably a draftee from the Bronx.

The (already briefed and practiced for riot control) 503rd MP Battalion from Fort Bragg is arriving, maybe with some of our classmates from the officers' course at Fort Gordon last year. Elements of the 101st Airborne Division from Fort Campbell, Kentucky, and the 82nd Airborne Division from Bragg are coming in, even a marine helicopter company. The base is in a frenzy of noise and activity with planes landing by the minute.

Things are happening all around us and still no briefings. Maybe for the senior officers, but not the ranks, not even for the junior officers. No one within sight of us has a clue as to what's going on. I'm no smarter now than when I got on the plane last night.

State of Mississippi, September 30. The Mississippi Army and Air National Guard, with an assigned strength of 11,000 men . . . were now called up with no knowledge of what, precisely, they might be expected to do, although most of the men doubtlessly knew from the press and radio why they were called. By noon Sunday, at least eighty percent of the Guardsmen had reported to their armories and airbases [around the state].[1]

Wherever an army unit goes, it settles into its routine with amazing speed. With the repetition and the regularity of tasks in army life, we could have landed at any military facility in the country. We're a trained and portable military unit and habit takes over. Line up the men on the tarmac and move into quarters, in this case the base gymnasium floor. Get the daily report out, inspect weapons and vehicles, conduct sick call and mail call.

But the most important matter at this moment for the men of C Company is that they get paid. I find an unused office and disburse the payroll. Each payee comes up to me seated at a makeshift pay desk with an NCO standing behind me, salutes, and calls his name out. I disburse his pay in tens, fives, and ones. He counts it out in front of the two of us, salutes again, and walks out the door. One by one they come through this makeshift office at the navy base until it's all disbursed and, yes, in the words of that warrant officer back at Dix yesterday, to "every last penny." None of us knows this morning that we will have little opportunity to spend the money where we are going, except at barracks (read: tent) poker, so those who went off to the Navy Exchange on this payday were the fortunate ones.

Then it's over to the chow hall for breakfast, where one soldier comments about how the U.S. Navy treats its men. "Hey, real china . . . beats those plastic trays back at Dix. Lieutenant, I knew I should've joined the navy."

By early afternoon, we're able to get pieces of the news, some from local papers strewn about the hallways and from short accounts aired over the television sets in the navy's rec rooms. A black man, James Meredith, is about to register at the University of Mississippi in a matter of a day or so and unrest is anticipated in the college town of Oxford, some hundred miles away from where we are. Well, there it is. We've now had our "briefing," unofficial though it is, but it may be the only one we'll get for a while.

National Guard Armory, Oxford, Miss., September 30. The troop raised both the American and Mississippi flags at the armory, posted a guard to keep reporters away, and loaded equipment and duffle bags. With all vehicles loaded the troop could move out on short notice. By mid-afternoon all but three enlisted men were present and only one of these was unaccounted for. Morale "was no problem." With radio reports coming in of [out-of-state] cars headed toward Oxford, [Captain] Falkner conferred with his executive officer and decided to issue M-1 rifles—"as far as they would go." But he still did not think his unit would be ordered to the University campus.[2]

Reporters are suggesting that some of the trouble might come from occupants of the unusual number of cars with out-of-state plates that have been crossing the state lines from all sides into Mississippi. Earlier in the week, a controversial and outspoken segregationist, a retired U.S. Army major general, Edwin Walker, was urging his followers throughout the South to "meet me in Oxford" to oppose the admission of James Meredith to the school.

(Walker had commanded a unit of the 101st Airborne Division in 1957 when it was sent into Little Rock, Arkansas, by President Eisenhower to prevent any disturbances resulting from the city's school integration crisis. Of this episode, he is said to have later made the statement that he was "on the wrong side.")

General Billingslea [the Commander of the 2nd Infantry Division at Fort Benning, Georgia], of course, was now in the Memphis staging area, as was General Abrams. . . .[He and his staff] arrived at the Air Station at one o'clock Sunday morning, CST . . . about an hour before the arrival of the last aircraft bearing Task Force Alfa from Fort Bragg (Pope Air Force Base).[3]

The troops go about killing time. The base movie theater is filled on Sunday afternoon and the 101st stages boxing matches with fighters from its own ranks.

Other than the nonmilitary TV briefing, we have little detail of what is happening on the Oxford campus. However, there's talk among some of the troops that the presence of all the federal troops here in nearby Memphis is a sufficient show of force to deter any violence. We'll go back home from here, maybe even tomorrow.

By the afternoon, deployment back to Dix is what many in the 716th want, even though that means going back to buffing the wax on the linoleum floors in the barracks and other garrison duties. It's a time-honored task familiar to all GIs ever since electricity and sixty-pound stainless steel floor-buffing machines were invented. They're away from the familiar—many of them eighteen- to nineteen-year-olds—largely drawn from New York, New Jersey, and Pennsylvania. Their homes are no more than a short bus ride from Dix on a weekend pass.

After a few hours, even the accents of the civilian workers on the base amuse the troops. One private tells his sergeant that he doesn't speak "southern" and wonders if his lieutenant will let him go back to New Jersey tomorrow on "the Dog" (Greyhound bus). The remarks in the ranks about their new surroundings continue.

"C'mon, Quinlan, it's the same air we breathe up north."

"No, it ain't, Boomer, it's different down here, I'm telling you."

The men sack out on the gym floor and the day drags on. I'm assigned as the OD (Officer of the Day) for the 716th. I take a desk near the rooms where senior officers from the various units that have arrived at the base are meeting.

> Two complete MP battalions are on the floor asleep. It looks like a DP [Displaced Persons] camp. Outside are at least three battle groups of Airborne, with more coming in. The airfields are covered with heliocopters [sic] and transports. We hear the continuous roar of arriving and departing aircraft. A two-star general has set up his CP [Command Post] next door.[4]

Back at Dix, an OD for the battalion is "on call" during the day and evening shifts of MPs on patrol throughout the post. The desk sergeant will call him only if another officer gets into trouble on the post (speeding ticket or worse) or if there's a domestic disturbance (read: spousal abuse) in the military personnel housing on the post.

Here at the base on this Sunday afternoon, the various ODs serve as contact points for their units. It's a matter of handling the phones and monitoring radio calls that might come in from down the hall. Things are quiet. I pick up some magazines and whatever newspapers I can find scattered around the room.

Oxford, Miss., September 30. It was mid-afternoon. Sheriff J. W. Ford sat at his desk in the white stucco courthouse answering telephone calls. The sheriff was urging vigilante groups from Texas, Louisiana, Alabama and Georgia to stay home. They had called to offer armed assistance to Mississippi.[5]

It's quiet for a while. But into the evening the radio traffic picks up and the telephone calls both at my desk and down the hall increase. The callers are senior staff asking questions about the status of our units and where they're located on the base.

The corridors get noisy and busy with messengers coming and going and radio and telephone operators calling out, "The Pentagon is on the phone, sir," and "General Abrams calling."

I'm off to the side in my little room, but I can hear one radio transmission. It's a request for tear gas, from whom and to whom I have no idea. A senior officer comes into the room and says that my battalion colonel is to be in an emergency meeting in five minutes. I rouse Colonel Brice, who has retired to an adjacent room. He's tried to catch some sleep after thirty-six hours without any. He dresses quickly and walks out and down the hallway.

I feel a growing apprehension. How to respond to any number of questions. Where is my platoon? Are they ready for this, whatever it is? How are they equipped?

I'm interested, but somehow don't feel involved . . . still an observer.

"The eyes of the nation and all the world . . ."

The White House, 2000 hours (Oxford time), September 30. Someone down the corridor calls out that the president's on the television. I

do a few quick jump-steps from my desk and find myself standing
outside the door of an already crowded adjoining office. A TV set
on a table against a wall is on, loud. It's so packed inside the room
that I can't see in. I stay out in the hallway—staring down at my
boots—and listen to Kennedy's voice.

> The orders of the court in the case of Meredith v. Fair[6] are begin-
> ning to be carried out. Mr. James Meredith is now in residence
> on the campus of the University of Mississippi. This had been
> accomplished thus far without the use of National Guard or
> other troops.[7]

> Ole Miss Campus. This odd thing happened: Shortly after the
> President started speaking, the State troopers who had accom-
> panied the marshals drove off the campus. I saw 43 cars in one
> convoy, bumper to bumper, on their way out. They came back
> later and then left again.[8]

> Americans are free, in short, to disagree with the law, but not
> to disobey it. For, in a government of laws and not of men . . .
> no mob, however unruly or boisterous, is entitled to defy a
> court of law.
>   [The Court] made clear the fact the enforcement of its order
> had become an obligation of the United States Government. . . .
> My obligation under the Constitution . . . was and is to implement
> the orders of the court with whatever means are necessary, and
> with as little force and civil disorder as the circumstances permit.
> It was for this reason that I federalized the Mississippi National
> Guard as the most appropriate instrument, should any be needed,
> to preserve law and order while United States marshals carried
> out the orders of the court.

As [Kennedy] spoke, the campus exploded in violence. A
length of heavy pipe came hurtling through the air. It struck
a marshal's helmeted head. As though on signal, there

erupted a rain of rocks, bricks, bottles—anything that could be thrown.[9]

I deeply regret the fact that any action by the executive branch was necessary in this case, but all other avenues and alternatives, including persuasion and conciliation, had been tried and exhausted. . . . The eyes of the nation and all the world are upon you and upon all of us, and the honor of your university and State are in the balance. I am certain the great majority of the students will uphold that honor.

Inside the YMCA Building across an oak-shaded grove from the Lyceum, a group of students watched Mr. Kennedy on a nationwide television hookup. . . .

Listeners began to rub their eyes. The first wave of tear gas sifted into the building. Its occupants were startled and their coughing drowned out the President's closing words.[10]

Let us preserve both the law and the peace and then, healing those wounds that are within, we can turn to the greater crises that are without and stand united as one people in our pledge to man's freedom.
Thank you and good night.

I can't hear the speech very well, but it's another briefing of sorts and from no less than the commander in chief himself. He didn't mention us here in Memphis. It's a strange sensation to stand in this hallway and hear the president of the United States talk on television about a problem in a town not far from where we are. For the first time I sense that we may get further involved. Are we to be part of a story or not? The TV set in the now-emptied-out dayroom is still on, but it's only video. It's running pictures of a black man walking with two or three white men, with suits. He's wearing a dark suit and tie. I guess it's Meredith. He doesn't look like a college student, North or South. I look at my watch—2015 hours.

Another hour drags on. The TV in the rec room is now off. I go back to a copy of an old *Memphis Press-Scimitar*.

> *Millington Naval Air Station, Tenn., September 30.* Meanwhile, as early as eight-forty, Oxford time, General Billingslea [now formally designated as the field commander] . . . received instructions to move a force of 800 to 1,000 National Guardsmen to Oxford to reinforce the marshals. [One hour later.] As the general situation at the Lyceum worsened, the authorities called for more troops, and at nine-thirty-three . . . Secretary Vance ordered General Billingslea to initiate movement of Regular Army military police units in numbers he deemed necessary to support the federal marshals in Oxford.[11]

"We need more tear gas."

Colonel Brice comes back down the corridor from his meeting.

"Alert the battalion," he says in his Oklahoma drawl. "Have them saddle up, we're under a movement order."

His voice has no urgency or emotion in it—could've been telling me to pass on the name of the movie that's going to be shown tonight at the base theater. I send a battalion runner over to the gymnasium to relay the order.

> *Ole Miss campus.* By now, the mob was getting completely out of hand. You could hear the crunch of automobiles being wrecked. Someone commandeered an automobile and sent it, driverless, roaring full throttle toward the line of marshals. It swerved to the side and crashed into a tree.
>
> Out of the night, a bulldozer came grinding across the campus toward the marshals. Somebody launched a tear-gas bomb onto the seat, and the driver jumped off. The bulldozer stalled short of its target.[12]

I look at the colonel.

"Sir, permission to return to my platoon?"

"No, stay here a little longer, I may need you. You're still my OD. I've got to go into another meeting."

By now there's a lot of activity in the nearby offices, including loud voices and two-way radio noise. I catch bits of shouts: "marshals under siege," "the mob," and "we need more tear gas."

Ole Miss campus. Suddenly, around 10 o'clock local time, the whole character of the mob started to change. The students, most of them, left the campus and hurried away to dormitories and houses. Quickly, their places were taken by a nondescript-looking mob of toughs—rioters with ducktail haircuts who wore leather jackets and cowboy boots. They looked like professional bullyboys, and the riot took on a more menacing character.[13]

After a few minutes Colonel Brice comes back into the room.

"The movement's under way. We're going to Mississippi. You'll be my lead jeep in the battalion convoy." He adds, "One of your sergeants can handle your platoon. You're taking us down to Oxford."

All I can say is a very slow, "Yes, sir," as I stand up at the desk and look at him. *OK, here we go.*

My mood swings this late afternoon into early evening have gone from boredom to curiosity, then to concern, and, now, to apprehension. We're involved. What are we getting into?

A clock over on the wall says 2215 hours.

I pick up the phone and call over to C Company and give the duty NCO the name of one of my sergeants who'll take over the platoon. I ask that a jeep with driver report to me and with a radio operator. At the gymnasium, the troops are directed to turn in any live ammunition they may be carrying. Steel pots are passed around, platoon by platoon, to collect it all. Not everyone complies with the order. "Damn right, they didn't get mine," some would later say.

I follow Colonel Brice out into the crowded hallway and shout over the noise, "Sir, I need some maps to guide this battalion convoy. Where can I get them?"

A captain comes up with an urgent message for the colonel. I can't tell what it is. He turns. I stand behind him, waiting for an answer.

He turns back to me. A grimace is on his face.

"We don't have any maps."

"Sir?" *You've got to be kidding.*

He looks over my shoulder at a distraction. Runs a hand through his hair and looks at me. He's tired. Maybe he thinks that the matter (no maps) is resolved because I remain silent. Actually, I'm speechless.

"Do your best, Hank."

So, there it is. The familiar phrase sinks in. Heard it in high school from teachers and coaches . . . but here? And the use of a first name and not my rank sounds like asking a favor rather than giving an order. I stand there and can say nothing. *Colonel, this is game day and we haven't a clue how to even get to the field.*

The HQ (headquarters) staff officers are rushing back and forth in the hallway, but at the moment I don't see them, nor do I hear any of the clatter. I've just been in a lieutenant-to-lieutenant colonel exchange. Now, I want just an Emmett-and-me kind of talk. But I don't get one and can't have one. Colonel Brice just stares at me. I know. *You're the colonel and I'm the second lieutenant.*

He turns and goes down the hallway.

I just stand there. Here we are, about to embark on a sensitive mission in the middle of the night—to a town I'm told is a hundred miles away—and the U.S. Army has *no maps* showing us how to get there!

I like maps. I even teach a course on map reading back at Dix. I'm sure that the U.S. Army has maps showing where the Russians will be massed against the NATO troops on the plains of Central Europe. The maps will be in great detail, maybe even down to the location of fire hydrants and park benches.

But not here? A map for the U.S. A-R-M-Y to get to a crisis in our own country? I'm being asked—no, ordered—to *do my best* as I tell my driver when he should turn left, *no* right, *no* . . . I mean . . . *go straight* ahead toward this town one state down from here. OK, it's trial and error. Well, OK, that is, if we're one jeep; we can turn around and backtrack. But it's not so good when we're followed by 140 other jeeps and assorted trucks, all following bumper-to-bumper. *No wonder second lieutenants are so expendable . . . and in peacetime too.*

Who would've thought? Don't state highway patrols have road maps? They do and we don't? (I later find out that we won't be the first unit to leave the base for Oxford tonight. But they, the 503rd MP battalion, at least had some advance notice—and practiced riot-control formations back at Bragg. Bet they had maps, too.)

A sergeant overhearing the conversation with Colonel Brice comes up to me while I'm still out in the hallway. He says that the army did a series of aerial photos of the campus from a helicopter a few days ago and offers them to me. I thank him and say that we need to get to the town first. We're still someplace in Tennessee.

I walk down the hallway and out through a screen door to meet PFC Ronald Barrett, just pulling up. He knows nothing about the movement order, nor about his new role as the lead jeep driver.

"Private Barrett, we need a map to show us how to get to this town of Oxford that they've been talking about in Mississippi, not too far from here. We're at the southern edge of Tennessee. We need it because we're going to be the lead jeep in the convoy going down there. And guess who drives and guess who watches?" *OK . . . a little comic relief now and then, Barrett.*

It's hard to describe the look on his face.

"Seaman Jarrell . . . Get into this jeep."

My older brother, a former army enlisted man, told me how second lieutenants should act in front of enlisted men in moments when quick decision making is required. He said that the only thing I need to remember is that, in their presence (even if only one soldier), I shouldn't hesitate in the face of a problem. Don't show indecision. If I have to make a decision, just make one—right or wrong—but just do it. Hesitation is worse than doubt.

Barrett looks at me. From the doorstep of the barracks complex, I can see the neon lights of a Phillips 66 filling station just outside a base fence and across a multilane highway. Open late on a Sunday night.

"Let's go over there."

We drive out through the gate toward the station. Into the South. Not yet the Deep South, but border-state South. Upper South, I guess they call it.

Up to this time tonight, I might be on any military post or base in the country. Our battalion moved last night from an army post to an air force base to a naval air station, without a hint of a move from the North to the South. They're all look-alike enclaves, where lines of authority are clear to those inside the gates (or, walls to a draftee). It's all about uniformity.

There's a reason why our service clothes are called uniforms. Sameness and regularity. Armies don't go off to wars with men who get to choose their own wardrobes. This is one place where clothes don't make the man and no second lieutenant has to pick out a tie that goes with a shirt or suit that first morning on the job. The army tells him that everything "goes with" olive drab (OD) on olive drab.

The only individual identity each soldier can protect is hidden in his foot locker on the floor at the foot of his bunk bed. Other than that, uniformity is the order of the day and the leveler for everyone who enters the military. Doesn't matter if your family has money and you have a college degree, you're still sitting on a toilet seat in an open latrine (think: no stalls) next to a guy who has neither. The food in the mess hall is the same, North or South (although grits might be served more at Fort Benning, Georgia, than at Fort Dix, New Jersey). Vehicles, workplace clothes and accessories, tools, all are OD, the olive drab color of the service. (Before the T-shirts of the Vietnam era came out in OD, we at least had one hold on civilian life—the white at the top peeking out from behind the fatigue shirt.) Our life is OD. And the uniformity of army life continues as privates salute lieutenants and lieutenants salute captains and on up the chain, be they black, Hispanic, Asian, or white.

But now, if only briefly, I'm away from those familiar trappings and customs. I'm out in civilian land, where the rules are different, particularly in this part of the land. After six years, I'm back in the South.

By crossing the highway, I'm where I was when I hitchhiked through the South in 1956 with my best high school friend. This time I'm no longer the teenager I was walking into a filling station on the outskirts of Memphis, looking for a map to get me up to St. Louis, on our way back home to Minnesota before our money ran out. But I am once again walking into a gas station in the same town, again looking for directions.

We turn into the driveway that leads up to the station. In full army battle gear, gas mask strapped to my left leg, .45 in a holster on my right hip, steel pot on my head, I walk through the door to face a night clerk sitting behind a counter.

He looks up at me from his magazine.

"Hi, I need a Mississippi highway map . . . but the kind that also shows a small strip of Tennessee at its top edge, you know, this Memphis area . . ."

He keeps his eye on me as he does a quick jump-down from his stool.

"So I can get down to the Mississippi state line from here, starting from this filling station, OK?"

He scurries along behind the counter and mumbles something I can't make out as he reaches over to a rack of maps in front of me. He peeks around it and offers me a State of Mississippi road map and asks if it will do. He steps back, places both hands on his hips, and glances down at the .45. I take the map without looking at it. I trust him. I'm more embarrassed to be doing this than he is startled to be doing it.

Can you wonder what he's thinking? *A map? An army looking for its way? What's next, a free fill-up for his jeep from one of my pumps outside?* In any event, he'll have a story to tell his grandchildren—how he helped out a Yankee soldier in full combat gear find his way down the road one night.

I can't understand what he says, but thank him and walk back out to the jeep. I'd better learn how they talk down here. I guess where we're going tonight I'll be hearing a lot of words spoken the way this guy just spoke. But maybe to him and to the people down the road we're going, we sound funny.

As we cross back over the highway lanes and turn to go through the base gate, I see that it's being manned by an SP (navy shore patrolman). He's out in front of a small gatehouse, directing what little traffic there is moving in and out of the base on his "graveyard" shift.

"Ron, pull over where that navy man is."

We stop just in front of him. I get out and walk around the front of the jeep. He sees my rank, a gold bar from another branch of the military service, but knows to salute. As I unfold the map and place it on the hood, I look at the name stenciled on his shirt. OK, Jarrell.

"Jarrell, sorry, I'm army . . . your rank?"

"Seaman, sir."

"OK, can you point out Oxford, Mississippi, on this map?"

He looks young, maybe just out of high school, and appears to have manners that his parents gave him long before the navy got him. He quickly offers to help and says so in an accent that is thicker than the one the gas station guy had. He looks down at the map and points with his flashlight.

"Sir, y'all need to go south down this highway here—from my gate along the edge of Memphis [pointing]—then on to the Mississippi line right here."

Good, he knows the area.

A few cars come up to the gate. He looks up from the map and waves them through. Then looks back at me. I thank him and he salutes. I get back into the jeep and we start back toward the gate when I catch myself. *Wait, wait!*

Yes, that's it. *Jarrell! Seaman Jarrell. Southern accent. A local. Yes!*

"Ron, stop, turn back!"

I look back over. He stands half in, half out of his gatehouse. *Jarrell, you're our man.*

"Seaman Jarrell, I'm under orders to be the lead jeep for a large U.S. Army convoy that's to come out through this gate in a few minutes, on its way to that town in Mississippi."

"Yes, sir?" He's still so gawd-awful polite.

"See all those headlights lined up over there along that side road . . . just inside the gate?"

He looks at me out of his doorway and then glances over the fence into the base.

"Yes, sir?"

"Look, we're all from up north. We don't have the foggiest idea where we are right now or where this town of Oxford is in Mississippi. I know you're navy and we're army, OK?"

"Yes, sir?" A puzzled look was beginning to grow on his face.

I remember my brother's words about hesitation being worse than doubt. I start to hesitate—catch myself—and then make up my mind.

"You're coming with us," I blurt out.

I'm as surprised as is the sailor, Barrett too, at what I just said. I say it before I realize what I have just said.

"Sir?"

"Yes, you've got to come with us."

"Sir, with all due respect, you're an officer, but, you're kidding . . . right, sir? I can't do that. I mean . . . I'm on duty here at this gate. My watch officer, well . . . he'll go crazy wondering what happened to me when he shows up for his night check. It's an AWOL offense, sir. Besides you're army, I'm navy."

Jarrell's words come on fast, even for a southerner.

"I mean, I'll show you on the map again. I'll draw the way how to get there. I really will, sir." He points to the map that I still hold in my hands.

As he's talking, which begins to sound like pleading, he glances back at his tiny wooden guardhouse as if he could flee there for refuge.

Things are rushing in my head. I hear him, but I'm not listening. Too busy fast-thinking by now. Too much delay already. I look back over my shoulder at the string of headlights inside the fence waiting for Barrett and me to get the hell out of this base and on our way.

Awkward. *Say anything, but be forceful ... make it a direct order. Yes, that's it, an order.*

For good reason, officers are supposed to remove the word "please" from their vocabulary when talking to enlisted ranks. Never mind that I've just given an order to an enlisted man who's not even in the same branch of the service that I'm in.

Again, the voice of my brother: "Just do it!"

"Seaman Jarrell, we're under orders from President Kennedy. This is a direct order to you. Get into this jeep."

I motion to Barrett who comes up and around the front of the jeep and points the sailor to the back seat. Jarrell is too startled to say anything, much less protest anymore. It looks like MPs are trained to nudge otherwise reluctant people to do things. Ron appears to have nudged Jarrell right into the back seat of the jeep.

We race back through the gate, aiming directly at the front of a long string of headlights. One part of me says that I just got our insurance man for this uncertain drive tonight. The other part of me says that I just kidnapped a sailor.

"Hey, y'all, just what are we all getting into, anyway?"

The 716th, with the engines of all the vehicles running, is massed up along an interior base road. Ready. Barrett backs the jeep into place at the head of the convoy. Neither of us has ever seen such a gathering of the complete battalion before, except for maybe a few of the veteran members at a retirement ceremony on the parade field back at Dix.

The assembled body is made up of three fully manned companies, supported by a headquarters detachment, all in jeeps, with the deuce-and-a-halfs and smaller trucks behind, 140 in all, carrying 650 officers and men.

While in the line, we learn that a part of one of the other MP units that arrived at the base this morning, the 503rd MP Battalion from Fort Bragg, will be airlifted to Oxford by helicopter and that the balance of the unit will go by road like us.

I leave the jeep and walk over to a group of lieutenants on a grass strip near the front of the convoy. It's just us, the most junior of officers talking with each other. The time-honored military protocol "prohibits" nearby enlisted men from wandering over into "officer country" and joining us. And, for that matter, it's a custom that also prevents majors, and even captains, from joining in the lieutenant-talk, as if they would want to. No one really small-talks with lieutenants in the army—except other lieutenants.

We stand around, maybe waiting to see a major, or even a captain, come up in the dark and tell us what's going on. No one shows. In the army, senior officer types do the leader things, and we junior officer types do the follower things. For us, there's no box outside of which we might think, as there is in the civilian world or under the demands of wartime combat. Thus, with no leading in sight, there is no following.

"Hank, where'd you go off to?"

"The colonel's got me as the lead jeep . . .went out looking for a map. Found one at that filling station over—"

"They didn't have one for you?"

"A map to where?"

"To this town . . . Oxford . . . in Mississippi, where we're going . . . where this riot's going on."

"OK . . . hey, maybe someone should point me in the direction of Mississi—"

"So it's a riot now?"

"Been one for a while, I hear."

"Yeah? What's going on down there?"

"Where's Sergeant Connolly? He'll know."

"Where's the new colonel?"

"In meetings all day."

"I heard we even got some infantry-type lieutenants to help fill out our ranks."

"Sure, so what are we going to do when we get there, take some kind of hill behind this 'Audie Murphy' guy shouting, 'Follow me'?"[14]

So there it is! The uncertainty. The mind-boggling absence of any clear orders. That's the worst part. Just who and what is at the end of this road we're about to drive down? By now our senior officers must surely know the full extent of the crisis. The NCOs—the ones we rely on so often—are spread back up all along the convoy line. But even they have no clue tonight.

> *Ole Miss campus.* The mob pressed forward toward the Lyceum, jeering at the marshals. Eggs and lighted cigarettes arched onto the three army trucks parked before the building. A student wrenched the fire extinguisher from the cab of one of the trucks and fired it into the face of the Negro driver. Other students slashed at the tires. A state patrolman stood by, grinning.[15]

The mob seems to be a mixture of nonstudents and students, and not all of those who are students come from the University of Mississippi.

Our talk becomes strained and animated. I can't say that we're anxious, anxiety being a state of worry. Here, it's more like low-level nervous excitement, like high school kids in a locker room with pregame jitters. Adrenaline. But it's really worse than a locker room. The players at least have practiced out on the field for the kind of game that they're about to enter. We're trained, but for what? We don't even know where the field is, barely the name of its town. But whatever it is, we just want to get moving and do whatever we have to do when we get to this town. Movement itself will be reassuring.

Our talking is not really "conversation," any more than locker room babble is. The words of one speaker are stepped on by the words of another. We're not really talking to each other. The words just puddle up on the ground.

"Hey, Lieutenant Horten coming down with us? He'll love it. We're close to Texas, aren't we? He's—"

"Who's gotta light?"

"No, he got out . . . back in the civilian world. Last Monday. Driving that Mustang with the top down through the streets of Lubbock right now."

"Probably listening about this thing on his car radio. Wishing he was in on it."

"Thought you didn't smoke."

"None of this stuff's on the radio. This thing's super secret. Called my wife. She didn't hear anything and she thinks she always knows what's—"

"Didn't smoke until tonight. Gimmie your Zippo."

"Hey, you're right. No reporters or cameras last night over at McGuire?"

Darkness adds to the suspense and the anticipation.

Most of us are smoking cigarettes. It's a national pastime, more so in the military. Starts in boot camp, along with coffee. "*Smoke 'em if you got 'em.*" The army orders teenagers to become men and the culture encourages *real* men to smoke. Kind of like memorizing the first swear words you hear from the big kids on the playground. As for a lot of junior officers, we're simply continuing a college habit—for me even earlier. But tonight, we're not smoking them— just sucking on them, fast-puffing. Some of the choices are Pall Mall and Marlboro, or whatever there is at the Dix PX (post exchange) these days. I put a lighted cigarette in my mouth backwards. Excitement and nerves will do that.

Ole Miss campus. It was 11 P.M. when the first contingent of troops moved in. Troop "E," a 50-man unit of the Oxford National Guard, rolled onto the campus in jeeps and three canvas-topped trucks—Capt. Murray C. Falkner, a Jackson insurance salesman and distant relative of the late author, Oxford's William Faulkner, was in command of Troop "E." Lt. Bobby

Crow, a University of Mississippi student, was with the troops
who joined the marshals at the Lyceum.[16]

Another lieutenant, dressed in his usual baggy fatigues, comes
over. He goes through his cigarette ritual, this time with fingers
shaking. He keeps slamming the top of a pack into the palm of
his left hand. Then pulls at the cellophane tab with a fingernail,
finds it, and rips off the strip. Picks at the cigarettes inside, finds
one, and tears off a piece of its thin end paper. Tries again to pull
it out, moves on to a second one, gets it out and offers it around to
any one of us. No takers, so he lights it up with his Zippo, throws
his head back while sucking in the smoke, blows it out, and, in
Louisiana-speak, says, "Hey, y'all, just what are we all getting into,
anyway?"

A veteran staff sergeant in career-tailored fatigues comes down
the line.

"Well, let's go, Lieutenants. Christ, what's the stall now?" he
asks. "For God's sake, this guy Meredith may be dead by now." He
moves on in the dark.

"I heard parts of the 503rd went out by chopper a while ago, a
lieutenant buddy of mine with them told me that—"

"Hey, who are the bad guys?" a voice in the cluster asks. "Maybe
we're just going to get in front of a bunch of pissed-off white students who don't like a Negro in their school and us helping him do
just that."

"It'll be like Little Rock, right?[17] Not much, a little pushing. Just a
show of force, a few rocks thrown, no real violence, right? I mean—"

"Sure, a show of force," a second voice joins in.

"You know, like they did there, soldiers escorting students into a
school building, so this thing here's the same. Hey! It's just one guy
who—"

"B-o-o-l-shit! No violence? Hell! I hear some of the marshals on
the campus are getting hit pretty bad by a mob . . . out-of-state rioters, mostly . . . not students."

So here we are—one or two years from our college ROTC commissions—about to get into something we could not have imagined

eighteen months earlier when we were taking our senior exams in schools around the country.

Ole Miss campus. By now, the riot was turning into total violence. More guns appeared. Out in the dark night, we could hear the intermittent chatter of small-arms fire.

A sniper climbed into a tree. A marshal fell, shot through the throat. A newsman took a burst of birdshot in the shoulder. Someone shouted, "Burn the Kennedys and the niggers!"[18]

The newly called-up reserve captain in our battalion violates the lieutenants-only protocol and comes over.

"I have to take a shit I'm so nervous." Why he has to share that with us, I don't know.

One of the lieutenants said, "Captain, you can go over there in one of those ditches." He disappears into the dark.

Another lieutenant looks over at my jeep.

"Hank, what the hell's that sailor doing in your jeep?"

Before I can answer, a quick rush of words comes from outside our little circle of talk. It's one of the senior sergeants, warning us that another order has just come down from battalion. He looks over his shoulder and in the darkness another enlisted comes over to our cluster. In a tone meant to be hushed, but one that comes out loud, the second soldier says, "Sirs, all Negroes in the battalion are ordered to fall out of formation. Regroup over there on the side of the road" (pointing).

"Corporal Russell, what'd you say?"

He doesn't answer, but just rushes on down the line, his silhouette flickering against the headlights of the jeeps.

"I refuse to step back, sir."

No one speaks. We look up at each other. Silence. Then we break and move back to our jeeps. I go up to ours at the front of the line and tell Barrett and the sailor about this latest order. Jarrell stares at me while my driver jerks his head away and looks out toward the lights at the gate.

The highest-ranking black in our battalion, a respected captain and friend, is Captain Linwood Hardmon, a 1959 ROTC graduate of Howard University, one of our four company commanders tonight. Colonel Brice walks over to him.

"Linwood, I want all the Negroes in the battalion, officers and enlisted men, to fall out and form up under your command."

The Cold War U.S. Army is not the same one as its successor during the Vietnam era will be, weighted with minorities and high school drop-outs. It more accurately reflects the 1962 demographics of American society outside the Fort Dix gates.

Many of the enlisted men come from their cities' white ethnic neighborhoods—the Italian and Irish sections of Baltimore, New York, and Boston. While they may go their separate ways in off-duty hours to nearby bars and clubs in towns that surround Dix, the enlisted ranks, white and nonwhite, all go on patrol, train, complain, and laugh together. For many of the whites, it's the first time in their lives that they've been in close contact with blacks and vice versa.

> Many of us had never met anyone from other parts of our country, or, in some cases, other parts of the cities we lived in. Our civilian life revolved around the neighborhood that we lived in and the friends that we had.[19]

But to every private who enters the army, his sergeant is not white, black, Hispanic, or Asian. His sergeant is his sergeant. Their introduction to army life means not only a leveling of egos, but a suppression, if not elimination, of racial biases.

As for the officers of the 716th, white and nonwhite alike, we all work together while on duty. Race, at least outwardly, is not an issue. We socialize together off duty, at the officers' club and in our homes (on post and off post). While these occasions might be first-time experiences for many of the northerners, they certainly are new ones for the junior officers and their wives from the

South—and initially awkward for them. Such events might be seen by an outsider as a form of forced socialization at the colonel's call. But it is not forced. We're the U.S. Army. We're together as a battalion, black and white officers, and at parties we all drink from the same beer keg, even though such social race-mixing has yet to reach many of our hometowns, civilian workplaces, and residential neighborhoods.

So the new order about the step-back of blacks has a stunning effect on all of us.

In our battalion tonight, each of the three companies, as well as the headquarters detachment, contains a small number of African American enlisted personnel, from high school dropouts to college-educated men. In addition to Captain Hardmon, a disproportionate number are in leadership roles as NCOs. It's fair to say that many of them found a home in the desegregated army.

> In order to function as a cohesive unit there really was no place for the race card. We had to have each others' backs if we were going to get through this together. We did not see ourselves as black soldiers or white soldiers, but as soldiers just doing our job together.[20]

We stare over in silence while the black soldiers leave their jeeps and trucks and fall into formation off to the side of the road at the direction of Captain Hardmon's new and unique command.

All do so, but for one.

A mid-rank black sergeant remains in formation at ramrod attention, staring straight ahead. It's dark and we can hear more than we can see. Some of us nearby can pick up his words. He speaks in a voice both strong and pained.

"I'm a noncommissioned officer in the United States Army. I served my country in Korea. I took an oath to do my duty in this man's army. I refuse to step back, sir."

We try not to look over. The black captain comes over and walks up to the black sergeant. The white colonel joins him. The nearby ranks step aside to make room.

I hear them talking, some of it agitated. Then, Captain Hardmon lowers his voice and says something that none of us can hear, but probably something that these two African American soldiers will remember for the rest of their lives.

After a few tense moments, the sergeant falls out of the formation, tears running down his face, as he joins the other blacks off to the side. It's a group that includes two company commanders, a first sergeant, a communications sergeant, and several NCOs.

The officers are immediately concerned about troop morale and a breakdown of small unit leadership within the battalion as a result of this last order.

(One of our sister MP battalions, the 503rd, disobeyed the desegregation order—for them, called the "leave-behind" order—that it received while still at Fort Bragg. Their senior officers said that such an order would decimate the battalion of first sergeants and platoon sergeants. "In violation of direct orders approved by the attorney general of the United States, [it] took off for action . . . with every one of its black soldiers."[21])

We're puzzled, but can only guess why the order was issued. Someone from headquarters comes along and tells a few of us that the situation has gotten so bad on the Ole Miss campus that to send in the army with black soldiers in the ranks would inflame the mob even more. They might be singled out by snipers who reportedly have positioned themselves high up in trees at the riot site.

So it may not be like Little Rock. This time the army is going into an unstable situation, one that has already resulted in many injuries. Apparently the command wants no more flash points.

At that moment, we're not aware of another MP troop movement occurring over on a runway of the base at that same time (2350 hours).

Millington Naval Air Station, Tenn. Nineteen single-rotor Sikorsky Mojave helicopters stuffed with MPs [Co. A, 503 MP Battalion] began lifting off for Oxford in three-minute intervals. Inside the aircraft [the men] struggled to open boxes full of chemical gas grenades. . . . The MPs stuffed the grenades into their pockets and checked their M-1 rifles, riot shotguns, and gas masks. . . .[22]

I walk over to the colonel to see if there are any last minute instructions. No, that's it. Minutes later, a directive comes over my radio.

"Golf 1, this is Example 6. Commence the movement. Over."

"Example 6, Golf 1. Roger. Out."

The now all-white 716th Military Police Battalion, with the addition of one white sailor, slowly angles out through the gate of the Millington Naval Air Station on its way to Mississippi.

My watch says 0015 hours, Monday morning, October 1.

3

THE DEEP SOUTH

Welcome to Mississippi—the Magnolia State

Barrett angles the jeep slowly through the gate and turns left out onto the highway. We're guided by newly posted navy shore patrol where minutes earlier one of our passengers had been on duty. Jarrell is hunkered down in the back of our jeep, trying not to be seen as we pass out of the base.

Civilian traffic is being held back. We're escorted by a navy truck and a few Tennessee highway patrolmen on motorcycles. As a rule, long military convoys move slowly in the far right lanes of highways. Now occupants in civilian cars, few in number, slow down and stare over at us as they pass by. They may be used to seeing weekend convoys of Tennessee guardsmen on their roads, but not at this hour. Had they been listening to the evening news, they might have found out why we we're on the road tonight moving south toward Mississippi.

I tell Jarrell that we won't take him very far, only until I have some assurance that we're on the right road after we cross the state line. Even though we have a Mississippi map, it might be an old one. I want real-time human help. A few miles later, the headlights catch a sign that says, *Welcome to Mississippi—the Magnolia State.* Our Tennessee escorts drop off. We're on our own. No transfer to any Mississippi highway patrolmen waiting to pick up the escort duty. I wonder why. One of the missions of a military police unit is "to provide liaison with state and local law enforcement agencies." Well, for some reason, none here. Maybe farther down the road.

When we cross the state line, I finally feel that I've gone from the North to the South. And if there is a Deep South, we have just arrived in it after passing through the Upper South.

Jarrell tells me that he can take me to a town called Holly Springs. His voice is a confident one now, as he says that the town is a few miles down and east from where we are. Then, it'll be a direct route south to Oxford. He's sounding more like one of us now, only a little less confused than we are. But beyond the immediate task we've asked of him, I wonder what he's thinking about all of this, our coming down here into his South. Is he navy tonight, or a southerner? Or both?

Mississippi. We're now on the same road that I took on the 1956 hitchhiking trip when my friend and I cut through the northeast corner of this state. Before that, the only sure thing I knew about Mississippi was how to spell it. Well, that and the one football poll that had Minnesota and Mississippi sharing the national collegiate title in 1960.

But earlier. It was something that all of us in Hiawatha Grade School had to memorize and repeat out loud as we stood alongside our desks. We spelled the letters out in unison for Miss Horkey, MISS . . . ISS. . . , the big river of our childhood that flowed by our school but three blocks and one woods away.

Ole Miss campus, October 1, early morning. The madness grew. Lights shining from the Lyceum illuminated clouds of gas and silhouetted wave after wave of attackers running behind Confederate flags. The flare of burning cars would catch a student in full Confederate uniform. It was not James Meredith who was the target that night—it was the Yankees, the Federal Government that had conquered the South and was about to inflict James Meredith on them.[1]

Here we are, a large U.S. Army unit moving down a highway. To the untrained eye looking at us on this night, that's all we are, a bunch of soldiers in a convoy. But in truth, we're a self-contained, self-sustaining community, a completely organic village.

We have our own food, supplies, water, clothing, and sleeping accommodations. Add to this our own radio/communications network, POL (petroleum, oil, and lubricants), and vehicle repair shop. Membership "benefits" in this army battalion also give us a restaurant (mess hall), a preacher (chaplain), even a barber, and, of course, our own police force. In military-speak, our mobile village has become fully "augmented," now that we have included other army branches, that is, a lawyer (from the Judge Advocate General Corps) and a doctor (from the Medical Corps) with an ambulance.

The only missing components of such a village are women and children. This "Army of the North" is a portable town about to move into (and on top of) a permanent town down the road.

Yet, with all the confidence that such a "community" can have, and even with the aid of a map and the advice of our local kidnap victim, it's still a bit unnerving. We're moving along a dark, empty, two-lane Mississippi highway, now well beyond midnight. No taillights in front of me and more than 140 pairs of bright headlights behind me.

By morning we will become an unwanted visitor to a small college town of sixty-eight hundred souls. We will end up like the house guest who stays well beyond the socially acceptable three days after which even fish begin to smell.

Fragments of voices sputter in and out over the radio net from platoons reporting their benchmark locations along the way. It's normal communication procedure and it's reassuring at least to know that the battalion vehicles are still closing in behind us. Well . . . it's reassuring if this is the right road. The radio is the only comforting sound now. It's like the comfort one had as a kid on the long car ride home at night, squeezing up into the front seat with Mom and Dad to listen to the sounds coming from the radio that glowed plastic-yellow on the dashboard of the old Chevy.

Conversation in the jeep is minimal because of the constant radio chatter that we have to monitor, no clearer than the scratchy voice of a bus station loudspeaker. The noise from a faulty muffler makes the transmissions even harder to understand, not to mention the leaking exhaust fumes that make breathing uncomfortable. But we're also quiet for more anxious reasons—keeping our thoughts to ourselves, each of us trying to imagine our role when this convoy arrives at its destination. Jarrell, our guest passenger, is also silent.

We soon reach the outskirts of a town marked by a sign that says Holly Springs. A few lit street lamps on the approach, but no lights on in any of the houses. The South is asleep. A couple of barking dogs come out to welcome the Yankees.

Jarrell leans up. "Lieutenant, all you have to do is turn right once you're in the town center and then keep on that road. That'll be state Highway 7. You can't miss Oxford."

"Good, Jarrell . . . thanks."

"Sir, can I get out here and return to my base?"

"Can you find a way back hitching a ride at this time of the morning?"

I don't want to let him go—my one human link to the South tonight—but I have no choice.

He says he can.

"Ron, pull over up there, slowly. Give everyone behind us a chance to see what we're doing."

I turn back to our guest passenger.

"Well, good luck and thanks, Jarrell. We really appreciate the navy helping the army tonight."

Barrett slowly edges the jeep over onto the shoulder. In turn, the convoy vehicles begin to curl over in a slow bumper-to-bumper chain reaction. Our sailor friend jumps out and runs across the oncoming lane. I look back and think that here's another southerner, besides that guy back at the Phillips 66, who'll have something to tell his grandchildren. Even more so in the case of Jarrell—how he was kidnapped by a bunch of Yankee soldiers one night.

From the far shoulder the seaman turns around, stands at attention, and salutes me with a shout. "Good luck, sir."

There are some moments in life that one will hold onto for a while. That's one of them. We start up again. Years later, I'll wish that I could send him a thank-you note.

Ole Miss campus, October 1, 0100 hours. The battle rages on, with snipers added. Four bullets embed themselves in the paneling around the Lyceum's white front door. "Get away from that door," a marshal shouts. "He has us zeroed in."[2]

The convoy slows down again and rolls into Holly Springs. We come into a square in the center of the town, dark but for dusty circles of light on the street from the overheads at two of its corners. It seems that we're the only people awake during this crossover Sunday night–Monday morning. All sensible God-fearing people in the town are asleep in their beds, unaware that Yankees are sneaking through. But I'm sure that lights will be switched on after some of the big deuce-and-a-halfs in the vehicle-train rumble through the square and downshift around the corners, and when the sputtering from the exhaust pipes comes in through bedroom windows.

A Necklace of Headlights

We turn out of the square at a Highway 7 marker and pass a sign that reads, "Oxford 31 miles." It's the first tangible evidence that I've not gotten the battalion lost. I think of Jarrell's "Good luck, sir." We've had luck to this point, into Mississippi as far as Holly Springs. But I also know that there's more miles to go to get to our destination on this country road. In the dark. We're going so slowly—maybe on the road for more than two hours now, not even the sound of a barking dog. But at least we have the comfort of movement. At least we're not standing in a circle of talking lieutenants back at the navy base; we're going toward some place up this road.

"Ron, looks like we're late for this party. Do you think they'll leave a light on for us?"

"Sir?"

"Never mind."

It starts to rain, a cold drizzle. Back at McGuire the canvas tops for the jeeps had to be removed for the C-130 load-on. The tops were not stowed in the jeeps. To avoid soaking in the slow drizzle, some men cover themselves with poncho liners while others zip up sleeping bags around themselves and try to sit upright, cocoon-like, in their seats.

We find ourselves moving down another two-lane road, but now a narrower one that follows the contours of the hill country of northeast Mississippi, unlike the straight line we took from Memphis to Holly Springs back on Highway 78. It seems that this "highway" hardly deserves an official number. So narrow.

Back roads in New Jersey outside Dix are not like this one. Nor is this like the roads out from Minneapolis into farm country. This is truly a back road, as if it belongs, not to the state of Mississippi, but to some farmer around here and we're trespassing. And he's up the road a bit hiding in the weeds—with a shotgun.

I don't know . . . maybe the whole state is a cobweb of roads like this. I wonder if this is the only way to get to the big state university that I've been told is Ole Miss. Or maybe we're just coming up to a side door.

Pitch black, except for what we see in front of us with the headlights that keep sweeping back and forth as Barrett rounds the curves. The convoy rises up and rolls down, twisting over and around the small hills. We're on a roller coaster at some county fair—the hills are too low for one at a state fair. From a view high above in the darkness it must look like a necklace of headlights, 140 sets of them, a lit-up, accordian-like caterpillar, whose body bunches up in the hollows and then stretches out when we go up and over the hills.

There's a smell whenever we drive down into the little pockets between the hills. It smells swampy. Old wet meets with new wet now with the light rain. It's a kind of a decaying, damp, close-in-on-you smell that I later find out one would expect farther over in the bottomland of the Delta.

As our headlights go around curves, we catch masses of dirt-embedded ground cover. It's so full against the side of the road that you can't tell when the low cover scrub stops and the bushes begin and when the bushes stop and the trees begin—all so close in on us. It's just one blanket of dull green growth unaffected by the rain. The same dried dirt's probably been there for years.

> *Ole Miss campus.* "Shoot the Yankee, shoot. Give me your gun if you won't shoot," one boy implored three state patrolmen running before a gas barrage. As two other boys hurried toward the battlefield, their arms loaded with rocks, one said to his red-headed companion, "I'm with you, Red, you know I'm with you. If we can just kill one, I'll be happy."[3]

All I can do is look straight ahead and follow the path of our headlights. There's no urge to look left or right. That would be sightseeing. We hunker down in our seats. After a while it seems that we've been staring more than looking. Fine, we're the lead jeep . . . better get it right. No local traffic. Maybe the word is out about this latter-day intrusion by northerners into their state because no one is venturing out.

But we soon discover that some have ventured out.

"Hey, nigger lovers!"

About five miles farther down the road, two or three carloads of young whites, maybe locals, come out of nowhere and move up alongside us in the passing lane.

"Hey, nigger lovers!" they scream out from rolled-down car windows, back and front.

They quickly move up ahead and turn over into our lane, jamming us down to a crawl.

"Ron, step on it, try to pass them."

We move over into the passing lane.

"Sir, I have to pull back, hill coming up," he shouts out as he slap-taps the brakes.

We retreat back into the right lane. It now becomes a game of "chicken." Are we going to pass them on a hill? Most likely few oncoming cars tonight, but we can't chance it. After we go over a low hill and we're driving on a safe flat road again, one of the cars moves back over into the passing lane, blocks us, and stays there alongside the other car at the same crawl speed. Kids, angry kids. Only when a rise in the road or a curve comes up does the blocking car scoot back into our lane. The harassment goes on for about two, maybe three more miles. I look over at Barrett.

"I want to fire a warning shot, do any good?"

(Pause.)

"Yes, sir . . . please, sir."

I thumb the button on the radio handset, to contact the colonel in the convoy behind us.

"Example 6, Golf 1. We're being jammed and hassled by three civilian vehicles. Can't pass them. They're blocking us. Slows the whole convoy down. Permission to fire a warning round in the air. Over."

(A long pause.)

"Golf 1, Example 6. Are the civilian vehicles hitting your jeep? Over."

(Sounds like his voice.)

"Example 6, Golf 1. Negative, sir. Over."

(Longer pause.)

"Golf 1, Example 6. Permission denied. Do you read? Over."

"Example 6, Golf 1. Roger that. Out."

I turn to Barrett. "'Permission DE-NI-ED!' Did you hear that?"

I jam the handset back onto the hook of the radio frame. Shit! What the hell is this? Only if they're damaging G-O-V-ERNMENT property? I should've said, "Hell yes, Colonel! Three bullet holes and counting!"

He probably asked that JAG guy in one of the jeeps with him.

All Military Police regulations state that a member of the Judge Advocate General's Corps [JAG] will accompany the commanding officer when the Military Police are entering a riot area or one of civil disobedience . . . . I rode the jeep with our commanding officer [Brice] on the trek south to Oxford.[4]

Minutes later the three-car convoy of angry whites drops off onto a side road. As quickly as they had come on to us. They don't come back. This is becoming more and more bizarre. First, no Mississippi State Highway Patrol escort. Now this scene.

What the hell is going on? The incident is unnerving, sobering. But we can only keep it on the surface, no deeper, no time to get angry. Maybe I will later. No time to reflect. Maybe I'll do that later, too. For now, just react. The mind races. OK, OK . . . catch up to this. What's happening?

This sudden hostility on the road seems surreal. At the moment it stands out as a shock to us. Here we are, the U.S. ARMY! Are we not here to break up some kind of fight between two sides? Some kind of standoff? And then we escort the student, as one of the lieutenants said last night, like Little Rock.

OK, so maybe more ugliness up ahead. Well, we're trained for this kind of stuff, but we never thought it would happen on a small winding road like this one. I guess we're no longer on the sidelines, about to referee a civil rights disturbance. Opposing players in a game don't usually try to beat up on the umpires (well, except for South American soccer). We're part of the fight now.

We know what we have to do if confronted or threatened again like this. We have the means. I can only hope that we don't have to use them. If the harassment back there on the road had turned violent, that poor carload of teenagers would not have been prepared for the kind of response that a U.S. Army unit—MPs at that—could've brought down on them. No, we're not giving out traffic tickets at Fort Dix. Will something like this happen again later on down the road?

Ole Miss campus, October 1, 0300 hours. The arrival of [various units of the National Guard] meant the regiment was complete, with more than 500 men. When combined with the force of 117 MPs, the 503rd's A Company and the two hundred or so federal marshals who were still battle ready, Billingslea at last had a force capable of taking the offensive against the rioters.[5]

A radio message comes from the colonel to slow down because the convoy is beginning to stretch out. We pull up a bit. Still raining. The wiper on my side starts to do a stop 'n start dance on the windshield. Glad it's on my side only. But for sound of the jeep's engine and the occasional message coming in on the radio net, still quiet on the road.

Mississippi. This is all so weird. We're not in some foreign country. The few road signs that our headlights can catch are still printed in English and Barrett is still driving on the right side of the road. A Burma-Shave sign would help or at least another Phillips 66.

There's still no other traffic on this rural road, no sign of any locals. Finally, at one lighted crossroad we come upon some humanity. Bystanders. I look over and keep looking over, turning my head back as we pass. The people in the small cluster are all black—grownups and kids, standing by the side of the road, just staring back at us. It's spooky. They make no gestures of any kind, arms down at their sides. Who knows, maybe they're a bit awestruck at the long line of military vehicles slowly moving past them under the dull light of the one hanging street lamp. Nothing but our faces looking back over at theirs in the night. How did these Mississippians know about us when that town back there was asleep? A white-black thing?

Farther down the road we pass through a town called Abbeville. On most country roads back on the edge of the prairie in flat Minnesota, we might have some warning of an approaching town. Maybe some far-off lights. But not here in this hill country. You don't know you're there until you're right there. The sign says "Oxford, Home of Ole Miss." We pull off the road onto a shoulder. It's almost 0400 hours.

"Is that clear, Lieutenant?"

Colonel Brice comes over from his jeep. The look on my face asks, "OK, what next?" My instincts are dulled, on hold. I can offer nothing. I look at him.

He stands there on the shoulder of the road in ill-fitting fatigues. They're probably the same ones I saw on him back at McGuire. The bottoms of the pant legs are crumpled down around his ankles. I always associated majors and colonels with crisp, tailored, photo-ready uniforms. Maybe he wore mostly Class A's during his crime-solving career. He seems so out of place with all those colonels I saw him with back at the navy base yesterday.

He's right at the edge of being tall for his generation and with the kind of craggy face that one associates with rural people, out in the sun more than city people. Maybe he inherited the face from a father who worked in the Oklahoma fields. He probably stayed in the army because of the pay, rather than go back home to those fields after World War II.

Many of the junior officers in the battalion like the colonel to the same degree that they feared his predecessor. The combat-ready major would've relished his role as commander of the 716th now.

One of the enlisted in the battalion, a stand-up comedian, said that the gung-ho major would've had us lay down a protective field of fire, using mortar (which we didn't have) and small-arms rounds as we approached the "enemy territory" last night at the state line. (Take our ammo away like last night at the navy base? Hell! He would've loaded us up with more.) Worse yet, the jokester continued, when approaching the "enemy" deeper into the state and near Oxford, he would've ordered an airborne drop, that is, after artillery rounds—fired from Abbeville—and an air strike from the few fighter jets up at Millington had softened up the Ole Miss campus.

Instead, thank you, we have the battalion's less aggressive command successor, the new colonel. And while he's hardly a sympathetic figure, there's something about him that makes us want to win one for him.

Maybe it's the face, passive, not active, almost sad. In the military, command colonels are rated by how well their line captains and lieutenants perform and then on down to the troops. We want to support him in this sudden and unexpected challenge coming so late in his career.

In his soft, unflappable drawl he says, "Hank, our orders are to report to a general officer. He's set up a temporary CP at the Oxford town airport."

"Where is that, sir?"

"Well, we don't exactly know. We have to find it and him," he adds. "He'll give us more instructions. Take two recon [reconnaissance] jeeps with you into town, find the airport, get the orders, and report back here. A major from the 101st will go with you. He's been briefed as to its location. He'll be present as the senior officer. But you'll be reporting on behalf of the 716th."

If you're lucky in a situation like this, you get people like this colonel whom you want to see and hear in such moments, ill-fitting fatigues or not. Calm and direct. Colonel Brice could've been sitting on a fence back in Oklahoma telling me about the crops.

I turn back to the jeep and find a major sitting next to my radioman. His name tag reads, "BEACH." I salute.

I wonder. Here's an RA field-grade officer in the back seat of my jeep. Infantry. Where did he come from? Did he come down from Memphis with us in the convoy? What's his role? I'm impressed. Airborne too. What's he doing with us?

He lets me talk first.

"Major, we've got this Mississippi road map and it looks like we've come into this town from the northeast."

"Lieutenant, the airport is off to the north and west of the main part of the town," he says, breaking the ice with an indirect reminder to me of his rank.

Good. Another guest passenger. *I hope you're as good as Jarrell was.*

Just then, two other company jeeps pull up with three MPs in each. Our little recon party sets off, leaving the convoy back on the highway monitoring our progress over the radio.

Moments later, I can tell that we've entered the town limits because Highway 7 has become a street that's named after somebody. It leads up to a low-lighted intersection. We can see a cloud of smoke and hear noise coming from the left and a few blocks down. Through a haze we can see shadows of a crowd. My only thought is to avoid it. I look over at Barrett.

"Take a right at this intersection and then veer off to the right again at any large street that comes into us. Keep looking out for any crowds that may pop up ahead of us."

A quick right turn, straight on, another right turn. Now, we're in a quieter part of town. What I'd give for a map now with one of those "You Are Here" arrows pasted to it, marking that intersection back there.

"Sir, see that sign up ahead?" Barrett blurts out.

"Yes, I got it, 'Oxford Municipal Airport.'"

Minutes later we race up an access road at the airport and pull to a stop in a parking area. The major and I walk over to a large combination truck/van and know it's army because it's painted OD. We're met by a major who escorts us over to a portable ladder with steps that run up into the interior of the van.

I find myself in a cramped office-like compartment surrounded by communications equipment. I try to focus, to be alert. An officer is sitting at a small field desk. I stare at his uniform, one star on each collar.

I'm surprised that I'm not nervous. Actually I'm relieved that I've found him. And relieved also that my newly constituted "team" has a major who'll take over. The general looks up at me. I sense that I, and not Major Beach, have to be the one to speak first.

"716th Military Police Battalion reporting as ordered, sir."

Before now, I've never been in the company of a general officer. Not even from the back row of the movie theater at Dix that sometimes doubles as an auditorium—much less front-and-center and addressing one. I remain at attention, still relieved, in one sense, that *my* job is over. I've delivered the battalion, well, almost.

He looks directly at me, not at Major Beach. Only now do I realize that the major will not be central to the conversation. It's just me—a lowly second lieutenant who was coaching a softball team to a losing record in upstate New York last week—and a U.S. Army general.

He stands up. He's tall. He has to bend his head down in the low-ceilinged trailer. I can see that the general's fatigues have stayed starched even though he's probably been in them for a day and a night. He finally speaks.

"Lieutenant, welcome, you are to send a platoon from your battalion immediately to the Lyceum building on the campus. It will support the army units already there [Mississippi National Guard and Company A, 503rd] in relief of the U.S. marshals. They're under siege from a mob. You are to disperse all crowds from the campus.

"We have reports of at least two fatalities and serious injuries," he continues. "Be equipped with tear gas and ammunition." (I didn't know about the ammo "turn-in" back at the base last night.)

"Is that clear, Lieutenant?" He was looking at me and, of course, expecting only one response.

"Yes, sir."

A "No, sir" at such a moment, even though very little is clear to me, is not an option. My response is but a reflex. Junior officers are conditioned to say, "Yes, sir" more often than "No, sir."

In the civilian workplace, orders from one's boss are often incomplete and a junior employee is left with questions to ask. OK to do so if it's an immediate supervisor, but not if it's the chairman of the board. One walks out into the hallway, hoping for the executive secretary to come running over to fill in the holes. So too in the army, the "Yes, sir" salute comes early on in a lieutenant-to-general meeting. Only later does one seek guidance elsewhere. In this case, that guidance comes in the form of the major-in-waiting out in the parking lot when we leave the van. He comes over.

"Lieutenant, the Lyceum is a large building with tall white columns on the university campus about three quarters of a mile south of here. Go up onto the campus and move toward the noise and the smoke."

"Yes, sir."

"Just get your men in the front of that building to protect the marshals from the mob if they're still there. Other soldiers, MPs included, have preceded you, but there may still be pockets of violence. You may run into some remnants of tear gas, so make sure your men wear masks."

"Yes, sir."

The mind races again. OK . . . the Lyceum is a large building. And this campus is down that way less than a mile? I even look over my shoulder as if I could see it. Which platoon will go? Pete's? He has a wife back at Dix. Do we have ammo? Or at least tear gas grenades? Major Beach and I return to the recon jeeps.

In this one instant it all becomes so real. As I thought back on the highway, no, we're not going to be a mere show of force or break up a street fight between two sides. We're going to be a *part* of a fight. The local TV news broadcasts back at the base yesterday and then President Kennedy's speech were up to now our only overview "briefings." Now we get the real stuff.

The orders from him. No paragraphs of detailed instructions—just three sentences. I find my mind suddenly clear. All thinking is pared down to a few essential "things-to-do." If you're lucky, the brain squeezes out all the other stuff and allows just those messages to stay. You focus on one thing and not on a scramble of four or five. Also, there's no time to reflect—just react. It's kind of easy after that, actually, a bright-line sort of thing. You don't have to think about finding a bathroom or if you're hungry.

I thumb the radio button and send the order to the waiting battalion to prepare a platoon. We start back toward the highway. Time: 0430 hours.

Maybe I'm in a Movie.

Our three jeeps rush back down the access road and start to retrace our steps. Then a mistake. We turn right when we should have kept on straight. Within a few blocks we come to the dead end of a small lane that overlooks a street leading down under a railroad overpass. A lot of noise and smoke. Damn, how'd we get into this? Make a wrong turn?

Barrett slams the brakes and I get out and take a look. A column of army jeeps is stalled below on the road that leads down under a railroad bridge. A small crowd, a piece of the mob, is on top of the bridge throwing railroad ties, rocks, debris, anything they can find, down onto the jeeps. I can't move away from my stare, ten seconds that seem more like thirty.

I don't think they can see us, this high up and over from the bridge about fifty yards.

I look down at the soldiers trapped in their open jeeps. Farther up toward the front of the stranded convoy I see a disabled deuce-and-a-half right under the bridge with a sergeant alongside it trying to get it moving again. That's what's stalled the convoy. They're going at him too.

I run back to the jeep.

"Ron, let's get out of here. Go back the way we came!"

He grinds the gears into reverse and turns around as quickly as he can. Too late. I hear a muffled *whack* and see a brick falling on the floor of the jeep. It's just hit Barrett across the face. I can hear other sounds, *thwack, thwack*, against the side of the vehicle. Something crashes into the windshield. So they're up high on this street as well.

I look out to see where it's all coming from, but it's a blur because the jeep is jerking around, making the turn. More rocks. I fare better because I can duck below the windshield. The major and the radioman hunker down in the back.

"Everyone! Get down!" I shout, for a second forgetting that Barrett has to drive.

I look up at him and see a little blood at the side of his mouth. Doesn't look serious. With the two other jeeps trailing, we speed up a hill trying to find a street back out to the highway.

I try to process our past movements. OK, retrace the steps, go back to where we made the wrong turn. Can't believe it, but my body craves a cigarette. My mind's too busy.

I hear nothing from the major. By now, he's just a passenger "along for the ride" and not my superior officer. It's my jeep, my recon, my battalion, and—my problem. I don't look back at him for any orders, nor does he give me any.

There are more bang-thuds against the sides and on the hood of the jeep. Crowds pop out into the street, throwing whatever they can pick up. Young kids too. I see one in our headlights—couldn't be more than thirteen—lean over and pick up a piece of broken concrete to throw as we rush by. We turn and try another route. My God! It's a residential lane that dead-ends into a cul-de-sac.

The major finally speaks up.

"Lieutenant, call back to your battalion. We can't find our way back to them. We have to bring your convoy into town over the radio. There's no other way."

That sounds like an order.

"Major, let me try one more time. It'll be too confusing for them—too risky—to bring them in over the radio. We can't, sir! All those vehicles, street by street! We don't even know how we got here ourselves—where we are now. It's still dark. They'll run into what we just did or what that other unit did down under that bridge."

He doesn't say anything.

Think! Think! Where were we fifteen minutes ago? What looks familiar on this street? Hold on . . . focus! Again, my brother's advice. *Don't hesitate. Make a decision.*

We find a small driveway alongside a house, running back to front. We go down it and out an end that empties into a large street that rises on the left.

"Left, Ron, keep going left!"

Things begin to look familiar. My "wounded" driver turns the jeep into another street that leads to a wider one that has a sign pointing to a highway. A second sign reads "Holly Springs 30 miles."

Bingo! Jarrell's good luck wish for us is holding.

We drive up to the waiting battalion where Pete Frechette's platoon from B Company has formed, up at the front of the convoy.

I repeat the general's orders to Colonel Brice and Pete. I have that cigarette.

We get back into the jeeps and the battalion convoy lumbers into town behind us. The return route is fixed in my mind. Back down to that residential street and then a right turn into and down the driveway against the house. By now its occupant is standing out in her front yard, in a nightgown, staring at us in disbelief. Like the angry whites in the car out on the highway, this scene too is surreal. I don't know . . . maybe I'm in a movie.

Movie or not, here's another story a southerner can tell for years—how a convoy of Yankees swept down along the side of her house and out the back driveway one night.

4

THE ARRIVAL

"Sir . . . just where is this downtown?"

At 0500 hours, on October 1, 1962, the 716th Military Police Battalion from Fort Dix, New Jersey (less than full-strength since the "step-back" of the black soldiers), with 140 assorted vehicles, including an ambulance and a mess truck pulling a water trailer, rumbles through an Oxford citizen's side driveway and out the other end. One can only wonder how long it took for the convoy to clear her property.

We've arrived. An Army of the North. A bit less dramatic than Sherman's arrival in the South almost one hundred years earlier. Yet in some quarters down here (and surely in that woman's house back there), we are just as unwelcome now as the Yankee was then.

The convoy pulls up along a tree-lined residential street just short of a big intersection. I sense that we're on the edge of the university. Across the street I see a lane that I guess runs up onto the campus and to the noise and the tear gas and the reason why we're all here this morning. By now the sun is about three fingers above a stand of trees off to my left. I don't know much else at this moment, but I know which direction is east.

I can see better now. And can reflect for a moment, and only a moment. I could do little of that when we got lost back there. Must be just a few blocks over from here. At the time I felt a charge of excitement—but the fear kind. Bricks, concrete chunks, whatever could be thrown. And then a rush of adrenaline followed. It was the kind that soldiers will feel five years later in Vietnam, only, for them, a rush jacked up by a multiple of fifty or more. Mine was a minor one, but a rush of something. Whatever. (That's a Minnesota word that one says for a lot of things, like when you don't know what else to say—you say "whatever.") When I saw two of them ready to throw concrete chunks at us, but a few feet away, it was a quick down-up sensation that came on—first, fear, and then, well, that rush of whatever—not unlike that first fight you had in the alley as a kid.

Pete brings his platoon up in jeeps. His NCOs check out the men. Rifles at the ready, bayonets fixed and unsheathed, gas masks on. His small group passes us, crosses the intersection, and rolls up the lane in the direction of the campus. In so doing, the 716th (Task Force Charlie) has entered the fray. The platoon, as regular army MPs, has trained for such emergencies, yes. But, except for my bare-bones radio message and quick jeep-side briefing to the colonel and Pete, it lacks both practice in dealing with and knowledge about what it will confront at the end of the lane.

Later I find out that the MPs in the 503rd (Task Force Alpha) and the soldiers in the 2nd Division (Task Force Bravo) knew their missions ahead of time.

Task Force Alpha (Fort Bragg, N.C.). The battalion [503rd] rehearsed airplane loading combinations for nine days. . . . Company A, which, as it turned out, would play a leading role in the Oxford affair, organized two platoons for riot control . . . [and] was able to practice platoon formations. . . . [Its commander] briefed his officers and non-commissioned officers concerning the company's possible employment in Mississippi and had his unit practice. . . .

Task Force Bravo (Fort Benning, Ga.). The 2nd Battle Group, 23d Infantry Regiment [2d Infantry Division], had "had very little riot control training." Upon notification of its possible role in a civil disturbance, therefore, the battle group began intensified training in riot control.[1]

Once the platoon reaches the campus and finds the Lyceum, Pete is led over to a general officer who's seated in a folding chair at a card table. It's Brigadier General Charles Billingslea, Commander of the 2nd Infantry Division at Fort Benning, the same one-star officer to whom I had reported at the airport earlier this morning. The top army officer in the operation in a folding chair! Field expediency. Must've been the one he had back in the van at the airport.

The general orders Pete to have his men clear the area near the Lyceum of any remaining rioters that may still be on the campus and to move to the downtown section of Oxford.

> *Town square, Oxford, October 1.* At 6 a.m., with a light drizzle chilling the air, a mob of young toughs gathered on the corners of Lamar Street and University Avenue, near the town square, pitching Coke bottles at jeeploads of soldiers hurrying by. A few yards away, a group of state police leaned languidly against their cars and watched.[2]

Unlike me, who hesitated to ask questions, Pete has the good sense to seek further advice from this general. He turns back to ask the one critical question that's on the minds of everyone sitting out in their waiting jeeps in front of the Lyceum.

"Yes, sir, but now, sir . . . just where is this downtown?"

He gets back into the lead jeep and heads down University Avenue toward the square.

> *Mayor's office, Oxford, October 1.* Even Oxford's mayor, Richard Elliott, could not get help from the Highway Patrol. "They said they had no authority. That's when I called for the Army." On Monday morning three carloads of troopers sat passive in a filling station while a mob threw rocks and bottles at passing army trucks.[3]

Pete has his platoon dismount from the jeeps and fall into a straight line, riot-control formation, south of the square.

Regulations say that you have to warn the crowd first, "read the Proclamation." The [lieutenant] got as far as, "By the authority of the President of the United States . . ." when a Coke bottle shot by his ear and smashed into his radio operator's knee. "Gas 'em!" went out over the loudspeaker.[4]

Billingslea's soldiers are elsewhere on the square confronting some of the mob. By now, it's around 0900 hours. A corporal in Pete's platoon, armed with a backpack-mounted tear gas dispenser, moves toward a store entrance. He sees a quick movement off to his side, turns, and discharges some of the gas. An elderly shopper, on her Monday morning errands, shrieks and runs off down the sidewalk. Poor woman—just trying to go about her Monday morning errands as if nothing had happened in her town overnight.

As on the campus, the mob on the square is broken up. Some of the rioters are detained and led back to the Lyceum to be interrogated by the ГBI; others flee for the streets leading out of town.

"Loyalties . . . at this time uncertain."

Meanwhile, I pull our lead jeep up closer to the intersection and stay on the radio net. Another squad of our MPs is deployed on foot, crossing the intersection, in the traditional riot-control wedge formation. I watch as they approach a lane. Then stop. Moments later the squad's sergeant, a veteran of service in Korea, comes running back. Sergeant Geitz blurts out, "Sir, a group . . . looks like highway patrol" (stepping on his words as if two people were talking at once).

"Maybe six or seven [quick breath] . . . they're just [quick breath] leaning against their patrol cars up that street." He looks back.

I look over at them. He continues, "About twenty-five yards in front of my squad. Just staring at us . . . they're not moving."

"What do we do about them, Lieutenant?" he shouts.

I look over at them again and take the radio handset.

"Example 6, Golf 1. Down here at the intersection . . . about to deploy one MP squad across street on up to campus. A group of civilian police . . . look like Mississippi Highway Patrol staring at us. Six or seven troopers total. Please advise on squad assignment . . . go around or confront and disperse? Over."

(Long pause before radio crackles back.)

Then, "Golf 1, Example 6. All nonmilitary personnel to be moved out of the area."

The monotonous no-name voice on the radio continues, "Loyalties of local law enforcement units at this time uncertain. Over."

What the. . . ? "Example 6, Golf 1. Say again. Over."

"Golf 1, Example 6. Loyalties of local law enforcement units at this time uncertain. Over."

"Roger that, Example 6, Golf 1, out."

I turn to Geitz. He's heard the order and stares at me, eyes wide and disbelieving.

"Sergeant, move them out."

Geitz's squad members, most in their late teens and early twenties, are about to clash face-to-face with other police—in uniforms as well. Our soldiers are everyone's next-door kids, not veteran police as most likely these state troopers are. Three days ago these draftees were directing traffic and handling drunks at Fort Dix. Now, suddenly, this morning, they're ordered to do this. It feels even more like I'm in that movie.

The sergeant's role is critical. Even though the squad members share a sense of protection because they're grouped together, the men still need their sergeant. Thank God for army NCOs.

Sergeant Geitz is no longer nervous, or at least he doesn't show it. He has a job to do and experience takes over. He runs back to the rear of the small V-shaped wedge and growls off the cadence for his men as he executes the orders almost with a relish. They advance toward the patrolmen, who by now are somewhat incredulous of what's coming up the lane toward them.

It's all so morning-quiet, but for the bark of the sergeant's cadence count: "Hut . . . hut . . . hut." The wedge of soldiers moves up the lane toward the small cluster of patrolmen in their custom-fitted khaki uniforms. One of the MPs stumbles on some curbing that he doesn't see because of his limited view behind the gas mask. Then, Geitz's bark comes out, strong and clear. "HEAR THIS, MOVE OUT! All personnel are to leave the area!"

Are we really doing this? Against our own?

Some of the highway troopers get into their cars in reaction to the sight of the MP squad—anonymous faces hidden behind gas masks—slowly closing on them. Rifles pointed upward, bayonets fixed. Others stand their ground, staring at the approaching soldiers. Two or three hold their arms out wide open. The gestures are clear, as if to say, "Hey, we're police too, just go around us."

From the jeep I can only stare. This is what our people are trained to do. I'm surprised that the squad members are doing so well. The first of Geitz's MPs to reach a patrolman lowers his rifle and prods him with his bayonet. No doubt now as to the army's intentions.

"You better not stick me with that thing, boy!" He stuck him. He moved.[5]

The other MPs quickly close in on each other as they're trained to do, while not breaking the discipline of the wedge. I watch as they use the butts of their rifles in order to move out the remaining patrolmen.

The Mississippians curse as they move toward their squad cars, get in, and drive off. They circle back around us at the intersection. I know that that's not the peace sign I'm getting from one of Mississippi's best as he raises his middle finger from behind a passenger window.

This one scene tells me a lot. I now know why the highway patrol didn't meet us back at the Mississippi state line last night to escort us. And they're no longer playing a role anywhere on the campus here in Oxford, if they ever did last night.

So this is how it's going to be.

I react to what has just now happened across the street in the same way I did to the earlier road incident, something between surprise and anger, with no time to think it over. Emotion comes before thought and reflection.

We still know very little of the bigger picture, only what we've just seen in front of our eyes, and this doesn't tell us much. We can place nothing into context and know of nothing else that might've been going on around us in the town over the last twelve hours.

We're still in America, right?

We'll Pillage and Plunder . . .

I take a look at our battalion convoy, jeeps and trucks, all lined back up the residential street. Drivers who have come down from Memphis during the night are slouched against their steering wheels, trying to catch some sleep. Once again, the constant crackle of the jeep radios is strangely comforting and a reminder that we're still military on this morning in civilian-land.

The residents along the street, now standing out on their front lawns, stare at us in their housecoats and robes. For the moment, many of the soldiers have little to do but sit in their jeeps, so they just stare back, except for the napping drivers. A neighbor is walking his dog up the street alongside our parked convoy and a paper boy looks over as he ambles by. It's a sudden and odd coupling of two groups, one a local civilian populace on what they thought would be just another morning—normal—the other a military intruder on a morning that is anything but normal. We're an army out of place.

After a few moments, I look over at the houses. A tired mind on a workplace break has a tendency to wander.

Hey! Maybe we should send a raiding party over to that woman standing out on her front lawn. Ask her to step aside. We'll pillage and plunder her three-bedroom colonial. Like Sherman's troops did a few states over a hundred years earlier.

Yes, confiscate her oriental rugs and her whisky. Have target practice with the household china. Maybe torch the place after we raid her refrigerator. And while we're at it, tell her to quiet her barking German shepherd or we'll shoot it.

Why stop there? We can raze the block. After all, to some of them, aren't we marauders from the North? Can't we forage like Sherman's troops did? The men are hungry—no mess call at that base last night.

But then again (looking back up the line of parked jeeps), I see that we didn't bring any foraging-party wagons down from the North as Sherman had done. Also, I remind myself that as a self-contained village we have no need to live off the land as they did. So here's "Billy Yank" in the Grand Army of the Republic arriving once again to strike fear into the heart of "Johnnie Reb." Well, maybe not the whole Grand Army. But, as Sherman had his Army of the West, we can say we're the Army of the North this morning. Well, if not that, at least the Army of Central New Jersey.

Just then, reality snaps me back. A long convoy of jeeps, many with broken windshields, goes slowly by in front of us. That's them! The unit that we saw getting battered under the railroad bridge, Companies B and C of the 503rd that came overland as we did. We just stare at them in silence and they stare back at us. No waves, no nothing, just looks of fatigue and puzzlement traded back and forth. If looks had words—"What the hell *IS* this?"

A civilian comes running up to me. In heavily accented English, he asks if I can direct him to the town morgue. He says that he's from the French Consulate in New Orleans and has heard that a French citizen was killed during the night. All I can do is direct him up to the battalion CP a few jeeps back. Later, I find out that he was referring to the reporter Paul Guihard of *Agence France-Presse*, one of the two fatalities from last night.

Now with the morning light, we're able to get a better picture of the part of the town that we're in. We see clean sidewalks, cut grass, neat front lawns. After a night of bizarre and violent incongruities, both back on the highway and here in the town, it all looks so harmless now, almost normal, almost familiar. Just like small-town Minnesota.

Yes, just another Mississippi morning.

There's nothing Deep South–different about this town compared to small towns outside Minneapolis. Except for the huge magnolia trees, we can't tell that we're in the South unless we hear a local talking. And no local this morning is offering to come over to the jeep to strike up a conversation.

Some of the Walls Have Bullet Holes . . .

I request permission to go up onto the campus and Barrett drives up the lane that both Lieutenant Frechette and Sergeant Geitz had taken earlier in their separate trips. We turn right at a tree-lined, parklike clearing that leads to a large building fronted with huge white columns. I guess it's the Lyceum building where Pete had reported with his platoon. Soldiers on the curb are taking a break and having a long overdue meal of C rations. Some call them World War II leftovers, no navy china this time. A few among them are trading the meat offerings for the peaches and pound cake. We park the jeep and go inside.

Civilians whom I guess to be deputy marshals are kneeling or lying on the floor in a main hallway. They're tending to injuries sustained during the night. There's a pile of shotguns and rifles stacked against a wall in a corner, no doubt confiscated from the rioters. Back outside, exhausted deputies are gathered in small groups along the side and front of the building. Some of the walls have bullet holes in them, as do a few of the massive columns.

Two men had been killed, both of them noncombatants
gunned down in the darkness of the campus. Paul Guihard, a
French newspaperman [and] an Oxford workman named Ray

Gunter. . . . A total of 166 marshals, 30% of all those sent to Oxford, suffered injuries or wounds, along with some 40 soldiers and National Guardsmen.[6]

A couple of the deputies come over to express thanks to us for arriving when we did. I thank them, but add that we weren't the first army unit on the scene. One says it was like the cavalry arriving at the last minute. OK, we're still in that movie. It's a John Wayne western and we're the good guys in jeeps instead of on horses, coming to protect the townsfolk.

The area around the Lyceum looks like a battleground, with a few burned-out cars in the approach lane, tipped over on their sides, one up against a tree. A stranded bulldozer. Debris all over. Marshals and soldiers are corralling apprehended rioters and leading them into the Lyceum for interrogation. A few of them look like students, if not from this place, from some school.

Lyceum, University of Mississippi, October 1, 0700 hours. It is chilly. The marshals are up from their fitful sleep, eating C rations. The Army is in control. FBI agents are beginning to interrogate the 93 prisoners—only a handful are Ole Miss students—and cataloguing their weapons: a .22 automatic rifle, a Swedish Mauser, an eight-inch auger and a 30-inch length of rubber hose. . . . Most of [the prisoners] are young, rough-looking punks.[7]

5

THE TOWN

We leave the campus and go toward the town center. There's little sign of any local car or foot traffic, most citizens choosing (more than being ordered) to stay inside their homes or shuttered stores. What little civilian traffic there is just gets bogged down behind military convoys that are swelling into the area. But where would the occupants of the cars be going . . . to a class? To get a morning paper that wasn't delivered? Our battalion is but one of many moving in and setting up camp. Forget the stand-alone self-sufficiency of the army units. I think that all this has to be a huge strain on the municipal services of this small town. But that's a problem and a challenge facing those well above my rank and pay grade.

I see a couple of cars with out-of-state plates over on a side street. A piece of what looks like a Confederate flag is draped over an open window in one of them. No one seems to be around who wants to claim the car and the banner, get in, and drive away.

Later I hear that U.S. Army numbers have reached nineteen thousand in the overall Oxford area. We're the latter-day equivalent of General Grant and his army in their visit to the town years earlier.

In the fall of 1862, Gen. U.S. Grant had driven deep into Mississippi. By December, Grant's Federal troops had reached the young and prosperous town of Oxford. They billeted on the fourteen-year-old campus of the University of Mississippi— then almost deserted by the exodus of students to the Confederate Army. Grant's troops settled in Oxford until Christmas

Day . . . and their wounded lay . . . as the Confederate casualties from the battle of Shiloh had lain before them . . . in the university's Lyceum building.[1]

We find out that many of the late-arriving demonstrators did not even make it into town. The 101st and the 2nd Division soldiers set up "stop, search, and turn back" roadblocks on roads leading into Oxford.[2]

The searches of the cars net a small arsenal of weapons, from shotguns to automatic rifles. Their owners say they're going "coon hunting." By midmorning two or three perimeters of roadblocks have been set up to seal off Oxford.

I hear from one of our senior officers that the 716th, along with some non-MP units, has been assigned to be in charge of the campus. Another MP battalion (the 720th from Fort Hood, Texas) also with non-MP units, has been assigned to the town.

I also find out that the student, James Meredith, accompanied by marshals, registered for the semester at an office back in the Lyceum at 0800 hours this morning.

"Hey! I'm white, you're white, OK?"

Later in the morning, a B Company MP comes back and tells me that his platoon confronted some of the mob downtown.

From him I find out that three of our jeeps are on patrol circling the town square in a close bumper-to-bumper line. Remnants of the mob are congregating because they have heard that General Walker has been arrested and is being held in an upstairs room at the courthouse on the square. Not true, as we later find out that the disgraced general was taken to the Lyceum after his arrest at 1130 hours at a roadblock, as he was trying to leave town. But the rumor continues to feed their passion once they are chased off the campus. They have clustered on corners leading into the square. According to the soldier:

Suddenly a brick came arching out from one of the groups. It bounced off the hood of a jeep, hit its driver in the face, and bloodied him. The squad leader, a veteran 716th corporal, called an immediate halt to the moving patrol on a side of the courthouse.

Corporal Diaz stepped out of the lead jeep. He started walking toward a small group gathered on the corner from where the brick has been thrown. The lanky MP, ramrod-erect with his M-1 rifle at port arms—moved slowly toward the crowd. Two of his men dismounted and stood ready by their jeep. The rest remained in their vehicles.

Just then, a man came out from the crowd and started to walk toward the corporal, arms stretched out, palms open. Maybe the thrower, maybe his proxy.

"Corporal, I know what it's like to be in the army, I'm a vet."

Diaz slowed down even more, keeping his eyes on the approaching man's hands. To him that was all that counted. His hands. The MP corporal was familiar with this stuff. The civilian was not.

"You gotta know we don't mean no harm to y'all," the man shouted out. "No, man"—looking back over his shoulder at his crowd—"we don't hate y'all. We hate the nigger."

A few voices sounded out from the crowd in support. Then the man said, "Hey! I'm white, you're white, OK?" A few "yeah, yeahs" sounded from the crowd.

The T-shirt guy continued on. A weak smile came across his face as he moved toward handshaking distance of Diaz. The civilian was looking at the soldier's eyes. Maybe he was a bit anxious, but only a bit. It's OK, he probably thought, two white guys, one army and one former army.

The civilian saw no reason to look down at the corporal's wrists as they started to rotate so that the stock of the rifle came pivoting up.

The army calls it a "horizontal butt stroke." In boxing it's called a right upper-cut punch. It glanced across the man's jaw.

He crumpled down onto the pavement of the square. There were sudden gasps from the corner and then . . . silence.

The civilians were stunned. All eyes remained fixed on the corporal, who looked over at the corner.

"OK, everyone . . . all of you! Now! Leave this area. GO! Now! Godammit!"

They did, slowly . . . but they did.

Had the phrase been in use at the time—a "teaching moment"—it would've fit this scene, ugly though it was. It was a signal to all who witnessed it on the square and others like them. Regular U.S. Army units, not local National Guard (although they had performed well), not Mississippi Highway Patrol (whose nonperformance was as surprising as it was unprofessional), had taken charge. There was a new sheriff in town. In this one incident, the lesson was clear. One of this corporal's men had been bloodied and someone was going to pay for it—if not the perpetrator, then his stand-in. And that man, if he had been in the army as he said he had, should've known better. Should've known there'd be payback.

No symbolism here . . . the brick wasn't thrown at the U.S. Constitution, at a court order, or even at the Kennedys. NCOs don't think big picture and the army doesn't want them to. The army wants them to protect their men and if Corporal Diaz wasn't in a position to do that he did the next best thing. One just doesn't throw bricks at a soldier and surely not a Regular Army MP.

As with the loose talk that Walker was being held in the courthouse, rumors are the norm on the street this morning, as they were on the campus. They swept through the crowd as fast as a Texas grass fire the night before: "They've got machine guns!" And "They shot a coed! She's dead!" All proved false. The daylight rumors ran a feverish close second: "Prisoners taken . . . being held in a basement without food or water." And "Soldiers . . . lining up people and beating them with rifle butts." All shouted into the ears of the mob in order to fuel their rage.

The Detainees

By 1100 hours, many of the demonstrators have been forced out of the downtown area and have been detained by the army and the deputy marshals over at the Lyceum or at the town armory.

Back on the campus I look over at some of the ones who are being held. My God! Are they the reason that we were ordered down here? I stare over at a skinny guy whose eyes are fixed on me. Hatred. I think. Yes, we're here because of *you*?

It's a bit odd to me that so many of them are skinny, as if they haven't eaten for a while. Maybe it's because many of them rode across the South last week in their beat-up Chevys and their Ford pickups and passed all the drive-in fast-food shacks along 78. They didn't stop because the racial hatred in their heads was so much stronger than the hunger in their bellies. They raced across all those counties at the call of General Walker and the radio stations to get to the Mississippi state line and then to go a few more counties before they finally got to the one called Lafayette (Faulkner's Yoknapatawpha). And then . . . to the nigger who dared apply at the "We Serve Whites Only" school. Maybe that's why they look so skinny this morning.

Some need shaves and haircuts. Although I'm still passing through my so-called young adult years, I have never seen such a collection of sorry-ass looking people before. I guess that this is what they call "rednecks" down here. One of them looks over at me and yells out of a mouth that has a few teeth missing, "Hey soldier, up north a nigger is fuckin' your sister right now, y'all hear?"

Some in the press will call them "thugs." No, this ragtag group of underfeds can't be called thugs. The word implies muscle, weight, brawn. Maybe it's a northern word, or at least a city word, and conjures up back-alley fights, car thefts, and street gang members hanging out on corners with lead weights inside their winter gloves.

A few look like students who didn't get back to their dorm rooms in time last night. White shirttails hanging out, khakis wrinkled.

They lost their innocence, if indeed they had any, when their curiosity, if that was what it was, got them into trouble. They became, by choice or by chance, participants in a *mob*.

It's clear that most of the detainees are not students. They don't look like students, not a button-down collar or khaki pant on the lot of them. Some have the greased-down, "duck ass" hair style of the late '50s and packs of Lucky Strike or Camel fold-tucked under their T-shirt sleeves. They wear the tight Levi's uniform of their class and workplace (clothes that only a few years later will be adopted by collegiate middle classes in both the South and the North).

They look tired, defiant, and bitter. Now it's my turn to be angry. Which one bloodied Private Barrett's face? That kid with the pock-marked face in the second row? I look over at him. Forget all that "southern way of life" crap, you little bastard. Did you throw the brick at us early this morning?

Or that one up front who keeps staring over at me? In a fantasy moment, I see myself picking up the chunk of concrete that's lying by the curb—probably first thrown last night—and heaving it into the line of them. But, as I look down at it I realize that that I'm in a U.S. Army uniform. So in my fantasy I have one of my buddies from Minnesota throw the brick. My stand-in.

So these are the violent ones who came to Oxford from all over the South this past weekend. I look over at a Mississippi Guard officer. *Boy! If this is your South, it sure is fucked up.* Then I look beyond him at this beautiful campus. How incongruous it all is. It just doesn't fit.

"Dixie" and "I Can't Stop Loving You"

By noon, I'm able to get a better picture of what happened last night from a student who comes up to our jeep. He's one of the few who'll approach us in the coming weeks. He confirms what I have heard, that Meredith registered this morning. He says that the town and the campus were overrun by out-of-state troublemakers over the weekend. When I ask him about all the students I heard were in the crowd, he says that they were from other schools or, "if from Ole Miss here, they were just curious."

I respond, C-U-R-I-ous!!! He adds that some of them may have acted out their curiosity in a "more animated" way.

And the lack of local law enforcement! Who among us is ready for this, we northerners from Vermont and New York, Wisconsin and Pennsylvania? We can understand the need to be called in to help put down a riot in the streets of a quiet college town. That is, to *assist* the local police or *state highway patrol*. Sure, call on us . . . we've got your backs. But this? I still can't get over the brief radio message a few hours earlier about the Mississippi Highway Patrol: "Loyalties uncertain."

I return to the convoy at the edge of the campus. Food arrives for the men who have not been sent out on patrol onto the campus, and Barrett gets medical attention for his injured jaw. I drive back onto the campus with Major Beach and it remains a strange scene. The leftover smell of tear gas is heavy in the air.

The campus is slowly coming alive with students trying to continue their fall semester. Some are crossing the grounds holding handkerchiefs to their faces to ward off the lingering stench of the tear gas.

I catch a whiff of it. Yes, the smell . . . the memories of my one-week course at Fort Dix's CBR (Chemical-Biological-Radiological) School, when even we younger lieutenants were all led, sheeplike, into a wooden shed, wearing our gas masks. Then at the directive of an instructor (a sergeant, of course) that we remove our masks, we took in the half-acrid, half-sweet aroma of the gas before we bolted, gasping and coughing, for the doors and out into the fresh New Jersey air.

Some students look straight ahead as we drive by; a few stop and stare at us, not a friendly smile among them. I wonder if any of them were part of the crowd last night. If they were, I'm sure they'll say that they were out on the campus just curious, watching—not like those "out-of-state rowdies." Of course, for us there is no distinction

as we recall the frenzy of the mob hours earlier, even though we saw
but a small bit of it. When one is a part of a crowd, in a common
rush of violence, even the most passive observer becomes a par-
ticipant in it. The observer can play as dangerous and destructive a
role as the guy standing next to him with a shotgun. The advancing
soldier—in a dark place, in a strange venue, within earshot of gunfire—has no time to sort out the bad guys from the near-bad guys.

The more violent troublemakers, it seems, have been driven out
of the town, but something still nags. A bit later it comes to me that
we're really on one side—we invading Yankees—and the students
and some of the townsfolk are on the other.[3]

A student yells over, "Hey, y'all loving that nigger, now ain't
y'all?"

Some students have returned to their hometowns at the call of
their parents to wait out the week before they trickle back to the
campus to start the semester.

Meanwhile, the Confederate battle flag, the "Stars and Bars," is
on display, hanging from a dormitory window. Through another
window I hear "Dixie" being played over and over on a phonograph.
Farther down the street, Ray Charles is singing "I Can't Stop Loving
You." I put the two together in my mind—"Dixie" and Ray Charles—
and smile. Ironic, I think . . . they'll listen to their music, but not go
to school with them.

6

THE ASSIGNMENT

The Assignment

By midmorning, the headquarters of the 716th is established in the town armory. Shortly after I arrive there, I run into Colonel Brice, coming out of a meeting he was in with the overall army command. He says that, at the recommendation of Major Beach, I've been assigned to be the OIC (officer-in-charge) of the security detail for the student, James Meredith. Maybe the 101st major forgave me for getting him lost and battered with bricks and chunks of concrete earlier this morning.

The colonel tells me to report to some U.S. Department of Justice officials at 1800 hours at a place on the campus called the Faculty House, where I'll be briefed on my new assignment. He adds that the authorities in Washington want only a military police presence on the campus. All non-MP units are to be removed from the town.

Moments later I'm ordered to escort a hearse that has come down from Memphis to Oxford to pick up the body of Paul Guihard, one of the two shooting victims. In my brief journey through the streets, it looks to me like martial law has come into effect (though never declared). I see troops all over on foot and mobile patrols, and we're not even in a foreign country. In some areas, local pedestrian and vehicular traffic is blocked or is off limits.

A few days from now, some residents will be issued passes to go about their daily business, one given to a part owner and manager of the venerable 1839 landmark J. E. Neilson's Department Store on the square. The man's daily habit it is to walk to and from his residence a few blocks away. (Years later that pass will be displayed by the man's son, current owner of the store, behind a glass frame that hangs on an office wall.[1])

We move into what we hope will be a peaceful coexistence with the townsfolk. Other than the mobile patrols and the manned roadblocks leading up to the campus, the army tries to keep a low profile by moving the rest of the troops to the outskirts of Oxford. Nevertheless, some of the citizenry will come to call us an occupier—no coexistence for them. Yet, while I still think we're the good guys, I begin to realize just how complicated this sudden military presence is for them. As with the students, the locals don't want us here any longer than, say, five hours ago. The reach of their "occupiers" is slowly beginning to spread through this small southern town like an oil slick moving over an army exercise map-board.

"He passed . . . this summer."

I sense a winding down by early afternoon and most of the men take well-deserved breaks in place. I request leave from the colonel to look around the town a bit. I call for Barrett and a radioman. I tell him that we have to find the house of a famous writer from this town. He looks at me, puzzled. I add that it's something I have to do. We set out in the jeep.

On that 1956 hitchhiking trip, taken to get away from a Minnesota winter that lingered even into our Easter holiday break, we came down through Illinois, Indiana, and Kentucky. I knew we were closer to the *real* South, the one of my Yankee imagination, after we crossed into Tennessee. We slept on newspapers in a jailhouse corridor in Chattanooga and then went on to Atlanta the next morning. It's about this time that we started to see the "White Only" and "Colored Only" signs. We listened to Lonnie Donegan sing the "Rock Island Line" ("I got all pig iron") on a trucker's radio while stopped at a rail crossing. After we got to Georgia, we turned west and hitched through Alabama and Mississippi, passing through Tupelo, Elvis Presley's hometown, on our way up to Memphis.

In a college paper a few years later, I wrote about the trip, mentioning the Elvis hometown highlight. My literature professor had another hometown in mind and could not believe that I had passed up an opportunity to visit William Faulkner's nearby town of Oxford when I had been that close. In a feeble attempt at humor, I said that the next time I was in Mississippi, I would visit his hometown. Little did I know that I would have that chance just a few years later.

Now, maybe it's a bit foolish to be going on this excursion to find the house of a famous writer in the midst of all of the chaos. But I think that things have calmed down enough to allow this break. And I don't know how long I'll be in Oxford, even in my new assignment. A few more days and maybe we'll leave a quieted-down campus and be back at Dix. I need to do this.

We leave the campus and drive down to the square. I have a better look at the downtown now and it's as if we've stumbled onto an outdoor movie set that's waiting for a crew to arrive for a shoot. It's a southern counterpart to the Bedford Falls of George Bailey (James Stewart in *It's a Wonderful Life*), only this town has a few balconies. There it is again! Evidence of the movie I kept thinking I was in this morning.

We turn out of the square and go south down a major street. Faulkner's home, called Rowan Oak, is hidden away on a large plot of land not too far from the downtown area. I know that the author died earlier this summer up in Virginia. We turn off the main street and suddenly find ourselves surrounded by trees on a small dirt lane that ends at the side of a house. If anyone is looking, the three of us in the jeep make quite a scene as we arrive, with the scent of tear gas on our uniforms, packing gas masks and holstered pistols. As we pull up, an elderly black man comes out of a work shed behind the house and walks over to us, rather tentatively. Must be a caretaker. He gets up to the side of the jeep as we step out and looks at us. Then, just a simple sentence: "He passed . . . this summer" (looking down as he pushes some dirt with his foot).

He must have known what went on last night, but then again, maybe not. It becomes clear that he has nothing more to say. I have no reason to mention anything about the events that have overtaken his town. Nor do we offer any explanation for our sudden appearance at the Faulkner home. He stares down again at the dirt. Is this his way? In front of white strangers? I look at him and then over at the house. We say something that is of no consequence, trying to make small talk. There's nothing more to say or do.

Yes, I've accomplished what I set out to do.

The radio in the jeep comes alive. It's a commo (communications) check. They want our location. Our radio man advises that we're returning to their location.

I thank the old man, almost in an embarrassed manner, I guess, because of our abrupt jeep-laden and armed arrival. I go to shake his hand. Limp. Our little three-man party turns back down the lane and out onto the main street.

"Now, you get out of there right now. There's trouble down there."

As we drive up the street toward an entrance to the campus, a half mile away, I realize that I have another "errand" to run. I ask Barrett to pull over at a pay phone that I see next to a Dairy Queen.

I put a dime in the coin slot and dial an operator. I wonder if an already overworked telephone exchange system in the town is even on duty after last night. A sweet southern voice comes on and doesn't disconnect me when I ask to place a call up north to Yankee country, Minneapolis. After my mother accepts the collect call, I tell her that I'm not in New Jersey as I had told them I would be. I add that I have to be quick.

"Mom, I'm down here in Mississippi . . . in Oxford, and I went through the riots last night."

Before she can respond, I say, "And tomorrow I take over as the officer in charge of the security detail for this Negro student, James Meredith."

There's a long pause during which I can barely hear something spoken in a hurried voice in the background to my dad. She quickly returns to the phone.

"I just spoke with your father. We know all about this. We heard it on the news last night. Now, you get out of there right now. There's trouble down there."

She keeps on as I try to interrupt and remind her that I'm an officer in the United States Army under orders.

"Now you go to the Greyhound station in that town and we'll wire you money to come home."

OK, let's end this.

"Mom, I'm in the army. Don't worry, I'll write in a few days. Bye, I have to go now."

I hang up and get back into the jeep. I'm glad I called. Even though I'm out on my own—in the army and all that—I'm still at an age that I check in with my folks from time to time.

We start up a street that leads back to the campus. We begin to slow down for a red light at the next intersection. Ron, should we just go through? *Isn't the army in charge of everything in this town now . . . detained rioters and traffic lights?* Somehow it feels odd to obey a traffic signal after the chaos in this town last night and this morning. If we stop at the red light, does our little act of civil obedience signal that law and order is returning? We stop.

I glance over to the opposite side of the street and see a man, maybe in his early thirties, coming out of a small store. Yep, this guy is no Ole Miss student, nor is he a townie. He's from the mob last night. His ensemble is a tight-fitting T-shirt, a bit wrinkled, a pair of somehow-still-creased Levi's, and a head of neatly combed, greased-back hair. A cigarette tight in his lips. He sees us. He stares. We stare back. He bends over and picks up a large rock at the curb. The hair stays in place. Nope. Can't be the Brylcreem of my teenage years. Never held the wave. Must be some kind of drugstore hair grease they sell down here in the South. He flips the rock back and forth in his hands while his body sways back and forth. He looks at us.

"Ron, OK . . . look at him, no, not just look, stare . . . stare at his eyes . . . lock onto them. Make the stare a warning. Don't look down at his hands . . . forget the rock. Just lock onto this sonofabitch's eyes."

The newly named "sonofabitch" puts his hands back down to his sides, but still holds the rock in one of them.

I glance at the light. Still red.

He's not really going to throw that at us, is he? *Hey, we're the U.S. Army!*

The light changes, we start to move.

The hand holding the brick starts to come up.

"Step on it!"

The rock skims off the hood of the jeep and bangs up against an already cracked windshield. We race through the intersection, up to and inside the perimeter that the army has set up to seal off the campus.

OK, even in daylight there's still brick throwing. And not at the marshals. At us! Again. Fine, just so we know the ground rules around here. Bring it on!

"Barrett, next time if we get the chance and we have two jeeps, we pull over, jam up against any one of them and pull out the night-sticks. Mullins [MP radio operator in the back seat], you too, be ready with your stick if this happens again."

Yankee Football Next to a Confederate Cemetery

In the afternoon the battalion moves to a field out near the airport. The site gives off a surreal impression. Here we are, invading Yankee soldiers, setting up a bivouac on a Mississippi hillside, next to a town whose citizens have met us with indifference and cold stares, if not outward hostility. Someone says we've set up camp next to a Confederate cemetery. Yes, we're still in a movie and have just relocated for another camera shoot.

Once again the army goes about its business of housing and feeding and otherwise supporting its troops with tents and a field mess. Wherever the army goes, there's food, be it served in a mess hall at Fort Dix or on a hillside in Mississippi. If not in combat, a mess sergeant promises three-a-day hot meals to the troops.

The men try to put the events of last night and early morning into some kind of understandable framework, struggling to make sense of what happened. Here we are, U.S. soldiers in our own country, clashing with our own people.

This afternoon, we play a pickup game of intrabattalion touch football on the hillside, both officers and enlisted. I quarterback one of the teams. Something's missing. We're all-white on both sides.

"He is to have no less freedom . . . than any other student will have."

At 1800 hours, my new driver, Spec-4 John Adams, drives me over to the Faculty House to report for my new assignment. (PFC Barrett, nursing that injured jaw, is off duty). I was a bit tired and distracted when I got the word this morning, so I can't recall if I'm to be meeting with civilians (Mr. Doar and Mr. Katzenbach) or with military. I think that the Department of Justice (DOJ) might have some kind of senior military liaison officer for this sort of operation and I assume that I'll be working under him and he'll be there to represent the army. And, in turn, he'll work with the DOJ people. So, I turn to a captain at the armory and ask him about the rank of the officer I'm to meet along with the civilians.

It's a harmless and routine question, particularly when one is about to report to a senior officer, and, in my case, report to *any* officer whose rank is above that of a second lieutenant. The captain tells me that I am to report directly to two civilians and that they both work at the Justice Department in Washington, D.C. He says he has heard that one guy works under the other. But he snaps at me a bit and reminds me that I won't be working for the civilians. I'll be working for the military.

Good. The protocol in the military world in which we operate is a comfortable one and its observance can be quite insular (read: no civilians). One is concerned only with its chain of command. Fine, I'll report to civilians, but I'll be working for the colonel.

The Faculty House is not too far from the Lyceum, down and across from the Grove. It's a Victorian structure that doesn't look like it belongs on the campus of a big university. It looks like a home more than a workplace. I walk up a long sidewalk, through the entrance, and turn into a large Oriental-carpeted room off the main hallway. Outside, the tear gas still lingers in the air, the riot debris has yet to be removed by army engineers, and here I am—walking across someone's Oriental with caked mud on my army boots from last night's rain. Too bad this room won't be in any of the photos about the Ole Miss crisis.

It's a bit strange going into a meeting with senior military officers in the background and civilian suits front and center—and here I am, a second lieutenant. Do these civilians outrank my colonel? Where is Colonel Brice? The officers look at me. I represent their team (and maybe their careers), the one military guy who'll be the closest to Meredith. I'm sure that some people are thinking, *"Don't fuck this up, Lieutenant."*

The unusual mix of military-civilian authority has caused confusion among the military since the outset of the crisis over the weekend. The National Guard officer in charge of the newly federalized Oxford contingent, Captain Murray "Chooky" Falkner (a nephew of the late writer, whose family chose a different spelling), was called last night at his command post at the armory to bring his men up to the campus immediately. The order came, not from a superior officer, but from a civilian, no less an authority than the Deputy Attorney General of the United Sates, but nevertheless . . . a civilian.

"I just got the craziest chain of command," Falkner said, explaining [to Williams, his immediate Guard superior] the presidential command that had just managed to bypass the entire U.S. military command structure. "Better do it," Williams noted, "JFK is the commander in chief."[2]

In the front line of the civilian suits is John Doar, a trial lawyer in the Civil Rights Division in the Justice Department. He's a lanky man with an easygoing manner about him, almost casual, but determined. He could have just walked off a movie set as a stand-in for James Stewart. It's more than a passing resemblance, the result both of his appearance and his delivery.

Next to him is Nicholas Katzenbach, the Deputy Attorney General of the United States and Attorney General Robert Kennedy's right-hand man. He's a large man, with an apparent nervous and awkward friendliness. I hear that both have just come through a horrendous experience last night with the marshals at the Lyceum building. Colonel Brice steps over and introduces me as the newly assigned officer-in-charge of Meredith's security patrol.

Well, we don't salute civilians and I've been away from handshakes for a while, saluting being the norm in my army world. In that world we salute people or they salute us, simple as that.

The two Justice Department officials tell me that a military police presence is the only visible force they want on the campus now that some degree of order has returned to the area. They say that the immediate concern of President Kennedy and the Justice Department is to protect Meredith and any deputy marshals or staff attorneys assigned to him. They're concerned about any violence or physical harm that might come from troublemakers, be they from within the student population or otherwise.

Mr. Doar speaks first.

"Lieutenant, we don't want Mr. Meredith to be moved from classroom to classroom with an armed escort of your military police. [Think: images of soldiers escorting students at Little Rock.] He is to have no less freedom to move about the campus than any other student will have."

The look on his face is a determined one and he uses a minimum of words that are direct and to the point. No rhetorical flourishes from this lawyer. He speaks in the no-nonsense flat delivery of a midwesterner. I'm familiar with that.

After Mr. Katzenbach makes a few remarks, they both look at me.

I'm surprised that I don't feel nervous, maybe because they're civilians. (If I can speak clearly to a general officer, as I did at that long-ago time this morning, this should be no problem.) Or maybe because there's not much I can say anyway, this being all so new to me, as it is to everyone else in this room.

Although I have little idea of what we're getting into, I have to say something.

"Sir, we'll do the best we can." (At my rank, I say "sir" to everybody in the room, civilians included.) "We have hand-picked sharpshooters in the patrol and they've all been briefed on the sensitivity of their assignment."

I shake the civilian hands again and go to leave the building to rejoin the battalion out on the hillside. Back where I belong. I continue to feel out of my element. It all started with that Oriental rug. I'm exhausted. Had there been a coatrack in the hallway on my way out, I probably would've saluted it.

On Tuesday morning, October 2, Adams and a radioman and I go out onto the campus where other units of the 716th are already on patrol. We want to get a sense of the building layouts and the streets in order to prepare for the Meredith assignment. At an intersection, we come across a small batch of booklets piled on a bench. I go over and pick one up and notice it has a campus map printed on its back cover. Some passing students are carrying around the same book. It's a fraternity orientation guidebook for freshmen.

I know that I need some kind of a guide or map if I am to be with Meredith every day on the campus. Here we are again, looking for a map for guidance.

We approach a student walking along a sidewalk with a copy of the booklet in his hands, slow down, and stop the jeep. I ask him where we can get a copy of it. I notice a slight pause on his side of the conversation, for we're part of the *them* who have just taken over his campus. *C'mon guy. I was one of you just a few years ago walking across a campus.*

He remains as polite as we are as he points to a building in the next block. And he calls me "sir," even though I'm probably no older than his brother. Must be the uniform. A good start.

We drive up to the building and Adams goes in and comes back out with fifteen to twenty copies meant for the first-year students. He hardly looks like an incoming freshman in his fatigues, holstered .45, and gas mask. He grins, "Sir, this is the closest I'll ever get to a college education. But at least I got the rules."

The discovery of this tiny campus map on the back page of the booklet, with each building highlighted in black silhouette and numbered, is a stroke of luck. The building numbers are the key. The map becomes an integral part of the patrol's operations. We'll use it to protect Meredith throughout his tenure on the campus.

Later in the day, I ask the battalion sergeant major to select twelve of the best MPs in the unit who, under my command, will constitute the security detail that we'll begin operating tomorrow morning. I ask for men who have qualified on the rifle and pistol ranges at the level of "sharpshooter" (or higher, "expert"), who have performed their police duties back at Dix in a commendable manner, and who have demonstrated mature judgment.

> The troops must have a very high sense of discipline. . . ; troops should be well-informed, particularly in . . . holding their tempers, not engaging in arguments with civilians, etc. They should be prepared to accept abusive language calmly and resolutely, and wherever officers or noncommissioned officers observe soldiers losing control of their emotions . . . [such soldiers] should be immediately removed from the scene of the operation [Gen. Abrams, citing Army Chief of Staff Designate General Wheeler's views].[3]

Above all, I ask for MPs who, in the opinion of this veteran sergeant, can handle tense situations with patience and restraint, realizing the unique assignment that they are about to undertake. I end by asking Top to give me a few men who speak "southern." He laughs and says that most of the troops in the battalion are from the North.

7

THE STUDENT

"AT EASE, men! I'll be in the area. . . ."

At 0700 hours the next morning our security patrol of four jeeps, three men in each vehicle, moves out from our hillside encampment toward the campus and Baxter Hall, where Meredith is housed in a separate end unit of the dormitory building. A sergeant and Spec-4 Adams are in my jeep.

Our mission? The army doesn't deal in nuance. Simply put, just keep this guy, the lawyer, and the marshal alive.

We pull up alongside the dormitory and I go in to meet Mr. Meredith. Lieutenant Frechette is on the grounds with a small contingent of MPs. There was a bomb scare reported this morning at the dormitory that causes some understandable tension, along with the jeering students who have gathered on a corner across the street. One of them yells over, "Hey, where's the nigger?"

A few of Frechette's men are posted on the way up to the door and, as I go up the steps, I say, "AT EASE, men! I'll be in the area all day!"

It's a phrase normally used by senior officers who suddenly appear when enlisted men are engaged in a work detail or eating in the mess hall. The arriving officer understandably does not want them to interrupt whatever they're doing by having them snap to attention.

We second lieutenants use it among ourselves for its affected self-posturing humor, a humor that enlisted men often find amusing. Pete's people acknowledge my remark and I hope it relaxes them a bit, particularly after what we've been through the last few days.

I should've ended my attempt at comic relief at this point. I go up to the door of Meredith's apartment unit. I think that only more of our battalion enlisted men are inside. I walk in.

"AT EA . . . SE . . . EE," I begin and suddenly stop. I quickly realize that I'm in one of those uh-oh moments.

No sooner do half the words come out than I find myself face-to-face with Mr. Katzenbach, Chief U.S. Marshal James P. McShane, General Billingslea, a bird colonel, my colonel, and assorted sergeants in the background. I catch Colonel Brice's eyes. Can't read them, but do read his mind and it's sending one of those "We need to talk, Lieutenant," signals. I'm too embarrassed to offer an apology or explanation and I move quickly toward an adjoining room. I walk in and hurriedly say "Hello, good morning" to three men, two of whom are whites in blue suits.

As was the case with the meeting over at the Faculty House, it's been a while since I've been around civilians in suits. I speak the words so fast that it's almost impolite, for I'm focused on the third man in the room. I turn to the newly registered, twenty-nine-year-old student from Kosciusko, Mississippi.

"Mr. Meredith, I'm Lieutenant Gallagher of the 716th Military Police Battalion. I'm the officer in charge of the security patrol that will be with you when you are out on the campus."

"Pleased to meet you, Lieutenant," he says in a quiet voice that fits his slight stature.

It's followed by a soft handshake from him, not a grip. So this is the hand that has started it all. He looks so out of place and I don't mean by the color of his skin. He's not in the campus fashion of the day, button-down collar, khakis, and penny loafers, but wears a suit neatly tailored to fit his thin, almost delicate, frame. His face is light brown with smooth skin. And it wears no expression that one can interpret one way or another. I don't see any immediate picture of strength or purpose. All that will come to me later.

He gives a well-groomed impression that suggests a lot of thought has gone into his appearance this morning, including the highly polished shoes. I sense a kind of in-your-face, conscious choice not to go casual or try to look like the rest of the student body. As he is six or seven years older than his classmates anyway, his choice of dress is understandable, regardless of race. He can't blend in, so why even try?

In these first brief minutes I sense a quiet reserve about him. He does not appear to be a lead actor in the civil rights movement, a role that I find out later others will urge him to play. He does not want to be anybody's stalking horse or to be a part of anybody's movement. Whatever he accomplishes will be his individual success and his alone. And for his own purposes.

In this small room I try not to have my look at him turn into a stare, this person who is the cause behind the presence of twenty thousand U.S. Army soldiers, not to mention some elements of the Mississippi National Guard, in and around the town of Oxford today. So I turn and look around the room. While he and his room may be neat and orderly this morning, an adjoining room is not. My eye catches a table with half-filled Styrofoam coffee cups and an ashtray full of bent butts—signs, maybe, not of his long night, but surely of the night that the other two men have just spent with him.

We wait.

The moment becomes one of those awkward gatherings when strangers are thrown into close quarters by chance—as in a stalled office building elevator—and each one hopes superficial conversation will cover the wait. Whatever does one talk about at such a time? No one asks one of those "Where're you from, Lieutenant" questions. Maybe we should all just look down at our shoes as if we really are in an elevator. A moment later, a fourth suit comes into the room and says, "OK, let's go."

A simple "let's go." When we're so close to such an event, to such an incident, we never see it for what it is—out the door and into a little piece of history—but I find out later that that's what this morning will become. I stand back to be the last one out of the room. Protocol. I look at Meredith ahead of me. He stops for a second to look down at his shoes. Out of reflex I look down at mine. Army boots. Still a little mud.

One of the 716th sergeants who had been in the room when I entered held the door for me. As I pass, he has a big grin on his face. Nothing to do with the significance of the moment—everything to do with the "at ease" remark I made when I first came in here.

"My daddy says he better be careful."

We leave the apartment with Chief McShane as Meredith's principal escort, accompanied by a Justice Department lawyer. They get into a car and move off to his first class. We follow in the jeep, staying about twenty yards behind, weaving through the debris-filled streets. At each of the traffic stops, small crowds of students call out insults to the new student and the car's white occupants—and to us in the jeep as well. They're off the sidewalk and over on the grass strips, some on the curbs as we approach, others stepping into the street itself.

"Hey, here come the nigger and the nigger-lovers!"

As the car pulls up to a building where he is to attend his first class today, students gather and heckle Meredith as he gets out.

"Good morning, you black bastard!"

"Go back to Africa where you belong, nigger!"

Just as Ole Miss's first black student was expressionless back in the dormitory, he wears no expression on his face now as he walks forward through a cluster of angry whites. (His face will wear down a bit in the months to come.)

I look at them. The loudest voices, others too hoarse to be loud, are coming out the mouths of reddened faces. Wow! What anger. What hatred. They strain their necks out toward us as we (the military police, the DOJ lawyer, and the marshal) pass by a few paces behind Meredith. The curses are scattershot and some are directed at us as well. We're part of the package. What catches my eye are the few coeds who join their male counterparts in the rush of emotion. The contorted faces of southern belles, not just pursed lips of disapproval, but pinched faces . . . hatred. I have to adjust to this picture—no more duck tails, white-T-shirts-and-Levi's-wearing skinny whites. Now, it's crew cuts, khakis, and bright cotton dresses on well-fed whites.

"Hey, here he is all dressed up in his Sunday suit like he's going to that nigger church out towards Batesville."

"Y'all look at him with that smirk on his face, now that he's got all the soldiers around him. My daddy says he better be careful."

Others in the crowd have their mouths locked so tight one can barely make out the lines of their lips, much less the gritting teeth just behind. They just stare. The hatred is palpable. Still others seemed to be there simply to observe, maybe to tell their friends and family later that they were here this morning. And, years later, their children and their grandkids. But can anyone in this crowd do any lethal harm?

The words "My daddy" catch my attention. It will be the first of many times that I will hear the phrase from students. I learn that parents play a large role in the lives of these sons and daughters of Mississippi, more than they do in the lives of teenage children up north when it comes to racial culture. Parents of northern college students simply are not faced with the issue of race separation. While neighborhoods in northern cities may be segregated de facto, their college campuses are not. This embedded legacy is just not there. Nor is the passion and loyalty for a region that I'm beginning to pick up on. I have never heard of "sons and daughters" of Ohio or Wisconsin.

One student, detained and interrogated yesterday morning, said that he left the safety of his dorm room on Sunday night near midnight to go back out onto the campus at the height of the violence because "my pappy told me to go back out there and stand up for my university."[1]

"Daddy." "Pappy."

My parents continued to play a role in my life as I approached my college years. But the role was diminished on the day the family car dropped me off at the curb outside my freshman dorm. In many ways, that was a "goodbye" on both sides. I don't recall a role that they (or the parents of my classmates) played as cultural overseers once I started college. Sure, our grades, spending, and partying habits might come up as topics of conversations once we got back home on school break. But there wasn't any urging to uphold "northern" culture or the legacy of race separation. While we had racism in the North, we didn't have the kind of parental oversight that seemed to perpetuate the legacy.

On my campus, if any one of us had said, "My pappy said this" or "My daddy said that" (the titles are interchangeable), it would've invited fair ridicule from anyone within earshot. Best to leave those kinds of phrases back home in the closet along with the high school letter jacket. Or was it just semantics? Simple differences in local speech from region to region in our country? Or something else? The word gave one the impression that the hold by the pappy onto the southern son was a bit stronger than the hold that a dad might have on his northern son.

The students at Ole Miss are witnessing a dramatic change in their culture. Not to downplay the moment, but our eyes are simply watching a student go to class, even though he is a black student on a once all-white campus. The only other blacks in sight are sanitation and cafeteria workers and a campus landscape detail.

The first moments in the crowd seem to be less uneasy for Meredith than they are for us. He's prepared for this and expects it. He's used to it. We're not. A few days later when I'm with him in his dormitory room, he tells me not to worry, not to be concerned. While not excusing their conduct, he says that the students are just mouthing what their parents want them to say. *The daddy/pappy thing again.* He adds that it all comes from their background, their towns and communities, their way of life—he knows that he stands as a threat to all of that.

"Their parents." That's what he's trying to explain to me. Yes, all the prior pappies. Does there come a time when the pappy (not the mommy) tells the son that the colored boy with whom he's been

The student. James Meredith with his lawyer, John Doar (left), First Assistant, Civil Rights Division, U.S. Department of Justice. Mississippi Highway Patrol Collection, Special Collections, University of Mississippi Libraries.

The Lyceum. The center of it all on September 30, 1962. Author's collection.

The crowd. Deputy marshals and students outside the Lyceum before the scene turned ugly on September 30, 1962. Special Collections, University of Memphis.

The aftermath. National Guardsmen and deputy marshals examine two burned-out cars near the Lyceum. Special Collections, University of Memphis.

The debris. Empty tear gas canister cartons litter the street adjacent to the Lyceum. Special Collections, University of Memphis.

The detainees. Some in the mob were students, few of them enrolled at Ole Miss. Special Collections, University of Memphis.

The guards. Soldiers from the 716th Military Police (MP) Battalion stand guard at a gate to the campus. Special Collections, University of Memphis/UPI Telephoto.

A 716th MP at the entrance to the Baxter Hall dormitory, with James Meredith and press. Special Collections, University of Memphis.

716th MPs face-off with the residents of the Kappa Alpha fraternity house on the University of Mississippi campus. W. Wert Cooper Collection, Special Collections, University of Mississippi Libraries.

The MPs move furniture placed in the road by residents of the fraternity house. W. Wert Cooper Collection, Special Collections, University of Mississippi Libraries.

The bivouac. Army pup tents on the football practice field adjacent to Hemingway Stadium. Library of Congress, Prints & Photographs Division, *U.S. News & World Report* Magazine Collection.

James Meredith on his way to class from the dormitory, Baxter Hall. Author's collection.

James Meredith in deputy marshal's car en route to class (car used first week only). Library of Congress, Prints & Photographs Division, *U.S. News & World Report* Magazine Collection.

James Meredith exits car to enter building for class (Spec-4 John Adams and author in jeep). Library of Congress, Prints & Photographs Division, *U.S. News & World Report* Magazine Collection.

Class schedule, fall 1962. Henry T. Gallagher Collection, Special Collections, University of Mississippi Libraries.

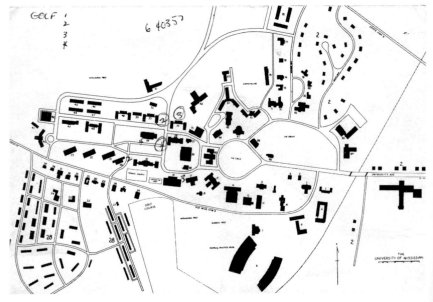

Campus map from the back cover of the freshman orientation booklet. Building numbers combined with 10-series radio codes assisted the Peanut Patrol in expediting the protection scheme during the first week. Henry T. Gallagher Collection, Special Collections, University of Mississippi Libraries.

James Meredith entering Peabody Hall. Author's collection.

Author, Spec-4 Adams (driver), and PFC Barrett (rear seat) watch James Meredith enter Peabody Hall. Author's collection.

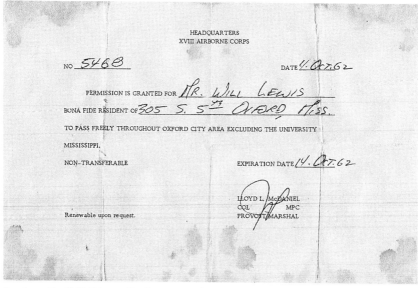

HEADQUARTERS
XVIII AIRBORNE CORPS

NO _5468_   DATE _4. Oct. 62_

PERMISSION IS GRANTED FOR _Mr. Will Lewis_
BONA FIDE RESIDENT OF _305 S. 5th Oxford Miss._
TO PASS FREELY THROUGHOUT OXFORD CITY AREA EXCLUDING THE UNIVERSITY
MISSISSIPPI.

NON-TRANSFERABLE   EXPIRATION DATE _14. Oct. 62_

                                    LLOYD L. McDANIEL
                                    COL   MPC
                                    PROVOST MARSHAL
Renewable upon request.

Pass issued by XVIII Airborne Headquarters to the owner of Neilson's Department Store on the town square. Courtesy Will Lewis.

REBEL —
Underground

Nov. 1, 1963

VOL. I, NO. 2   University, Mississippi
                                       October

FLASH

(OR SHOULD WE SAY "BANG"?)

WE URGE THE ORGANIZATION OF "REBEL UNDER-GROUND" TEAMS AND UNITS ON EVERY FLOOR OF EVERY DORMITORY AND IN EVERY SORORITY AND FRATERNITY HOUSE ON THE CAMPUS.

Our primary objective is to encourage James Meredith to transfer to some college where he would be welcome. There are many "Yankee" colleges which would eulogize him and make him "Tar Baby" of the campus.

His forced entry here has already caused two deaths, bloodshed, chaos and bitterness which will last for years. He has made his point and proved that our President is controlled by the NAACP.

While the Communist Party, USA, was wiring President Kennedy to send troops to Ole Miss on September 30th in a telegram, the Communists in Cuba were installing missiles aimed at the United States.

Russell Barrett, Left-wing professor, dined with James Meredith the other morning. It is in keeping with his philosophy to mingle socially with the Negro who has done so much for the Communist cause through the NAACP. (National Association for the Advancement of the Communist Party.)

We are looking forward to the day when the KKK (Kennedy Koon Keepers) will leave our campus.

Congratulations to Russell H. Barrett, Robert J. Farley, Harley F. Garrett and James W. Silver. In recognition for services rendered the NAACP has proclaimed these professors to be "Honorary Niggers".

Incidentally, we feel that these and a few other "racial perverts" now on our faculty would be happier teaching at Tougaloo or Tuskegee.

The "Rebel Underground" holds the Federal Court in "contempt". Those judges are indeed "contemptible".

Now, boys, don't upset Sidna. She may win a Pulitzer Prize.

BEAT LSU

READ AND PASS ON

The *Rebel Underground*. Leaflet distributed on campus. Special Collections, University of Mississippi Libraries.

Railroad overpass (since dismantled). At this overpass, a stalled convoy of a unit from the 503rd MP Battalion was attacked by a mob throwing debris from above. Author's collection.

Peanut Patrol outside Oxford Armory, author far left. Author's collection.

Aerial view of Camp USAFOX, spring 1963. An upgrade from the pup tents of October 1962. U.S. Army/Courtesy Richard Mitchell.

C Company Commander (716th) Benjamin Waldron and First Sergeant Ballowe. U.S. Army/Courtesy Richard Mitchell.

Work detail at Camp USAFOX, aka "Mud." U.S. Army/Courtesy Richard Mitchell.

USAFOX bulletin board. Courtesy David Steinberg.

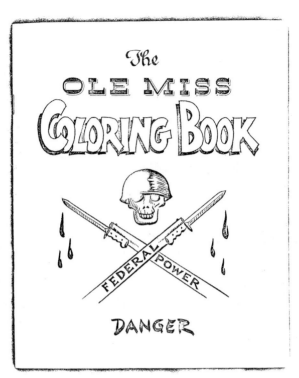

The Ole Miss Coloring Book. Author's collection.

Author (center) with 2nd Lieutenant Richard Mitchell (right), successor officer-in-charge, Peanut Patrol, and Corporal Gutierrez, C Company, Camp USAFOX, spring 1963. Author's collection.

James Meredith graduates from Ole Miss, August 18, 1963. Special Collections, University of Mississippi Libraries.

James Meredith with U.S. Congressman John Lewis at the 2006 statue unveiling ceremony. Author's collection.

Author Henry T. Gallagher, officer-in-charge (OIC) of James Meredith's security patrol (Peanut Patrol). Author's collection.

Letter to the author from James Meredith, November 1962. Henry T. Gallagher Collection, Special Collections, University of Mississippi Libraries.

TO: Lt. Gallagher

I know that your assignment over the past few weeks has been unique, if not indeed strange, I have enjoyed your presence and I hope you have not been too unhappy.

The processes of civilization are sometimes hard to understand. Yet, they must go on. In this development, sometimes we find ourselves (some of us) at the apex of a point of friction. Immediately we are harnessed with a great responsibility. We are all duty bound to carry out this responsibility to the best of our ability. This we will do.

Presently we are faced with a great and grave racial problem in our country. It points deep in many directions. I feel that it is essential that we solve this problem, if America is to hold the place among nations that it deserves. Finding a solution to this problem is my goal.

Best wishes, and lots of luck to you in your mission.

J.H. Meredith

playing down by the creek is actually a "nigger" and an inferior (or whatever adult-to-a-seven-year-old-kid word is used) human being? All this said so that the "Word," almost as in the Bible, is passed on? Does this chain ever break? What if the son goes north or out west to work for a while? Or to Europe for a year or so, to see how the rest of the world lives? Or does the son always stay inside the state lines, becoming a *pappy* himself?

> They [the Ole Miss students] remain, in general, close to their families and share their views. Signs of even routine post-adolescent rebellion are lacking.[2]

I can only wonder how far this kind of pappy-to-son talk goes back—from deep down at the base of the family tree and then up the trunk through all the successor pappies, ending up with the newest twig on the tree—the screaming kid out on the street corner the first day. How far will it go forward? This kid will be that pappy someday.

Not to worry, Meredith says. But . . . we're new in town. We're only hours away from the violence and we have to make adjustments that go beyond his perception of the situation. We have yet to get a feel for crowds, not crowds of violent gun-toting troublemakers, but of students, unarmed ones, we hope. Conversely, the students have yet to take their measure of us. But most of them avoid heckling the patrol members directly—something about a military uniform to a southerner.

I position the three other jeeps around the campus at various out-of-the-way locations, although there is hardly a way that an OD army jeep holding three OD armed soldiers can be totally out of the way. But the out-of-the-way sites are to lessen our campus profile as much as possible. Their relative invisibility is crucial if and when the soldiers have to come out from their "cover" in a rush to protect us.

A rule is set down that will remain the standard policy for months to come. While out of sight, the soldiers are to be on the radio with me and not more than thirty seconds from my location with Meredith (and any accompanying deputy marshal and DOJ lawyer) whenever we're out on the campus.

When the students move in a bit too close to us in the afternoon, we have to make our presence known immediately. We need to set a tone. With all due respect to the Mississippi National Guardsmen who acquitted themselves so well on Sunday night, we have to show the students that we're not Mississippi's own, once-a-month soldiers from nearby towns (and even their student body). It is a marker we have to throw down. We're not only from out of state, but we're trained regular U.S. Army military police. We have none of the divided loyalties that might have troubled some of their own Guardsmen, not to mention their highway patrolmen, that night. Some of the locals might even consider us mercenaries who've come down from the North, called in to do the bidding of the Kennedy brothers.

Although we're but one jeep of three soldiers slowly following behind Meredith, somehow the students have to sense (yet we can't show them) that fully armed backup is ready to move to us within thirty seconds. The students can never fully appreciate the seriousness of our role. I order the patrol members not to talk to the students unless it's essential for their work. This "no-talk" order to the patrol members will further signal the importance of our job.

Some tension remains throughout the day. We can't know for sure if all the rioters have been detained or have left town. And, if not, are they still mixed in with the students and intent on doing more than heckling and jeering?

"Lieutenant . . . we love our Nigras down here."

On Thursday morning, October 4, the battalion continues the mobile patrols on the campus along with our patrol. We transfer to another bivouac location, this time the football stadium practice field on the campus itself. Like it or not, we become a "part" of campus life.

The gag order in place with members of the patrol might not even be necessary. North and South do not talk to each other, even though we will become a constant presence on the campus and in the town. While senior university and town officials talk to senior military officials about law and order issues, as well as traffic control, telephone service, water supply and garbage disposal, there is no such dialogue down at our level.

However, the Mississippi Guard members who are still on federal duty this first week do speak to us. We are all on the same "team" and are tented together on the same football field. On Wednesday morning, while having a cold-water shave in one of the stadium bathrooms, a senior officer in the Mississippi Guard at the next mirror glances over at me.

"Lieutenant, y'all come back here again when things quiet down. We love our Nigras down here, y'all will see."

It's not a thoughtless sideways snicker, like "Hey, nigger lover"; it's the N-word said in an acceptable southern-accented form that I haven't heard before. A kind of safe in-between word, I think. OK, another introduction to South-speak, if that's what it is. (Years later a white Mississippian will tell me that it was the racist's way of never having to say "Ne . . . GRO," while his Delta-born wife standing next to him will say that "Ne . . . GRA" was simply the word "Negro" with the local accented overlay, no racial slight intended.) However, what strikes me is his use of the word *our* which precedes his *Nigras.* It was a possession kind of thing . . . our community, our football team . . . our *Nigras.* So, this is the cultural divide between us, one bathroom mirror away. There it is, the word—a slight or not—but combined with a paternalistic separation as he marks the line between him and the blacks in his South.

He says it with such apparent affection for the blacks and such hospitality for me. And "southern" hospitality it is. He really means it, where a northerner might not really mean it, if he even gets around to saying it. But, with this Guard officer, who could've been a local farmer or a car salesman last week before the call-up, it's a long-standing affection for the blacks provided there is distance between the two. Separation. That's the key. And the affection will continue as long as he stays separated and "in his place." And surely one of those places this Mississippian hasn't expected a "Nigra" to be this morning is on the Ole Miss campus carrying books and not a rake or a broom.

Also, the *down here* from him is a subtle reminder that I'm from *up there* and maybe I have a few things to learn in this new land. It's but the first of many times that I will hear the invitation to come back to the state, combined with this odd paternalistic boast. Southern hospitality coupled with a social commentary.

I seldom heard any mention of "blacks" on that hitchhiking trip through the Bible Belt in 1956. It was never part of any conversation we had, not with the city jail keeper in Chattanooga who let us sleep on newspapers in the hallway. No, not with the Salvation Army clerk in Birmingham who gave us two couches in the lobby. And surely not with the truck drivers who picked us up on Highway 78 (the one we just convoyed down) as we went west from Birmingham over to Tupelo and on up north to Memphis. And if the "Negro" did come up in conversation, it was "nigger," said as easily as we would say "Swede" up in Minnesota.

The conversations with local police, truck stop waitresses, and truckers were all white-on-white. The only outward displays of the racial separation were the *Colored Only* or *White Only* signs at the bus stations and roadside cafes where we would stop. Of course, no blacks driving cars or trucks dared (or probably wanted to) pick us up, only white drivers. It was simply their way of life—SEP-AR-ATE—and some things just did not need to be talked about with two teenagers from the North; some things were unspoken, taken for granted, just under a southerner's white skin. The black was not a visible enough feature of the white man's world to be talked about much.

Other than these few kinds of exchanges with Guard members, the North and the South continue not to speak to each other after the first week. On the topic of race relations, it seems that the two groups remain separated by years of post–Civil War conditioning. New Jersey talks only to Massachusetts and New York—not to Mississippi, who talks only to Georgia and Alabama.

But we do have a few southern accents in our Army of Central New Jersey. Jimmie Dukes is having a good time talking to the girls with his Georgia accent, though these conversations may be a risk for the coeds because we hear that the dean of women has ordered expulsion for anyone in her charge caught talking to soldiers. If any other southern accents are heard from the military on campus, they're more likely to come from the career-bound officers in the 101st or the 2nd Division units—West Point and Citadel graduates, and the enlisted men under them.

One morning as we drive up to Baxter Hall, we hear the chant *"Airborne, all the way . . . Airborne, all the way"* from the 101st soldiers as they run their morning exercises up the lane past the sorority houses. Word is that a few of the occupants, risking ridicule from their coed sisters or censure from the dean of women, lean out of their windows and wave towels, or even more intimate items, at the passing troopers.

"Where are the Negro soldiers?"

By midday, Meredith has become aware that no black soldiers are in our detail or on any others on the campus.

"Lieutenant, where are the Negro soldiers? There must be some in your ranks."

What do I say?

"Mr. Meredith, I think some of the units were ordered to hold back Negro troops from coming to Oxford Sunday night and Monday morning. I mean, things were pretty bad. I heard there were snipers in the trees. Maybe Negroes would've been singled out."

I don't think my answer resonates with him. Later in the month I realize that he never really appreciated the scale and impact of the violence that raged over the campus that Sunday night. He was hidden away in Baxter Hall, most likely asleep, waiting for his first full day of classes and the first real day of his mission. He hadn't a clue.

As a result of this and other comments from him that will follow in the weeks to come, I sense a disconnect between his view of it all and the real-world situation. It's the beginning of a pattern of indifference or feigned ignorance of the reality of what's going on around him. In either case, it appears to be a necessary survival trait that I will see over and over again throughout the time I'm with him. What he can't anticipate, appreciate, and make sense of can't bother him. He can tune out, simply not comprehend how a sniper might be on a roof of a building down the street, holding a high-powered rifle. Keep the blinders on so he can accomplish what he set out to do. For him, it works. He's "pushing the envelope" years before the phrase comes into usage.

I quickly pass his comment up to headquarters. He also makes his views known where it would count.

> Meredith complained to Deputy Attorney General Katzenbach that the troops guarding him and seen elsewhere on the campus were segregated. [After some discussion among senior military and civil officials, including the president], General Howze issued instructions to his subordinate commanders to use their Negro soldiers in all duty assignments with two exceptions. Negro soldiers would not be used as "individual sentinels or on isolated individual missions" [the president's words]. . . . He added that "this policy must be applied with great care by all commanders to assure that our men are not placed in situations exposing them to undue risk or where the possibility of conflict with the local citizenry is high."[3]

Apparently Meredith was still not satisfied with the restrictive use of black soldiers and made his views known to the press:

On Monday, October 8, 1962, Negro soldiers were indeed seen among the [other] soldiers. The ones I saw, however, were on a garbage-detail truck and unarmed. The white members of the detail were armed. This condition constitutes a dishonor and a disgrace to the hundreds of thousands of Negroes who wear the uniforms of our military services.

. . . My conscience would not allow me to go on observing the situation without, at least, letting the Negro soldiers know that I did not like them being dishonored.[4]

I found out later that one of Meredith's operational tactics is a frequent resort to the press, a press that's all too hungry for something, anything. He must have a sense for the benefits of such media coverage and public relations.

Shortly after the troop segregation issue was raised, the black members of the 716th who were pulled from our ranks are brought into Oxford and integrated back into the battalion. One of them, Sergeant Brooks, is assigned to our patrol as the NCOIC (noncommissioned officer-in-charge). I brief him, saying that the students are going to shout out "nigger" and throw all kinds of "racist shit" at him. He says that he can handle it, that it's his job . . . simply adding that he's a soldier.

A few days later, when the sergeant, due to a personnel matter back at the camp, arrives late to his assigned jeep on the campus, he is dropped off by a white private driving a jeep belonging to the orderly tent. The nearby students can only stare at the scene. It's probably the first time they've ever seen a white driving a black in the state of Mississippi. God only knows how they might react if military protocol required that lower ranks salute NCOs and this white driver salute this black sergeant.

The students with whom I came in contact at Ole Miss could not believe that I was . . . that we were . . . blind to the racial make-up of the members of our unit. It never occurred to us to be any other way.[5]

Meredith's complaint about the absence of black soldiers on the campus went to the right official. A civilian. He didn't suffer the confusion that the Guard officer, Captain Falkner, did on Sunday when he was ordered up onto the campus by that same civilian, Nicholas Katzenbach. The Department of Justice is in charge. The U.S. Army is in a supporting role and has known that from the outset. But as the roles are played out on this stage, some uncertainty and confusion do arise, as they did when I went to report to the two DOJ civilians on Monday night. Not only is it a matter of who the players are and what their roles are, but what their authority is. Easy to tell in the military. Rank. One need only look at the metal symbol on a collar or a shoulder. But the military officer can't determine rank when the individual in front of him is wearing a suit and a button-down collar. It's easy back at the Pentagon. When a civilian employee has a cubicle next to the colonel's, either one of them can refer to the DOD publication, "Military and Civilian Schedule of Equivalent Grades" and see that it shows the same pay and housing allowance due the colonel and his civilian counterpart. Equals. It's a management tool used by the various personnel departments in the services. One might even take a peek at it to see who in the office "makes the coffee." Does the one-star general walk down the hallway to meet in the senior civilian official's office or vice versa?[6]

"Who let that coon in here?"

Late Wednesday afternoon, I go over to the student cafeteria for a briefing to learn of the plans for Meredith to eat his evening meal there tomorrow night. Mr. Doar and others meet with the cafeteria manager, Mr. Bounds. The plan is to have Meredith enter the dining hall toward the end of the supper period so as to cause the least amount of notice and disturbance. He will be accompanied by Doar and a deputy marshal and sit near the main entrance.

Meredith's presence in the student cafeteria will be another step in his integration effort. To many of the Ole Miss students, it's one thing for him to study and sleep in a dormitory room closely guarded by the military and the marshals. It's quite another thing to eat meals in a large common dining hall filled with whites. His decision to do so simply underscores his stubborn insistence that he will conduct himself as any other student will while out on the campus.

Later in the day, the few students who are in the cafeteria for early supper are caught by surprise by his arrival. We're concerned because, in contrast to a classroom, it will be the first time that he's in a large open hall. He's with but one deputy marshal, who is armed, and John Doar, of course, who is not. Adams places our jeep at the front entrance.

A moment later, my radioman says, "Sir, we've lost radio contact with the marshal inside. We can't raise him on our freq."

Another jeep calls in. "Do you want us to come closer to the steps of the building?"

"No . . . not yet. Wait."

Students walking by the cafeteria outside see Meredith through the windows. They begin to shout out curses at him. They've never seen a black in the dining hall unless he was busing dishes or standing behind a serving counter. The domestics in Mississippi dare not eat in the family dining room. They eat back in the kitchen. So, too, do some of the students think that their cafeteria is where the Ole Miss "family" eats. How dare he eat here? Before tonight, the hecklers thought that the "nigger" in their midst could carry on his bizarre mission inside the four walls of his cell down at Baxter Hall, eating his meals under the watchful eyes of the "Kennedy coon keepers."

And what alarm might course through the disbelieving onlookers if he should dare to get up from the table to go over to a drinking fountain or, worse yet, to the students' bathroom down a hallway? No need for a "White Only" sign over either, for he was already in a "White Only" building. Mr. Bounds would not have had enough time to run around and get signs made and hung up. My God! What if he sits on the "White Only" toilet seat . . . a seat for years dedicated to bringing comfort and relief to the bottoms of white male southerners?

> The fight in the South over desegregating restaurants has been long and bitter, and has become one of the focal points of the whole civil rights controversy. So it was a shock to the Ole Miss students when, for the first time, they saw a Negro take a tray and start down the line of steam tables. . . . In the cafeteria, a student said, loudly, "Who let that coon in here?"[7]

The curses continue. Bounds comes out of the building and runs over to my jeep. He keeps looking back over his shoulder at the front door of his cafeteria as he asks for "protection" if things get out of hand. I tell him that we'll just have to see how it plays out. He runs back up the steps and into the building.

No incidents. After another fifteen minutes, Meredith and Doar come out the front entrance and move on to Baxter Hall.

As we move through this first week, we try not to focus attention solely on Meredith. This seems simple enough, but in the beginning it seems unnatural. He's our charge. Won't we just want to watch him as he walks, so he'll come to no harm? Like a concerned parent watching a child amble on ahead? When his class period ends, all we do is eyeball the front door of his classroom building, like the family dog waiting for its owner to come out.

How wrong . . . and dangerous! But we have no specialized MP training, no starter kit, in this art of guarding a body. No army field manual for such a task. Prisoner escort is the closest to any training model for MPs and that's hardly the case here, although Meredith will come to complain that he's just that, a prisoner, surrounded by army captors.

We just learn as we go along. We begin to move our gazes back and away from him, at a distance from where we can see left and right, no longer center. We perform eye-sweeping—quick eye movements over a crowd. I start to look, not for any potential small-group violence, but for a single gunman. I remind Adams not to look at Meredith, but to look around him and beyond him.

It becomes instinctive. We do a quick glancing survey of bystanders as Meredith (and the deputy) wade though a group of students. If they're all looking at the "subject," then that's the context in which we will work. But our concern intensifies if we spot certain other kinds of individual behavior, such as eyes fixed on us and not on Meredith. Checking us out to see how we work.

It's also important not to concentrate solely on the immediate crowd around our charge, but to look at individuals who might be standing off a bit in the distance. We learn to look at the upper floors and rooftops of campus buildings.

Our stares go deep into the crowd to look for people who seem out of place now that the more violent ones have left Oxford. Are there any "nonstudent-looking" observers whom we can spot by checking out their dress, their demeanor? This is not too difficult for some of us on the patrol who were college students ourselves only twelve to eighteen months ago.

If we see anyone standing out from the students—is he just there out of curiosity or for other purposes? We can't forget that we're still in the early days of this forced racial integration of the university, an event that remains a deeply traumatic one for many here in the South.

> In spite of the relative calm, the visceral emotions that had boiled over into bloody insurrection were still inflamed. On Friday [Oct 12], as Meredith walked to the library, still guarded, a coed shouted out: "Why doesn't somebody kill him?"[8]

It's at this time that we construct the profile of a Meredith stalker (the killer "wannabe"), whose persona will become part of our daily briefings and the clear focus for our sharpshooters. He will be the face on the poster that will remain with us throughout our time at Ole Miss. The bad guys have left the campus and we realize that the students will bring no lethal harm to Meredith. In the days and weeks ahead, they'll become irrelevant. It's the "Man Wanted" guy we begin to look for.

The threat, we think, will come from outside the student population, a very public and violent attack on Meredith by one gunman. It is this one ominous theme—waiting for the lone gunman—that will hold and keep our attention. We give him a name, the "crazed gunman" (we're not at a point yet where he deserves his own radio call sign). He will most likely be a committed segregationist, an extremist who will come onto the campus and get close enough in a crowd of students to get off one round from a rifle or a handgun. (Think Byron De La Beckwith in 1963 and James Earl Ray a few years later.)

Or, maybe no need to get in close. I come from a boyhood culture of game hunting. In that sense, Minnesota is like Mississippi. In the fall it's a hunter's country and hunters wait for "opening day" with the same impatience that their kids wait for Halloween. Rifles and shotguns are commonplace in small towns, and SUVs and pickups parade down main streets with trophy kills lashed to their trailers and hoods. So there's nothing unusual about a rifle on the streets of Oxford this fall. Our gunman might be one of them. And it's even possible that no one would know of him in the community of those who are of similar mind, the Klan, for example. Just a law-abiding good ole stay-at-home racist. And, when not at home in front of the TV set, he might be at a deer camp in the next county over, practicing. No opening-day wait for him. He has his own calendar. He's not a trained assassin, but a trained racist who can bring down a buck at two hundred yards. All he needs is a high-powered rifle and a bent mind.

If we're lucky, we might be able to see him before he gets off that long-distance round. But without that opportunity, we can only try to catch him before he flees the campus. In a sense, all we can be is a visible deterrent who might give the "nut case" pause once he sees us. But a lot of hunters get illegal shots off outside the views of game wardens. So too here, that's all we really are. And to him the campus is a hunting ground over which his prey freely wanders.

62 Olds White Ark 31-1898

MPs in the field are trained to keep notes. So too their officers. Mine are recorded in a Woolworth's ("Nifty Notes, 10 cents") spiral tablet that I keep in a chest pocket of my fatigue shirt.

For example:

"I'm warning you, Mister, we're gonna have a party tonight." (student remark to deputy marshal)

black & wh Ford Tenn 2C-8910

(at cafeteria) 20 min meal/me to marshal (signals to window) (gestures) "stay in . . . go out back"

62 Olds white Ark 31-1898

2 men (near) Conner Hall Fla 19W 939850/short/glasses/black hair/brown pants/grey jacket

One never knows which bland tablet entry might be the first piece of evidence in an investigation of a tragedy on the campus.

Despite our constant presence and visibility, those of us responsible for his safety know that it is all but impossible to guarantee the life of James Meredith—freely walking across the campus—against the act of a determined sniper.

In the weeks to come, at the end of each day when Meredith is back in his dormitory on what he probably considers "lockdown," I'll receive regular briefings from an FBI unit which has taken up residence and is working out of an office in a downtown hotel. They'll advise me of any suspicious newcomers in town who may have checked into local motels or hotels—again, the specter of the person who just might be the one we're expecting. I'll include any FBI alerts in my briefing to the Peanut Patrol the next morning.

8

THE ARMY

The "Peanut Patrol"

The patrol needs a name for communication purposes. We're sitting around the orderly tent at the practice field and a commo clerk comes and tells me that we need a call sign for the patrol. Lieutenant Vince Farrell (Providence College '61) looks up from the comic pages of a local newspaper and says, "Hey, Hank, call it the Peanut Patrol . . . you know, from this Charlie Brown *Peanuts* strip . . . yeah, and you can be Peanut 1." From that night on, the name sticks and does so well beyond its original purpose. Over time the call sign will change but not the unmilitary-like brand name given the patrol. (At the time of the Cuban missile crisis later this month, even a deployment message to the Oxford command from the Pentagon will contain a reference to the "Peanut Patrol.")

As for assigning me, a lowly second lieutenant, to be the OIC of this security patrol—this is the military way. In contrast to the business world, where more thought might have been given to making such a critical personnel decision, the military simply throws young officers into the pool and they are expected to swim.

The patrol briefings by me at the morning roll calls are a mixture of the routine and the novel (including a court martial warning in the event of serious misconduct).

Excerpt from notes of an early October 1962 roll call:

1. campus assignments
2. seriousness of mission
    — be level-headed
    — Peanut 3 has "engine trouble" today
    — Peanut 4 will "malinger" today
    — appearance
    — manners toward students
    — radio procedure
    — incidents/court martial (Article 15)
    — inconspicuous
***
4. fatigue uniforms
***
7. no talking to students
8. wash jeeps
9. tonight's movie: *Let No Man Write My Epitaph*

Often the most important part of the morning briefing for the men will be that night's movie selection.

There is no need to advise them of the consequences of any soldierly misconduct. They're well aware of Article 15 and the court martial options that the U.S. Army has available to it if any one of them becomes insubordinate, undisciplined, or commits an offense under the military code. Moreover, they know all too well the daily scrutiny they're under—from the command, the press, the students, and others—while serving on this patrol.

". . . a lieutenant just waved a general off the road."

On Sunday I go on a helicopter recon out to Clear Creek, about nine miles west of the campus, to look over an area alongside a two-lane road that connects to an interstate. We do "contour" flying in a LOH Light Observation Helicopter) over patches of trees

and small rundown farmhouses. The noise brings out black occupants—a man and three trailing kids—probably seeing this flying
creature for the first time in their lives. All faces staring up. Do
they know what's going on? Maybe they're so far away from this
story now.

Meredith has left the campus to go up to Memphis for the
weekend. I'm ordered to meet the marshal's car that's bringing him
back this afternoon at a point on the road after it turns off Highway 55. There's concern that a sniper might seize the moment on
this small country road—away from the campus and the troops—
where Meredith will be traveling with nothing more than a one- or
two-car escort. After I get back on the ground we take the jeep
out onto the road to do a sweep, looking for anything unusual.
Nothing.

As we circle back toward Oxford to wait for the Meredith group,
I look in the rearview mirror and see a jeep coming up quickly
behind us. I turn to Adams.

"John, see that jeep behind us? Dammit! Who are they?"

"Don't know, sir." He stares into the mirror.

"Off-duty? What the hell! Are they out on a Sunday frolic? C'mon,
get out of here. What 716th jeeps are supposed to be on this road?"

"Don't know, sir."

The radio jumps alive. It's a message from the marshal's car carrying Meredith. A hurried voice comes on, mentioning the Meredith call sign: "Magnet, closing fast on your location."

I jerk my head around and motion with my right arm to the
fast-approaching jeep to get off the road. I point over to the dirt
shoulder.

Get off! Get off! Dammit!

The mystery jeep finally turns over onto the shoulder.

Looking back, I don't catch the three stars on its bumper plate
or the long whip-backed radio antennae as it moves off the road.

Adams does.

"Sir, I think a lieutenant just waved a general off the road."

What the fuck?

OK, I recall hearing that a lieutenant general had taken charge of all military forces in the Oxford area from Brigadier General Billingslea a few days ago.

We then pull over a hundred yards farther down the road. Moments later two black government-issue late-model Fords speed by us.

While still in the jeep on this country road on what started out to be a peaceful and uneventful Sunday, I begin to prepare my defense. *Sir, we had a job to monitor the road.* No one told us a general, or any military, would be out here this afternoon.

I look over at Adams. He's trying not to grin. He's of no help. It's one of those moments that enlisted men relish. One of those "Humor in Uniform" anecdotes for *Reader's Digest.* He can't wait to get back to his buddies to tell, in great detail, a "can-you-believe-what-the-lieutenant-just-did" story.

That night, without much warning, Meredith tells one of the marshals that he no longer wants to be driven to class in a car. On Monday morning, with a marshal and a DOJ lawyer, he leaves Baxter Hall and starts to walk to his 8:00 class.

Up to this point, we've tailored the patrol's operations to fit the shifting attitudes and conduct *only* of the students. Meredith was the constant. Now, we have to adjust to the new dynamic. Should've expected it. He not only thinks he doesn't need us; he surely doesn't want to be seen as a government charge being driven around the campus in a marshal's car. He wants to walk like any other student.

Our work becomes more challenging. It's too impractical for me to follow in a jeep behind him walking. I would clearly look like a handler, a sitter. He'll resent it and the students will ridicule such a scene. I decide to walk at a short distance behind him while Adams and the radioman stay in the jeep, watching our movement. This method too has its limitations, for it reduces the quick reaction capability of the other units to weigh in if an emergency arises. Our radio is thirty yards behind me. That's five hundred yards when seconds count against a gunshot.

We devise an operational plan that becomes the model for the duration of our time on the campus. One jeep simply will hold a line of sight on Meredith and then pass him on to another set of eyes in another jeep that will "pick" him up in their sight line. I no longer will move just because he does.

After I finish the walk to his first class, I stay nearby in the lead jeep.

4. DUTIES AND RESPONSIBILITIES

a. The Peanut Patrol will become operational whenever there is indication that Mr. Meredith will depart his quarters. Radio and telephone communications are established with the U.S. Marshals accompanying him. The officer in charge will direct and control all movements of the patrol. He will always position himself unobtrusively in the approximate vicinity of Mr. Meredith.

The marshal accompanying Meredith into the classroom has instructions to contact me in the event of any disruption inside the building. When they come out of the class, I go on the radio net to the other jeeps and report that "Magnet" has started walking toward his next class. This time, I stay in place and sight-track him until I lose him around a corner or down a street. At this moment I "pass" him on to another unit into whose line of sight he will appear. This jeep will then call in a "pick up" of him.

b. The remaining three (3) vehicles will be positioned in the general area of travel by Mr. Meredith, but out of sight of the subject. They will be inconspicuously parked in locations near enough that they can readily be concentrated at a given location in the event of emergency.

Each morning, the jeeps are placed in positions that conform to his class schedule for that particular day.

c. The OIC will always attempt to determine Mr. Meredith's schedule prior to his tour of duty and brief all personnel prior to their going on duty.[1] (Memo dated November 18, 1962. The SOP was in effect starting in early October.)

The virtue of this new method of monitoring in place is that Meredith *appears* to be freely walking the campus with but one marshal as an escort (and a DOJ lawyer at times.) Yet, he's in the line of sight of at least one of our units at all times. Seldom, if at all, are there any blind spots or gaps in the "pass on" and "pick up" scheme that we have developed. It's an "overlapping" of visuals, so that one pair of eyes is seamlessly lapping over onto another pair—like passing the baton in a track meet, the baton being Meredith, along to the next "runner." And the backup is always the battalion radio dispatcher monitoring this "track and field" event over at HQs at the practice field in case an incident arises that requires a response that is beyond our capabilities. Most important, the thirty-second response rule that we've trained for remains unaffected by this new security model. It's at this time that the campus map we picked up at the fraternity office comes into good use.

When communicating by radio, military police use the "ten code" system of radio communication (as did many civilian police agencies then), a set of actions or instructions running from 1 to 20 that are preceded by the number 10. For example, 10-14 is to designate a specific location, while 10-15 designates movement *to* that location. (We all remembered the late '50s television series *Highway Patrol* where Broderick Crawford would send his signature hoarse-voiced "10-4" transmission ["message received" or "I acknowledge"] over his police radio.)

The map on the back of the orientation guidebook for freshmen comes into play now. During these first days, we need only transmit a ten-series code number with a building number in order to designate a Meredith classroom destination. The use of the building numbers on the map coupled with the ten code numbers becomes a simple field expedient. Radio traffic is at a minimum and the messages are confidential. We play a cat-and-mouse game with the students. In the early days, before Meredith's movements on the campus become predictable and before they lose interest in harassing him, student ham radio operators routinely try to monitor our transmissions in attempts to locate him. If they find our frequency they only hear a jumble of numbers on their intercepts.

How important is all this? We'll never know. But it's one more tactic we use to make it a bit more difficult for anyone to locate and threaten Meredith. The use of a jumble of numbers is also helpful when students come up to the various patrol jeeps and try to listen in on the radio messages or talk to our patrol members.

We also begin to make novel assignments for the patrols (assignments that might give passing students a misleading impression of military discipline and equipment readiness). At roll call each morning, I order one patrol unit to malinger, a well-known army term meaning to "avoid work, duty, or service." I identify a specific campus site close to a Meredith-scheduled class location for that morning. The designated jeep will pull up behind a tree or building and its occupants will "relax" and appear to simply be avoiding duty. I designate another three-man unit to have "engine trouble." That jeep will pull over and the driver, not the designated sharpshooter, will throw up the hood and look for an engine "malfunction."

Without much notice to passing students, the radioman in the backseat in each of the two jeeps will be intently monitoring the radio traffic of the rest of us. The two "actor teams" for that given day, the malingering jeep and the engine-trouble jeep, will move around to various spots across the campus, depending on Meredith's class schedule, and continue their acts.

Why all the attempts at deception? Simply to comply with the instructions of Mr. Doar that we not escort the student Meredith from classroom to classroom with an armed guard or a visible shadowing team. He is to have the desired "freedom" that any other Ole Miss student might have. However, the army has its agenda (no approximate threat of harm). The patrol remains under the thirty-second "Rush to Magnet" rule to ensure that this student not only has the freedom that the DOJ so urgently wants to show the world, but that he has the continuing *opportunity* to enjoy that freedom.

Pity the reaction of the young Ole Miss Army ROTC cadet intent on a military career if he comes upon the scene of either cast of army "actors." Here are two jeeps, one with undisciplined soldiers and another one that doesn't work.

"Eat, nigger! Eat, nigger! Eat! Eat!"

On Monday night, Meredith goes back to the student cafeteria for his evening meal with a Justice Department lawyer and two deputy marshals.

The students inside ignore him. However, as the crowd outside grows, the mood changes. While many appear simply curious, a few start to shout out curses once again.

"Hey, the nigger's inside eating."

They move up close to the open windows and taunt him.

"Eat, nigger! Eat, nigger! Eat! Eat!"

The crowd turns more raucous. We drive up to the front of the building and watch from the jeep. I radio for more of the patrol to move in toward us, but not too close. I hear glass breaking. A rock has gone through a front window near the table where Meredith and the others are eating.

> Glass sprinkled the 29-year old negro student's table as he was eating. . . . [They] moved to another table. . . . [The marshal] grabbed the rock and ran outside. There he was jeered by the crowd, which grew suddenly in number to more than 100 [later to 300]. The marshal handed the rock to a Lt. Gallagher of the army regulars, who was in a jeep outside. The Army officer called for two more jeeps, which quickly arrived.[2]

Colonel Brice arrives a few blocks away in the dark and comes on the radio to say that if things get out of hand, he's nearby with the gas.

The gas. That means Corporal O'Neill with the double-canister tear gas (CS) dispenser. It's a menacing-looking piece of riot control equipment, backpack-mounted hardware that looks like a leaf blower. It was used on the town square last Monday morning when the downtown was being trashed. The colonel also reminds me that a reaction unit of the 101st is in bivouac a few blocks away.

Just then, one of the marshals comes out of the building and finds flattened tires on the government car that is supposed to take Meredith back to Baxter Hall.

"Hey! There's the nigger lover from Washington!"

He comes over to the jeep to give me the rock and the car keys. For now, the students avoid including us in their curses. We're in military uniforms. Again the southern heritage of respect for the military, but also a respect for our weapons, which are in plain view. The marshal is wearing the traditional government uniform, a dark gray suit. Harmless looking. They don't know that the suit coat covers a loaded .38 pistol. To the crowd he's a symbol of the hated federal government and the Kennedy Justice Department.

By now three of the four patrol jeeps are grouped in front of the cafeteria building and at the edges of the crowd, which has grown to two hundred. The fourth, ours, is in the middle. This is the first time students have gotten so close to us in the lead jeep, standing next to us, looking at Meredith through the cafeteria window . . . and then back at us. Not good. We've lost the comfort of control as we no longer enjoy distance from them.

It's important that Adams and I look directly into the crowd. And listen to them. It's part pep fest, part angry crowd. Well, OK, this is what the Justice Department wanted. He's free to roam and to roam right up into the cafeteria while we stand back. In a matter of minutes, "hands off" has become "hands on." I look over at the radioman in the back of the jeep. He's hunkered down and in contact with the colonel just up the rise of the hill toward Baxter.

OK, students only . . . I hope. What of the gunman? Is he in here with this crowd?

We've passed a tipping point, from demonstration to confrontation, and might be moving toward the next point—violence. It only takes a few in a crowd to confront while the others hold back and continue to demonstrate. We're not campus police, not even state highway patrol, who might share the anger—or at least have sympathy—for these students. Now lighted cigarettes are being thrown at us. A few bottles and rocks. I see one of the throwers. I start after the fat-faced momma's boy. Stupid of me, but for one flash I wanted to be back in that alley in Minneapolis and not in this uniform. I'm across the street and onto the lawn and see him duck into a dormitory. Probably to get to a phone and to call his pappy and cry. I catch myself and my breath. I shouldn't be doing this. Lieutenants order nonlieutenants to do this kind of stuff and, besides, this kid's got a hundred of his closest friends out here tonight and the other hundred are not ours. I return to the jeep.

We're regular U.S. Army with orders to use force, an option which might include the order to shoot for "maximum effect," if for a moment we see a serious threat of bodily harm to Meredith or a deputy—and a *moment* can be a split second. These kids just don't get it.

I look at the crowd. They have no clue that we will use lethal force if we have to.

Weapons may be loaded and fired to prevent an attack on Mr. James Meredith, U.S. Marshals, Representatives of the Justice Department, or guards, patrolmen, and other members of this command.[3]

OK, where is he? Is he still inside the cafeteria and we're out here with this crowd and a government car with flat tires?

One of our units calls in, using the ten-series. The twenty or so students standing next to us don't understand the message that

Meredith has been slipped out the back door of the cafeteria to a another marshal's car.

We're not sure he's back safely in Baxter Hall. With daylight gone, the crowd has gotten bolder, their numbers growing.

"Sir, do you need us?" Another radio voice comes up from another MP unit, this time uncoded. "We can see you from up the street. We have gas."

I look at one student, who has thrown something toward the steps of the hall. I point my night stick and direct him to come over to the side of my jeep. To my surprise he does. Just stands there. Obedient. I'm wearing a uniform. Two of us get out of the jeep and look around for instigators up by the steps of the building.

By then a voice on the radio from back at the camp comes on and demands to know if Meredith has been taken out of the area. The angry senior-officer voice comes yelling out of the speaker.

"I don't give a damn about your codes and call signs, is Meredith back at Baxter?"

"Yes, sir," one of my patrols responds.

Although we know that Meredith is back and safe in his dormitory, we stay on a bit to hold the attention of those in the crowd who do not hear this last message. We don't want them moving toward his dormitory just a few blocks up the hill. I look at them. They haven't "tipped" yet.

Ten more minutes pass and we back off and leave the area. The incident is the closest we had to the kind of violence we saw last week. The mood of the crowd changed quickly from verbal taunts to the throwing of rocks and lighted cigarettes, first, toward the building and Meredith and the marshal—and, finally, toward us. We were moments away from calling in the tear gas dispenser and the nearby airborne unit.

The frightening thing about the incident is the realization that there's no middle ground in these kinds of confrontations. It was dark. They had closed in on us, some only curious, others bent on mischief that could have escalated to violence. If a student had made even the slightest physical contact, hostile or otherwise, with any one of the patrol, the whole dynamic of our crowd tolerance would have changed. We have our orders. We have our "rules of engagement" for students, instructions about how we are to handle the noncombatants (the combatants have left the field). The crowd had no rules of engagement.

Until we were sure that Meredith was no longer at risk, we played the crowd. Played them. Their conduct approached the line, but didn't cross it.

On the ride back to the camp I think of what just happened back there. I can't believe what I just saw. My imagination starts up. A fantasy. I'm back in our high school lunchroom and L. C. Hester, a black star athlete and friend to all of us, is sitting with us at lunch period. A group of bullies comes over to our table, looks down at L. C., and shouts, "Eat, nigger! Eat, nigger! Eat!" while the rest of the students in the lunchroom look on. And then go back to their conversations and sandwiches.

After we return to our tents at the stadium, I thank the men for their restraint and conduct during the crowd scene. I'm also thankful that we didn't run into the man with the rifle.

"Yo, Lieutenant—just another day at the office," a voice pipes back.

Somehow, no southerner or midwesterner would have come up with this kind of a quip. The "yo" is pure South Philadelphia, from one of the 716th draftees of that city. I'll forget to tell his sergeant to have this private stop addressing the lieutenants as if we were buddies walking down his block back in Philadelphia.[4]

The words are a welcome vote of confidence from the patrol, a relief. Normally, an officer need not look for such a vote. The men have none. But this is not normal duty.

I doubt that they see what they're doing in the larger context. Later they might come to realize that they are on one of their country's civil rights "marches." But right now, their efforts are reaction without reflection. And, of course, that's what the U.S. Army wants tonight.

I'm not sure any of them stop, look around, and appreciate the significance of what they're involved in. Nor do I, really. We're here before history gets here. We live and work in the moment. Our only concern—at times an obsession—is to keep this guy alive. We have no long-range vision, just one day at a time.

But they do their job and did so tonight. This was their workplace, members of an American workforce. They "went to work" this morning, just as their buddies all over the Northeast (the lucky ones who didn't get drafted) went to work in the trades or in the shoe factories and woolen mills, some of them following their fathers. Or, the few who went on to the small number of community colleges. These soldiers tonight could've been back at Dix after a shift, ready to go into town or fall into their bunks. Here at Ole Miss, punch in, do the job, punch out. They're soldiers. They performed. No problems with them, just so long as they get their pay, their food, and their mail (which has begun to come down to Mississippi), all on time.

For our generation (and past ones) of Americans away from home in uniform, gathering in front of the company clerk outside the orderly room or tent for mail call is the highlight of the day. It breaks the monotony experienced by those serving in a peacetime army and the horrors of those serving in combat. (That moment may be diminished now when the soldier can receive news from home or a girlfriend, including an occasional "Dear John" letter, all by e-mail.)

I start to enjoy the job, if that's the right word under the circumstances. At first I can only experience the outer layer of what's going on. Later I begin to see the more significant parts of the drama. As I watch Meredith walk across the campus, I begin to see that we are also walking across a piece of our country's history.

"Lieutenant, this article says that you. . . ."

The next morning, Tuesday, October 9, the *Memphis Press-Scimitar* carries a story about last night's cafeteria incident under the headline "Meredith Is Almost Hit by Rock at Cafeteria" and "Rowdy Demonstration by Students at Ole Miss." The article generally reports the facts as they happened, but flavors it up a bit, a crowd of "500." My eyes catch a sentence in one paragraph that says, "When the Army grabbed one of the toilet paper throwers . . . Lt. Jack [sic] Gallagher jabbed a night stick in the youth's ribs. . . ."

On the way back to the stadium in my jeep that night, I receive an urgent message from the battalion radio clerk on night duty, saying that I am to report immediately to the "Charlie Golf" at the armory.

Charlie Golf? Charlie Golf? It doesn't sink in until I go to the letters "C" and "G" and then to "commanding general." He's hardly the subject of normal radio traffic for the Peanut Patrol or a second lieutenant. Yes! The general, Hamilton Howze, whose jeep I waved off the road on Sunday. Back at the stadium I don't have time to check with Colonel Brice. What's this all about? I drive down to the armory, wondering what I may have done that would call for a face-to-face with a three-star general. Or, are other officers there as well?

I park the jeep in the lot next to the nondescript armory building in downtown Oxford and go inside. *Think! Think! Why? What the hell happened? Why me?*

A main room is filled with junior officers and enlisted men on the general's headquarters staff. I guess that the officers are all career bound and most of them have the jump wings patch on their fatigue shirts. I'm sure I'm the only straight-leg (nonairborne) ROTC graduate in the place. It's a bit of an awkward scene. I'm not really one of them, but have been ordered to be here for some reason.

They're all doing whatever a general's staff does, although I can't figure out what that might be at this time of night. Meredith is back safe in his dorm room. But I forgot. The general's XVIII Airborne Corps headquarters at Fort Bragg has been moved to this University Avenue location in this now-quieted southern town and I've just entered it. It looks like a command center for a NATO exercise. The armory has become a mobile operations center for a wide range of military contingencies far beyond the immediate Meredith matter.

Everyone seems to be squeezing a cigarette between their fingers or their lips. I want one, but think I can't join them since I'm *not one of them.* The air is stale, warm, close, even though a few electric fans are working. Phones are constantly ringing.

I put my helmet down on the top of a nearby radiator and stand off to the side.

A few officers glance up from their paperwork and their phones and then go back to their tasks. I turn and see that a part of the long room at one end is separated by a portable curtain-on-wheels that functions as a room divider. I guess that it's a makeshift arrangement behind which the general sits.

Finally, a sergeant comes over. I introduce myself and say that I'm here on orders to report to the general. Moments later a captain comes up to me.

"Lieutenant, have you ever spoken to a general officer before?"

It was so obvious the answer he wanted.

"No, I haven't, Captain."

I feel no reason to mention the dawn briefing by the brigadier at the airport last week when we arrived. Maybe it's because the general on the other side of the curtain has two more stars on each shoulder. And a "yes" answer will draw the curiosity of this warrior into asking more hassling questions. I want him to finish his talking down to me, just a junior officer from some college ROTC cadet corps, surely not from his Corps of Cadets at West Point. He jaws at me inches from my face as if I'm a plebe back on the parade field while he practices a "shout-in-your-face" conditioning that he learned when addressing anyone below his cadet rank.

"Well, you answer only what General Howze asks and say nothing more, is that clear, Lieutenant?"

"Yes, sir."

As quickly as he has come over to me, he pivots and marches back to his task, doing whatever staff officers are doing this night in the armory. I sense that he's part of a select fast-track group of junior officers clustered around the general.

Of course, the captain, along with all the rest of the young staff officers in here tonight, is on his way to becoming a career member in one of our country's elite military tribes. Some of his academy classmates may even consider it a calling, like the priesthood, particularly if a father or a grandfather did the calling. For the career officer, whatever army post he's on is his home. Not so for the ROTC officer; it's not even a home away from home. For him, it's a "hotel" room away from home. He's just out of town on an extended "business trip." There may even be some of the two-year lieutenants who might wish they could wear civilian clothes under their Class A uniforms during the final week of their tour—so that they can be ready for their return to the civilian world.

At this moment, I must have nudged the radiator where I had carefully placed my steel pot on its wrong side, the bowl side. It twirls a bit before it falls off, crashing to the concrete floor. There's a loud noise—the kind that I heard the night of the riot—as it clangs around on the floor. Heads in the room jerk up.

They look at it.

A face peeks around the curtain. It's Katzenbach's. He looks down at it.

I join the onlookers, as if pretending for a moment it isn't mine.

Then I walk over and pick it up off the floor, claiming ownership for all to see. It's not a good start for a meeting with a general.

Moments later, I'm called in to report to him. I step around the curtain, walk a few paces left and turn to face the officer seated at a long table with an aide standing behind.

Here I go again. A second lieutenant meeting a general. But this time there's even more rank on each collar, a lot of stars to look at all at once.

I stand at attention and salute.

"Lieutenant Gallagher, reporting as ordered, sir."

"At ease, Lieutenant," he answers in a firm voice.

Lieutenant General Hamilton J. Howze III, Commanding General, XVIII Airborne Corps, Commander, Strategic Army Corps, looks every inch the part. Had we still been in that movie (the one that I thought we were in for a while back there) and if central casting were doing what its name implies, surely he would have been in this chair tonight. I can imagine that some general officers don't "look" the type; this one does. No hesitation in his dress. He was commanding-general neat to a thread. He gives the impression that he's been wearing a uniform since he was barely a teenager. His square jaw, handsome good looks, and bearing merely enhance the role. He was born at West Point into a military lineage on both sides of his family.

He begins.

"Well, Lieutenant, Deputy Attorney General Katzenbach had some commendable remarks to make about this security plan you have devised to protect Mr. Meredith."

Thank God he preceded me into this room.

Keeping in mind what I have just been told on the other side of this curtain, the rules of protocol with a general officer, I say, "Thank you, sir."

He continues, "I want you to brief me on this system of protection you have for the student Meredith."

I start to relax a bit, taking my eyes off those stars, knowing that I'm now at least moving over to familiar ground. I'm a bit more confident, just a bit. I begin explaining the "pass on, pick up" system that we use. It's not easy to describe it without a map. I pause.

"Sir, it might be easier to explain the method with the use of a map."

He motions to his aide to find a campus map. Moments later one is spread out on the table.

I'm now in my element. By chance, I am closer to the story than anyone else in this building tonight, even though Meredith is also the sole mission of all of these other soldiers. How ironic, how inexplicable this is. Here I am, a non–West Pointer, ROTC graduate from a small Minnesota college. I'm in the room briefing a three-star general from Fort Bragg, all purely by happenstance.

Ah! What sweet revenge it would be if he could also order that shout-in-my-face captain in here to listen to a recitation of my job.

I'm back in college at my senior orals for my B.A., standing in front of a panel of three inquisitors, now just one. I'll max this question. I've lived its answer hour by hour for the last week.

I explain the protection system as I have by now memorized its every detail, naming the classes Meredith attends, what schedule times, which buildings, how the security detail is positioned around those sites, on call by me in the event of trouble. I add that at least one of us has him "covered" on our radio net at all times with our pass on, pick up scheme.

He doesn't pause and stare at me as if tricking me into thinking I've given an incomplete answer—looking for some self-incriminating slip—like detectives do with suspects in grade B movies, in those small rooms with the one hanging light bulb. No, he's pretty straightforward. But little do I know that in a few moments I will be cast as a "suspect."

I tell him that I think it's the best the army can do in light of the fact that Meredith is free to walk the campus as is any other student. Because of this remark about Meredith's exposure, I decide to risk telling the general.

"Sir, we can cover him, but not overprotect him. The Justice Department wants it that way. Someone can come onto the campus with a rifle and take a shot at him from a distance. All we can do is try to catch the shooter."

He doesn't comment, but seems satisfied with the briefing.[5]

There's an awkward pause, so I say it.

"Sir, we didn't mean to wave your jeep off the road on Sunday. I had been advised that no other military would be in the area at the time."

"I understand," he says.

OK, I'm done. I want out of here.

I think I'll be dismissed. Surely, a three-star general has more pressing things at hand. He must be burdened with enormous pressures of command in this unique and politically sensitive mission.

Seconds later, I realize that I was called in here to see the general because of one of these very pressures. As he goes to move the campus map aside, I see a copy of the *Press-Scimitar* newspaper opened to the "Gallagher jabbed a night stick in the youth's ribs . . ." article.

In a breath, it becomes clear why I'm here and not back at the camp. So much for a briefing on the protection of the student Meredith. So this is why the urgent radio message to report to the "Charlie Golf." In sports jargon it's called a "game changer." No—worse than that—I never really had the ball.

"Tell me, Lieutenant, what happened outside the cafeteria on Monday night."

As best I can, I recite the story of last night's demonstration.

"Lieutenant, this article says that you struck a student."

So much for the confidence (even arrogance) that I had a few moments ago. My mind goes blank. I don't know if I heard the general's comment. Maybe I didn't. I look down at the floor. I hear phones ringing in the distance. Then, silence.

How could the paper get it so wrong? Damn reporter.

OK, so maybe I did hear his comment.

Finally, the lieutenant answers the general.

"Sir, I didn't touch the student with the nightstick, but merely pointed it at him and told him to come over and stand next to my jeep—which he did. We saw him throw something at the window next to Meredith's table. It would have been foolish to hit anyone with the stick as that would've provoked a response from the crowd that clearly had grown very large."

Then I take a chance.

"Sir, it's a southern newspaper. I know the reporter. He's up against my jeep every day. He wants a story. He exaggerates at times."

"Thank you, Lieutenant."

I salute, turn, and move back out from behind the "command curtain." I leave the building. I feel like running. Light-headed and relieved, I drive out of the lot and back to the football stadium.

When I see the *Press-Scimitar* reporter the next morning, I call him on his fabricating the use of my nightstick, as well as on his not getting my name right. He knows that I didn't touch the student, says so himself. I tell him that his version of the incident got me into trouble with a lieutenant general. He says that his editors want more excitement in the reporting coming out of Ole Miss. He adds that they have their own "viewpoint" about this whole crisis. I ask where his newspaper is located, forgetting its complete name. "Memphis."

9

THE CAMPUS

Just Moving On

I have not realized the extent to which this crisis has become a national story. When you stand in the middle of something like this and are caught up in its details, you don't have a view from the sidelines.

And while this may still be a story off campus and out of state, probably 90 percent of the student body has moved away from it. For them, it's yesterday's news and, if not over, it's happening on another part of the campus. It's quickly become a nonstory and the continued army presence has become an annoyance.

The few times I take my eyes off the immediate "Meredith crowd," I look down a few blocks at a flow of students crossing a campus intersection. They have absolutely no interest in him and what he's doing. The irony is that he is of the same mind toward them, as though to say, "Pay no attention to me and I'll do the same toward you. I'm here to get an education and, please, you do the same."

How oddly this small daily drama must be playing out against the backdrop of the rest of the campus. If, for a moment, one could view the larger part of the university from far above, above the heads of the immediate actors (main and supporting) in this story, above Meredith and me, our patrol, and the marshal, above the small cluster of heckling students, one might then have a better perspective.

From that lofty perch, one could catch a normal day in the life of a large public university whose students are just moving on, oblivious to what Meredith is trying to do, probably not supporting him but not obstructing him either. Just moving on.

This overhead scene would be more real than any snapshot of us down here at this street corner. How sorely Meredith must want to be lost in that larger group of students and not be with us in this daily drama that plays out from class to class wherever he goes.

Of course, he remains the story—just a shorter one—by mid-October. The reporters never cast the spotlight over onto those students at the intersection. They want it kept on the black student at Ole Miss. He's the news.

In fact, we have become as much of an annoyance to him as his hecklers are. Can't we all just go away? Even given the proximity between him and us, there is no casual contact, no friendly bonding that might occur between a "protected" and his "protectors."

The small mobile pockets of harassing students are a minor part of the day-to-day activity of the university. The rhythm of campus life goes on. Ironically, the hecklers themselves rejoin that rhythm soon after we pass by. For them, it's become a casual thing to do, like tossing a football or the new collegiate toy, a Frisbee, in between classes—there's nothing ominous or of any consequence about their behavior.

But there's other behavior on the campus that causes me to continue to make notebook entries:

Subj + 4/ white '62 Chev/ Miss 43212 Hinds

Chev green/wh '61 Miss /C22581 subj

Henry Hotel [new guest]/Riker/Calif male/70/ heavy set/ open yellow shirt/tan jacket

"Honorary Niggers"

Another form of campus opposition to Meredith comes with the appearance of a hate leaflet. In early October a one-page publication, *Rebel Underground,* anonymously circulated on campus and slipped under dorm room doors, boasts of:

Organization of "Rebel Underground" teams and units on every floor of every dormitory and in every sorority and fraternity house on the campus.

Our primary objective is to encourage James Meredith to transfer to some college where he would be welcome.

* * *

While the Communist Party, USA, was wiring President Kennedy to send troops to Ole Miss on September 30th in a telegram, the Communists in Cuba were installing missiles aimed at the United States.

In reference to a particular "left-wing professor" who "dined with James Meredith the other morning":

We are looking forward to the day when the KKK (Kennedy Koon Keepers) will leave our campus.

As for other faculty members similarly aligned:

Congratulations to Russell H. Barrett, Robert J. Farley, Harley F. Garrett and James W. Silver. In recognition for services rendered the NAACP has proclaimed these professors to be "Honorary Niggers."[1]

Of course, priorities being what they are on this campus, emblazoned across the bottom of the leaflet are the words

BEAT LSU[2]

I do wonder about faculty members here. Are many from out of state? In any event, are their opinions on race any different from those of the protesters? Do they have any influence over their students on this topic? I have the impression that this campus is an isolated place—from the world of ideas and the real world itself.

Mississippi U. Students Found Isolated in Culture and Outlook
By THOMAS BUCKLEY
Special to the *New York Times*

OXFORD, Miss., Oct. 20—Virtually all 4,638 white students at the University of Mississippi exist in an isolation more profound than that which they impose on the one Negro student, James H. Meredith.

This is the conviction expressed by many thoughtful members of the university faculty as they seek to assess the repercussions from the violence surrounding Mr. Meredith's admission.

To an almost incredible degree, many faculty members believe, most of the students are uninformed and little interested in events and opinions in the rest of the nation and the world.[3]

Dutiful Sons and Daughters of the South

I admit that Meredith is half right with one of his observations. He might have been caught by surprise at the level of violence that came from the mob that night. But he's probably correct in saying that hecklers are simply acting out their parents' opinions and prejudices. They are dutiful sons and daughters of a South that they want to preserve, not really thinking or speaking on their own. Some will say that, on this subject, they can't—or decide not to—think on their own.

After that first week, once the anxiety and excitement of what we are doing wears off, boredom takes over. It doesn't take long for me to realize that I'm on a campus of a school of largely upper-middle-class kids who put a lot of enthusiasm into fraternity and sorority life and football. Ole Miss is known for football and pretty coeds, the former I had heard about (coming from a Big Ten powerhouse state) and the latter I can see. Beauty is valued on this campus. That's it, football and girls.

Football. If you wanted a few weekend dollars you could hold up a convenience store in broad daylight in downtown Oxford during the third quarter of any home game. Actually, you could rob the whole university if the Rebs were behind by six in the fourth quarter. It would be harder for an away game if the TV set is in the front part of the store.

Girls. I don't know if the girls understand football. Their boyfriends probably tell them a little about it, but after a while they tire and turn back to the game. No problem. A girl goes to the stadium to see and be seen. But the game? Most likely she doesn't know the difference between a touchdown and a touchback. A safety? She thinks that's the thing her boyfriend carries around in his wallet.

> Thus the school remains largely as it has been, one for the middle and upper classes, for posting "gentlemen's C's," making "contacts" and finding a suitable husband or wife.[4]

No wonder Meredith broke the mold.

Racism Covered, Just Under the Skin

Toward the end of October, I begin to relax on this job. No one on the campus looks like those we saw early that riot morning. We look at the students. Many of them are Mississippi sons and daughters of parents who have instilled in their children a deep-seated sense of how their day-to-day societal and cultural lives should be arranged and lived out. And part of that arrangement is governed by the doctrine of racial separation.

Some of them look back at us with curiosity, some with annoyance for this intrusion into their way of life. And, finally, there are a few with real hatred in their eyes. Maybe some of them were out here late that night.

The overwhelming majority of the mob, the out-of-towners, showed their racism openly and without cover. They had no need or desire to hide it—violently honest, candid, direct. In any police lineup, they would've been easy picks.

Not so with the Ole Miss students who joined with them into the early morning hours. The few who did stay out on the campus had, in their daily middle-class lives, little in common with their country cousins—the three thousand other whites who descended onto the campus. Before then, the Ole Miss students may have harbored racism just under their skin. But on that one night, the students who called themselves "just observers" made common ground against the "nigger" who dared to attend their Ole Miss.

Skinny, Levi's-wearing, T-shirted, working-class whites from outside the town were embraced by well-fed, khaki-wearing, button-down-collared, middle-class Ole Miss whites, who finally let loose their festering racism. But once the out-of-towners were chased off the campus and out of town by the Guard and the regular army units later in the morning, these students could no longer do their wild mob dance. They dressed their racism down a bit and took it to wherever Meredith was walking on the campus.

What by now has become a constant is my surprise that no group—student leaders or otherwise—will intervene in these kinds of incidents, to at least tone down the ugliness, the rhetoric. Aren't they on the football team or at the head of the fraternities? But then again they too are "sons" of the South. It's as if the rest of the student body will simply walk by these sidewalk confrontations in the latter part of October and into November, roll their eyes and—you know the kind—give off those "boys-will-be-boys" looks as they move on to their classes. My God! Is it only a football and party school? Do they all think the same? Are there no high roads for student leaders on this campus to walk?

As we move toward November, even the harassment begins to lose its vitality; James knows that it's simply a matter of time before the more vocal hecklers will turn their attention back to football and Greek life. There is no longer any on-campus threat to him, if there ever was after that first ugly weekend. Now it can only come from an off-campus source, the ardent segregationist. We have to stay here in case the bad guy makes an appearance on campus. Hoping that it never comes.

After a while I even forget that the student we're protecting is slightly dark-skinned and everyone else around here is light-skinned. He's simply some guy walking across the campus, hurrying to a class. And I think that that's a scene that most everyone else on the campus has come to adjust to and expect, if not fully accept.

Many students feel distanced from him, even beyond the obvious. Years later, a southerner and coed at the time will tell me, "He was so different from the rest of the students on the campus and I don't mean by his color. First, he was older than us and he always wore a suit and tie. He didn't participate in any class discussions, at least not in the one class [history] I had with him. Some students, who might have approached him out of curiosity, if nothing else, were so turned off by his personality and his aloof demeanor. That had nothing to do with his being a black."[5]

"King" Cotton in Minnesota Instead of Mississippi

Despite the coed's assessment, I know that southerners have grown up with the legacy of the "peculiar institution." I try to compare this cultural fix Mississippians have on race with anything that I experienced growing up in my part of the country, to place it in some kind of context. My father, a quiet influence on me, may have mentioned from time to time that the "coloreds" in Minneapolis were moving south from Lake Street toward our neighborhood, but never with any anger or real discomfort in his voice. At most, maybe he had an unexpressed concern that such a drift would affect house values.

I didn't grow up with any institutional or state-sanctioned separation of the two races that led some in the South to cling to the deep-seated legacy of the peculiar institution. I don't feel a division in my loyalty between my state and my country. For them, it's a mind-set that in the early 1960s turned into a hatred of those courageous blacks who, along with some whites, began to challenge the status quo in the South through sit-ins and Freedom Rides. And, shortly thereafter, Meredith shows up to challenge the legacy, and the hatred becomes exposed, raw, and deadly.

Few of us in the battalion have any idea of what the oft-repeated "way of life" is all about. We're Yankees. (I'm so much a northerner I'm almost a Canadian.) Unlike the rioters that Sunday night, some southerners keep the ugly part of "the way" to themselves. It's there, but buttoned down, like the collars on their shirts. It's "under the skin," the skin of an Ole Miss student or of any of those truck drivers I met on my trip south in 1956. For that matter, James holds it all under his skin as well. Even the few southern-born members of our battalion probably maintain the same attitude under their skin, an early version of "don't ask, don't tell" that protects them from the possible ridicule or unwanted comment, maybe even hostility, from others in the 716th.

Most of the battalion members, though, come from the virtually all-white small towns or de facto segregated neighborhoods of large cities in the Northeast, where a black man might be safe, but still feel uncomfortable wandering into an Irish or an Italian section. If they're from New England's rural areas, all the neighbors are white. The 716th draftee in the Cold War army of the 1960s gets a tuition-free education in race relations. He may wake up that first morning at boot camp and look over at the bunk next to him and see it's occupied by a black man from nowhere near his hometown (or his knowledge of the world).

I don't know how the men in the 716th feel about this whole experience down here, as far as the race thing goes. Maybe back in the tents on the practice field they might talk about it, might speak their mind, one way or the other. But when on the street, on the campus, on the job, they do their job—not voicing any opinion about the change going on before their eyes.

In order to function as a cohesive unit there really was no place for the race card. We had to have each others' backs if we were going to get through this together. We did not see ourselves as black soldiers or white soldiers, but as soldiers just doing our job together. Most of us were of the mind that we were here to do a job regardless of race; Work together, put in our time, stay out of trouble (whenever possible) and return home, hopefully a more mature individual.[6]

I look at two of our jeeps parked curbside against the backdrop of this beautiful campus and think: what if our history had been different? What if slavery in this country had been a northern phenomenon, upside down on the map, and I had been born in a "Deep" North?

What if cotton had been "king" in Minnesota instead of Mississippi and slavery had become my state's peculiar institution? Would I have been out on a street corner in Minneapolis today, protesting the admission of an African American to the nearby University of Minnesota? And would some military police unit from Georgia be here in jeeps trying to keep the peace?

James will remind me that northern cities will eventually erupt with racial discord and violence: Newark, Detroit, Watts.

The patrol members keep contact with the students to a minimum. Once in a while army-student conversations do take place by the jeeps, but generally the divide between the occupiers and the occupied remains.

They are very much taken with our names. The Irish, German, Italian, Greek, and Spanish identification tags on our uniforms draw questions, "Don't y'all have any real *American* names?"[7]

Some of the soldiers hope that a student will come over and talk about the Ole Miss football team (unbeaten and eventually the nation's number 3 team in 1962). After all, we're in the South, where college football is the next "king"—after cotton. Private Barrett, an avid follower of Notre Dame football, would love such a discussion.

But, of course, it is not to be. Well into late October we're still *them*, the annoying presence from the North.

As we move toward November, the days get shorter and the level of boredom increases. Occasionally the men will speak up to test my patience about the army's rules regarding contact with students.

> Personnel are permitted limited conversation with male students, however, they will refrain from answering any questions pertinent to military operations in the Oxford area, the whereabouts of Mr. Meredith, or any activities in which Mr. Meredith may become engaged. Personnel <u>will not</u> offer personal opinions, nor discuss any matter related to the present situation in the Oxford area.[8]

"Lieutenant, we've been down here a long time, you know. Can't we at least talk to them [coeds, he means]? Meredith's OK, ain't he?"

"But the girls, sir . . . one of them . . . keeps coming up to the jeep. I'm from Puerto Rico. Maybe I can help her with her Spanish."

And, "Lieutenant, they keep asking what we're we still doing down here."

"Don't answer them."

"What do you want us to say because—?"

"Look, Maurice, I don't know. We officers are bored too. Just tell them the North won that war a hundred years ago and now we've had to come back down here. Because of a Meredith court case, something about equal rights, the Constitution, I hear."

Then there's the inevitable talk about rotation back to that North—going home.

"Lieutenant, when can we go back to Dix? Back home, you know, sir? This is like a foreign country. When's this bad movie gonna be over?"

Thank God for army humor. One Boston soldier jokes about asking the sergeant for our DEROS, the military acronym for "Date Eligible to Return from Overseas."

"Sir, let's go back to Dix, there's no Commies down here."

Missiles in Cuba

We're on the tented practice field on Monday, October 22, and someone sets up a TV on a field table. Loudspeakers are hooked up. President Kennedy begins to tell us about the discovery of Soviet missile sites in Cuba. We retire for the night. I wake up and see that at least half of the troops on the grounds, including those from the 101st, have pulled out during the night.

Maybe I should say "fled" during the night. The infantry soldiers were probably all too happy to leave this field assignment. There's not a hill on the campus that they could charge up and hold. The provost would be appalled if he came onto the campus some fine autumn morning and saw freshly dug foxholes around its perimeter.

It's as if a tornado, like the one in the *Wizard of Oz*, has come through and blown them out of—not Kansas—but Mississippi, all the way over to their Cuba staging grounds in Florida, South Carolina, and Georgia. We're on alert, DEFCON 3. A few days later I even see our battalion's name on a manifest for an assault craft to Cuba. But the Peanut Patrol is to remain in place.

Later in the week, Pete Frechette comes up to me.

"Hank, there's a Halloween costume party at my frat house tonight."

"What's a house?"

"It's my fraternity at Wisconsin. There's a chapter here on the campus. I talked to one of the brothers today. He told me about it. Some of them are calling it a Cuban invasion party and they'll dress in fatigues and bring cigars. Let's crash it. Wearing our uniforms, we'll blend right in."

We drive the jeep out the gate of the practice field and park it on a campus street a bit off from where Frechette has been told the frat house is located. We fall in with a line at the front door. As we enter, someone shoves a beer in my hand. I say thanks. We try to mingle as I hear Elvis singing "Return to Sender." It mixes with the party noise in the room.

I let Pete do the talking, the kind of brother-to-brother talk that goes on in this world of fraternities.

Boy, this is good, what a release, what a break!

With half of the first beer in my hand gone, I go up to a coed and ask, "Hey, how 'bout them Rebs?" A student told me this morning that such a question was always a good opener.

She's pretty. Maybe this is what a southern belle is supposed to look like. Now, even close up, she looks prettier than the girls do where I'm from. I don't know, maybe she works harder at that prettiness. I don't think there is such an expression as a northern belle. I guess beauty's a big thing down here. Someone tells me that it's a campus of beauty queens and their pageants. And Chi Omega is the sorority of queens here, with a boast that two of its sisters have won recent Miss America contests.

The football question works with her.

"Are y'all in this house?" she asks.

"Excuse me?"

"This house, this fraternity."

"Well, no."

"Oh, well, who are you with?"

"Well, I'm not with a fraternity here. I mean—" (I want to say I'm with a huge fraternity that we have to pledge—the U.S. Army—but hold back.)

Too many words together. Northern accent. Uh-oh! She takes a second look at me.

"Wait a minute, I don't think y'all from around here. I think I know who you are. Y'all with the army . . . down here for the Nigra Meredith, right?" (Smiling . . . with a "gotcha" look.)

My cover is blown. A second coed overhears the talk and comes over.

She teases, "Where's y'all's helmets?"

I try to change the subject. Guessing that every Ole Miss student is from some place other than Oxford, I ask her where she's from. She answers that she's from over in (some named place). Only

later do I come to realize that Mississippians usually make this their
first question.

"Pete, I think we should go."

We do, but it's a pleasant night away from our football-field
home. It's one of the few times I've engaged in an honest North-
South dialogue, superficial though it may have been. But not so
superficial when I think of her answer when I asked her where she
was from. "Place" to her was important.

Boy, this is good, what a release, what a break!

Two Different Sets of Whites

After a while the students stop staring at us. Maybe the novelty, if
you can call it that, has finally worn off. By early November, if someone does stare at us, it's a rare occasion and we make a mental note
of the individual. Sometimes he gets an entry in the Woolworth's
notebook. While we can never blend in or be accepted, our presence is by now tolerated as part of daily life on campus.

But the soldiers, even if wearing civilian clothes (one wacko idea
coming out of the Pentagon for next spring), could never blend in.
As surely as there's a racial divide between Meredith and his white
classmates this fall, there's a separation between the students and
our troops—two different sets of whites—looking at each other
across a cultural chasm that would never close. The student group
is made up of middle- and upper–middle-class sons of Mississippi,
the planters' kids. They drive around the campus in Delta-daddy-
given Thunderbirds and Buicks. They're in penny loafers and neatly
creased khaki pants, walking with the state's "coming-out" daughters, wearing pleated skirts and cotton dresses. The soldier group
is a mix of lower-middle-class (or lower) northeasterners from
working class families (a class no Ole Miss man would admit membership in, even if it were true), wearing ill-fitting cotton fatigues.
Many don't have cars back home, just subway tokens and bus trans-
fers. A few might have hand-me-down Fords or Chevys from an

older brother parked out in the street, or an aging Studebaker up on blocks in the backyard. Many of them first wore khaki when they went home in their starched Class A uniforms after boot camp.

During that first week, in this thrown-together pot of young American males, an Ole Miss student was overheard to yell out at a trooper, "Hey, soldier, if you weren't so stupid, you wouldn't be in the army."

I went to college at an all-men's university, so I'm not used to watching women cross a campus. But I get the impression that some of the Ole Miss coeds, once the curlers are removed in the morning, spend a great deal of time fussing over their "presentation" before they set out on the campus each day. One of them might even imagine herself walking down the runway of a beauty pageant and not a sidewalk next to Fulton Chapel. And with "poise." A big word down here. She might be thinking—like a Heisman candidate over on the football field—that scouts, in her case the beauty contest kind, are watching her every move.

Unlike some schools in the North, this university still adheres to a stringent dress code for the coeds, "skirts and dresses." Even traveling to and from the tennis courts, the female player is required to wear a raincoat over her shorts.[9]

My driver, a good-looking guy, cannot understand why coeds are not coming over to our jeep to talk to him. I remind him of the gag-order issued by the dean of women and by our command as well—men only, and then no controversial topics. But one day a very attractive coed, a quiet and daily passerby, finally stops, looks at me, and comes over to the jeep. I'm curious, even flattered, that she's approaching us. *Uh-huh. One of those Ole Miss beauties. Must be the water down here.* In a soft southern accent that will remain in my memory long after I leave this place, she says, "Lieutenant, I have one thing to say to y'all." (Her voice is as soft as Minnesota's own Land O' Lakes butter.)

"Yes?" I answer quickly.

(A pause.)

"Just fuck y'all!" (Spoken as her head snaps back.)

She returns to the sidewalk, regains her pretty coed composure, and continues on her pretty way. With that kind of language, this gal will only be in the audience for the beauty pageant, no runway for her.

Very few of our troops have gone to college. Most have high school diplomas, while a few had their last look at a classroom the day they dropped out of high school and enlisted (by their own choice or, in some cases, by that of a judge). For some of them, with no experience or opportunity to attend college, this is the first time on a campus. And a sobering view it is for them.

> Many of my platoon members, high school graduates, if even that, were surprised at what they saw once they found themselves on a college campus for the first time. They wondered how students in a university could spend so much time harassing Meredith. They'd come up to me and ask, "Sir, don't they have to study? They must be pretty smart to be out here doing all this stuff at night and then being in class the next morning."[10]

And, for some of our troopers, those who did go to colleges with broad statewide student populations, it was an eye-opener. They saw a university, a public-supported institution, that was more like a private school. The students seemed to give off an air of entitlement and superiority.

We settle into a routine that continues to be ruled each day by James's class schedule. We move back and forth across the campus like chess pieces on a board, moving into locations that vary depending on whether it's his 8:00 a.m. history class at Grad 24 (Dr. Marquette) or a 9:00 a.m. pol. sci. class at Conner (Dr. Fortenberry).

There is a bizarre contrast between minutes of intense focus and long stretches of boredom. The sharp focus lasts for ten minutes at the start of each morning.

He's out on the sidewalk . . .
    . . . crossing the street
        . . . up the steps
            . . . into a classroom building.

Then we pass fifty minutes of flatline boredom, with occasional glances to see if anyone's clustered around the doors waiting for him. At first it's the hecklers, then later into November there's no one.

The class ends and we're back into a bright-line focus. It's a focus sometimes edged with a spark of tension if, say, an unidentified adult appears in a crowd close to the door of one of his classroom buildings. Or he's been in a nearby parked car for too long a time.

"Golf 2, Peanut 3, why is that car still parked over there? How many occupants? Over."

"Peanut 3, Golf 2, one occupant, doesn't look like a student. Over."

"Golf 2 . . . get a full vehicle ID. Over."

"Roger. Peanut 3. Out."

(Back to desk sergeant.) "Peanut 3. Request vehicle check . . . '61 White 4 Dr Ford . . . plates Miss 42556 Calhoun County. Over."

Followed by me to patrol jeep: "Golf 2, Peanut 3. Do slow drive-by. Make visit if cause. Your call on this one. Over."

"Peanut 3, Golf 2, roger that. Out."

"Any Negroes in your hometown?"

It's during one of the periods of boredom that I turn to Private Barrett, who has rejoined us as the third man in the jeep since he recovered from the injury to his jaw.

"Ron, where're you from?"

"Kittanning, Pennsylvania, sir."

"Any Negroes in your hometown?"

"No, sir . . . all pretty much white. Closest town, I guess, with Negroes would be Pittsburgh."

"No seasonal workers, nonwhites . . . farm workers up from Mexico?"

"No, sir."

"What about when you got drafted? You got to know Negroes, right?"

"Sure."

"How'd you feel about that? I mean your attitude . . . first time Negroes next to you in the bunks . . . in the showers and latrines? Any discomfort?"

"Not at all, this is the army. But army or not, it doesn't bother me. In the barracks, on work details, on duty, we're all together . . . the same. On patrol we work together, I get along with them, they with me. Sure. But when we go out on pass, we don't mix together all that much. You know, off post into town. We hang out with our white buddies. So we don't really get together, but when we do on post, hey, it's OK. We do our job."

Thinking back on our mission at the University of Mississippi, I think about some of the irony presented by the situation. Our unit had black military policemen, but they were really perceived only as fellow policemen. We had black sergeants and black officers. Again, they were simply sergeants and officers who were military policemen.[11]

"How about the rest of the guys in the platoon?"

"Sir?"

"Attitudes among the white soldiers in the platoon, you know . . . about Negroes."

"I don't know, Lieutenant, a lot of the guys in our battalion come from New York . . . Philadelphia. Maybe their stories are different . . . you know . . . big cities with neighborhoods that had all Negroes. Then ones with all Italians, then they had Irish sections. I guess Negroes wouldn't go into those neighborhoods and vice versa. I mean, they had nothing to do with whites. They would stay where they felt comfortable, same as for whites. You know, sir? That's just the way it is."

He looks over at me.

"But, down here, I mean, sir . . . it's so different . . . you know what I mean? This is kinda scary here, you know, Lieutenant . . . that night . . . with those little kids throwing all that stuff at us? I couldn't see them very well because I had to drive and then the blood on my face. But I did see those kids and I'll never forget that. . . . And then the guy who threw that brick at us later in the morning. Geez. I mean . . . here we're just doing our job, right, sir?" He continues, "But I don't think this is what would go on in my hometown if we had Negroes, I mean, I don't think so, but this down here is so different."

"The Negroes who got stepped-back that night in Memphis. Anyone from your squad?"

"Yes, sir, Corporal Jones. I felt bad about that. I mean he's our squad leader and all. We never looked at it that way—that he's a Negro—he's our squad leader."

He continues, "That thing with the Negro soldiers back at the navy base that night was kinda strange. For morale, you know, sir? I mean, we left Dix all together to come down here . . . and then they break us up."

(Long pause.) "Are we doing any good down here, Lieutenant?"

"Well, he's still alive, isn't he?"

Just then he comes out of his class.

"Peanut 3, Golf 3, Magnet 10-15-67." We move down the street.[12]

Further into November, there's no hint of any impending violence that would resemble that riot Sunday and Monday in early October. No sentiment for it. Now, just words, no gunshots. But even if the anti-Meredith rhetoric has quieted a bit, our operations remain unchanged since that first day.

(1) Each member of the patrol will be armed with a pistol Cal. 45. In addition one (1) selected individual in each vehicle will

be armed with a rifle. They will carry two (2) magazines or clips of ammunition [now reissued] for every weapon with which they are armed. One (1) magazine or clip will be inserted in the weapon; however, no round will be inserted in the chamber. The safety on weapons will be in lock position at all times.

(2) Each vehicle will carry four (4) CN grenades, two (2) canister grenades, and two (2) baseball grenades.[13]

Reporters from local newspapers often gather around our jeep. And when story lines dry up, they press us for something, anything, to satisfy their editors. They want the soldiers' opinions on the race issue, Meredith, the students, Cuba, Berlin. What do their folks back home think? Their questions—"What do you think of this situation, Private?" and "Do you think you should be down here, Corporal?"—are strictly forbidden. We all know the sensitive soldier-citizen confrontation the army has just gone through. We just look back at the reporters and smile.

All such interviews are forbidden by the command. The men are not to have opinions, only orders. (When my college paper asks the headquarters here if they can do a story on me, the army refuses, saying that they do not want any retaliation or harassment toward my family back in Minneapolis.)

As a result, the press is left with asking the "Where are you from?" and the "How's the food?" questions . . . hardly stories to send back to their papers.

"I'm late for my Spanish class."

I can't say that I get to know our charge very well, even though I spend a lot of time with him. He's a private man, with a bearing and focus that are determined and mission-oriented, almost solemn. I stay with him over some lunch periods in his dorm room. The apartment is a series of small rooms in a row, shared by overnight marshals and sometimes a DOJ lawyer. You know when you've entered his space. It fits the occupant. Spartan. I guess a lot of firsts around here. First black to be in the room unless here to change a light bulb or fix the toilet. First black to sleep in that bed, use the bathroom and the drinking fountain down the hall. Ah! The iconic southern drinking fountain.

This from one of the lieutenants on duty:

> I was assigned the midnight guard shift at the dormitory hous-
> ing James Meredith and a contingent of U.S. Federal Marshals
> [Baxter Hall]. . . . One evening, Meredith tried to use the hall-
> way drinking fountain. The residents piled out of their rooms
> and pushed ahead of Meredith. He waited his turn, only to be
> pushed out of place again . . . as he tried to use the allegedly
> "White Only!" . . . Not for "Niggers!" . . . drinking fountain.
> The Federal Marshals escorted him down the stairway, back
> into his room and I was ordered to "Clear the Hall!" I had to
> push and shove the residents back to their doors and into their
> rooms.[14]

One day in his dorm room with him, I sit down and start read-ing some of the hundreds of letters he receives each week. (I didn't believe it, but someone years later will tell me that in certain parts of this state, a black man remains standing in a room with a white who's seated.) Some of the letters support his mission, others threaten his effort. I come across one that contains more than the usual racial slurs and invective. It's a death threat, with specifics on the location of his immediate family and their daily habits.

"James, have you read this one?" I ask. "They know about your house in Kosciusko. They say they're going to kill your wife and kids. Listen to this—"

"Lieutenant, we'd better go, I'm late for my Spanish class."

Other times, at the lunch break, we have short talks. But even at these times he seems remote, a divide existing between us, even in the small room.

However, if I were from his South—maybe an ROTC lieutenant from an Alabama or Georgia school—it might be different. At least they'd be from the same region and "way of life." Yes, two different backgrounds, but one common history, well known to the other. But I'm on the outside looking in, with my nose pressed up against the window of the South. I'm from Minnesota, no closer to this world than if I were a member of some Finnish peacekeeping team sent into the crisis.

When James does talk to me, it isn't on any trivial subject. No small talk. He tells me that cities in the Northeast and Midwest will soon explode with racial violence. At first I want to talk to him about the remark. But I hold back. Maybe I don't want to think about it. Maybe it's a topic as foreign to me (read: wish to avoid) as this is down here. But he tells me all this because—to him—I am the *face* of the North. Surely, the white students think so.

As for his remark about northern unrest, well, for now, I have a job here. And my orders are to act and react, keep him alive. Maybe I'll come back someday and talk to him about this, if he lives through it. And then I'll have time to reflect.

He also keeps to himself because I'm but an audience of one. Too small. He, of course, wants to talk to a larger universe of listeners about his mission. All I have is a loaded .45 pistol and twelve armed soldiers. I can't give out press releases. That's what he wants . . . to spread the word about his mission, as he did that day after he asked me about the absence of black troops.

After a while, I realize that all of his comments are well tailored, not just those made to the press and "suitable for framing," but the ones made to me in the privacy of his room. Even then they're well measured and deliberate; he's on message and on mission 24/7. Much of what he says sounds "on stage."

A Solitary Performance

Each day as I watch him walk across the campus, I see a self-contained, self-absorbed figure with a walk that is anything but college-casual. A fellow student might move over the campus grounds with a slower, more informal gait. His is faster and more focused, head down, on a straight line to his next class. Driven. It's as if he's trying to get to the room even before the bell rings letting out the prior class. Get to class, get to exams, get to graduation—accomplish the mission.

Yes, theater. In a throng of students he's doing a one-man show. No, it's almost as if two live dramas, his and then everyone else's, are being played out on the same stage at the same time. Two casts. The roles of one are oblivious to the other. Once in a while his solitary performance will be interrupted by a few courageous students who'll stop to talk to him as he crosses the campus. The members of the other cast watch this. I sense a slight annoyance from him at the interruption, but he's extremely polite at these times and doesn't discourage the approaches of the well-wishers. The well-wishers will have their dorm rooms trashed or clothes bleached shortly after speaking with James.[15]

He doesn't encourage them, just tolerates them. Once this brief intermission is played out—as an actor might step behind the curtain for a moment—he's back out on stage, continuing the performance.

Some students dare to have dinner with Meredith . . . at their peril.

University officials Friday pushed an investigation of the ransacking of a dormitory room occupied by two students who ate dinner with Negro James H. Meredith in the Ole Miss Cafeteria Thursday night. The room was broken into and its contents strewn about while [the two students] were absent.

Many students have shown an increasing anger over efforts of a few to be friendly toward Meredith, especially when it involves eating with him in a public place.[16]

I hear that there's an organized effort by some on campus to shun Meredith, to turn their backs when he comes toward them on a sidewalk. James might be happy to shun and ignore them as well.

Army Life

After a few unusually hot days, the weather turns. We northerners are wrong to think that the South has summer year round. The soldier is not allowed to know when the seasons change. The army tells him when they do, when summer becomes fall. We don't learn from the changing colors of the leaves on the oak trees in the Circle or the cooler weather coming over from Arkansas. We learn when we're told by a memo posted on the bulletin board outside the orderly tent that the uniform of the day has changed from cotton to wool. In this case, it happens in late October.

It is about this time that the total troop strength under the Oxford command is pared down to approximately five hundred (two military police companies). And, not unlike the Union troops who had come south a hundred years ago, we return the practice field to the football team and move into winterized quarters, in this case the armory and its adjacent tent city.

Army routine. At a certain level, a day in the life of a GI in Oxford is the same as a day in the life of that soldier at Fort Dix. This campus (like Camp Drum, New York, for some of us) is simply temporary duty (TDY) away from our permanent army post.

Mail call will be held once daily at 1100 hours. . . . Military police units will establish their own procedures for handling mail.

Personal laundry and dry-cleaning may be turned in to the Supply Tent (No. 3) on Wednesdays and Saturdays, between 1400–1500 hours. . . . All items of laundry and cleaning for enlisted personnel will be done at no expense to the individual.

Sick call will be from 0800 to 1030 hours daily at the Aid Station in the Armory.

Limited PX facilities are available in the Armory. The following schedule of hours . . .

The students' annoyance at our small but continuing presence in their lives is matched by the soldiers' boredom at still being here. The army tries its best to maintain morale in the camp while pursuing this unique mission.

Rest and relaxation visits are scheduled on Mondays and Wednesdays of each week to Millington Naval Air Station near Memphis, Tenn.

Nor is our spiritual life overlooked by the command.

Catholic mass is conducted each Sunday at St. John's Church in Oxford. Protestant services are conducted each Sunday at the Armory and also at the Airport. There are no Jewish services available in the immediate area.

A movie screen was set up on the practice field and *Breakfast at Tiffany's* was the inaugural showing that first week in October. However, I don't recall any music, prizes, balloons, or searchlights bouncing off the low clouds on that opening night. When we moved to the armory, the battalion moviegoers had to observe the requirements of peaceful coexistence with the locals and were advised that

Movies will be shown at the Armory and the Airfield each night at 1800 hours, <u>except</u> when the Armory showing conflicts with local National Guard drill periods.

As for proper military conduct in the town and on the campus:

Cat calls, whistling and other discourteous words and gestures toward local civilians, particularly females, will not be tolerated.

Another directive warns that we are subject to the local and state laws of Mississippi:

> Particular attention should be given to local traffic regulations. Military drivers may be apprehended and ticketed for . . .[17]

I wonder if Barrett would've gotten a ticket had we run the red light that first morning at the intersection when the brick hit us.

Such a warning, coming in mid-November, tells me that we're all getting back to some sense of normalcy. A month and a half ago we had no time to look around and be aware of traffic regulations in Oxford. Had we engaged in what now seems like a luxury, we would've seen a typical southern town, with a downtown and square, the seat of Lafayette County.

The Square

The square was the venue for the mob at the tail end of the riots. When they lost the campus, they came down here to trash the town in a violent temper tantrum. It was their last stand, before they crawled out of town on their way back to what was becoming less and less of their South.

The square was also the site of the last stand of the mob's bizarre standard bearer, General Walker. He came back here after he had sounded retreat (if only for himself) from the campus six blocks away. Then tried to make a run for it. Recognized at a roadblock, he would be arrested and whisked off to Springfield, Missouri, for a well-earned psychiatric exam conducted at taxpayers' expense.

Now swept clean of all the riot debris, the square might again be as Mr. Faulkner once saw it:

> A Square . . . quadrangular around it, the stores . . . school and church and tavern and bank and jail each in its ordered place. But above all, the courthouse: the center, the focus, the hub;

sitting looming in the center of the county's circumference . . .
musing, brooding, symbolic and ponderable, tall as cloud, solid
as rock; dominating all: protector of the weak, judiciate and
curb of the passions and lusts, repository and guardian of the
aspirations and hopes.[18]

Adams and I drive back over there. Along each of the four sides
of the square are the usual small businesses that serve the citizenry
and constitute the economic, political, and economic lifeblood of
the town and the region. A Confederate soldier is standing atop a
pedestal on the south side of the square. He's facing to the south.
How could they get it wrong? I thought they were all erected with
the soldier facing north and the oncoming Yankees.

The square is back to its pre-riot status and that means business
as usual off the square as well. But then again, some of that normal
never changed . . . segregated parks, playgrounds, libraries, motels,
and cafes. Even the drinking fountains.

There are separate schools for Negro children, separate drinking fountains and rest rooms in public buildings. No Negro
ever sits down with a white person in a restaurant. In clothing
stores owned by whites, Negroes are not permitted to try on
a hat or a pair of shoes before buying. If a Negro puts a hat on
his head in one of these places, it is "sold."[19]

As for blacks who venture down to the square, I've been told
that they had better be "moving," that is, be there for some commercial purpose, a bank deposit, for instance. OK to shop at Neilson's. (But for the day-to-day stuff the blacks felt more comfortable
north of the square at the Jitney Jungle . . . Mississippi's own.) But
to be on the square for a social purpose—to meet and greet a fellow neighbor who just might be black? That's OK, but no dawdling.
The few benches on the square were on the courthouse grounds
and were divied up by a process of "self-segregation"; the whites sat
here, the blacks sat over there. The separateness was evident in the

parks, libraries, motels, and cafes all over town. Do the blacks have their own "separate but equal" square in Oxford? Village and town squares have been important throughout the civilized world as venues for social intercourse. A half a mile away a black is sleeping in a bed at a university where only whites could sleep before, but he best not come over here—unless he wants to make a bank deposit or buy a hat, which, if tried on, is sold.

> The most disturbing thing about Mississippi is its superficial resemblance to the United States. We would feel much more comfortable if it did not have the same institutions and symbols that we are used to. It would be better like Canada, with different cars and mailboxes and cigarettes.[20]

"Sir, I'm not a redneck ..."

Things have normalized sufficiently that male students begin to approach our jeeps and talk to patrol members. The students know about the "soldiers to male students only" exception to the army's gag rule. One day, two come up to us where we're parked outside a class building while Meredith is attending a class. I've been told about one of them. A bit of a talkative pest; every campus has them. Even though he wears the predictable campus uniform—plaid shirt, khaki pants—something about his demeanor matches the description of the student who's been approaching other members of my security detail in the past weeks.

He's a bit hesitant at first, possibly when he sees that I'm an officer. But seconds later he starts walking toward the jeep. He wants to tell me about the South. He doesn't offer his name, but "gadfly" will somehow fit.

"Sir, I'm not a redneck as you Yankees might call some of the people here in the South," he starts. "I'm not white trash, the kind y'all saw a few months ago when you first came to Oxford."

I do a quick look back in my mind and think about the angry whites from that night.

"I come from a good family over in Greenville. You have to know that, Lieutenant."

Funny how they all say that about their families.

"But y'all came down here from the North and forced your ways onto us. President Kennedy, he's your boss, right? I know your soldiers don't want to be down here. They'd rather be fightin' Communists in Cuba or at the Berlin Wall, but Kennedy sent y'all down here, right? And he's pro-Communist."

I don't say anything—even if I could—just look over at him and listen. He rocks back and forth from one foot to the other as he talks. Not aware of this quirk.

"Lieutenant, sir, y'all don't understand . . . I mean, we have a sacred doctrine here in Mississippi. It's called states' rights . . . rights separate from federal laws. And it's the Kennedy people who are pushing these federal laws down onto us. Your states in the North have these rights but you don't seem to care about them. Well, we do."

"John, Ron, keep your eyes on that guy over there by Peabody."

"This thing about Nigras is our way . . . it's our heritage. We don't mean any harm to them, not like those troublemakers that night did. They weren't from around here. I mean . . . we love our Nigras. They didn't."

There it is . . . that "love" stuff again.

Former U.S. congressman Jim Symington, as an administrative assistant to Attorney General Robert Kennedy, traveled to the campus during the first week of the riots in October at the request of his boss. In random conversations with students, he often came across the "love" remark as well. He turned to one and said, "Oh! Well, that's fine, then. If you love them, then you'll let them go to school with you, right?"

"Oh, no, we don't love them that way."

Do I stay with this guy?

"Lieutenant, we respect your uniform, but we resent y'all being sent down here by the Kennedy people."

OK, let him talk.

"But, we're not upset at y'all . . . you're military. It's a part of our tradition here in the South, you know? My daddy served and my uncle served. But y'all shouldn't be here. Look at Cuba and Berlin . . . being down here makes y'all not ready for trouble if it breaks out there."

I think he's waiting for a conversation, but it remains a monologue. He's warming up, covering everything I've heard since I've been in Oxford.

"Sir, we love Mississippi, our southern way of life. Y'all needn't have come. It's a conspiracy by them to keep y'all down here and off guard, right?"

He grabs at his belt buckle with both hands and steps back, still rocking side to side. Smiles and looks over at his friend.

The companion steps in.

"Y'all come back in a few years," he says. "We'll work this thing out. Maybe better than y'all will up north. I mean y'all got racial problems up there too."

OK, here it comes.

"Sure, we southerners don't conform to your ways."

"Your ways?" Wait a minute. Whose ways? Hey! What am I, some kind of spokesman for the North, the "voice" of the North? Or, did he read my thoughts from that first morning when I mused, "We've arrived, an Army of the North." My accent would betray me if I tried to tell them I'm from Alabama.

But, truth be told, I'm thrown off a bit, not prepared for such a conciliatory opening. The word "conform" is not an anger word or one of confrontation. And no nervous body language from this guy.

"John, make sure we're on freq."

"Y'all are serious about this. Well, so are we. You push this onto us. We know we have some race issues down here, pretty bad. But we know we'll solve them. There's more to the South than what you saw that night."

Now both are trying to talk at the same time. They know they've lost my ear, so the lead guy starts to work on Barrett in the back seat. All he can do is smile and listen. Then he turns to Adams, who's not as polite as Barrett. Adams has an edge on him. Maybe it's a class thing . . . toward the students. I like that in case of trouble. He'll be ready. Now Adams has no time for either one of these guys. His eyes are fixed on the one over at Peabody. But he does turn his head to give one of those "I don't-give-a-shit" looks and go back to his stare. Now, they can only lecture to the jeep.

The nonconfrontational companion continues.

"Y'all in the North won't know how to solve your problem because y'all don't think you have one. Y'all too busy looking down here."

(I'm reminded of James's remarks to me about impending racial tension in the North. Years later, a journalist friend will remind me that self-righteous northerners thought the 1960s civil rights movement in the South was a noble venture, a high-ground moral undertaking, that is, until the movement started *moving* north.)

The radio crackles alive, "Peanut 3, Golf 4, Magnet 10-14. Over." Adams pulls the jeep out of its spot and we head down the street.

The comments from most of the students who approach our jeep follow a similar pattern. They say that it was outside troublemakers who caused the violence. (Under their breath, they might like to include the Department of Justice and the U.S. Army in that group as well.) It's always "they" and "them," not "we" and "us."

That's fair enough . . . to a point. But they seem to ignore the fact that some of their fellow students were a part of the late-night crowd that became a mob. By their very presence alone, these students shared equal billing with the outsiders. They say they were "observing"; the army says they were "participating."

But openly participating that night or not, the under-the-radar connection between some of the Ole Miss students and the rioters is an undeniable and sad reality. Strange bedfellows they may be, but in that bed they share a common passion. For the students, it's a low-level burn born out of the "My pappy told me" antipathy toward the "Negro." For their country cousins it's a more open and violent "nigger-hating" anger. One at low heat, the other at high flame.

But both share the same goal, no better articulated than by the Mississippi governor the day before the riots at an Ole Miss football game in Jackson. He screamed into a microphone, "I love Mississippi . . . I love her people, our customs [read: separation of the races]. I love and respect our heritage [read again: separation of the races]." The forty-two thousand fans in the stadium went wild, particularly the ones who believed that code words were being used.

Maybe no one will even tell them.

Shortly after that, it just comes to me. It's as if we look up one day and realize that we're here on the campus of a school that, yes, cares about learning, but that also cares a lot about football, fraternities, and sororities. More than about Meredith. It's time to go home. The army and the Justice Department have a different agenda, but, at least for now, it will no longer involve any troops from the 716th.

The orders come in late November. B Company, the last of the battalion that's been left in Oxford, is scheduled to deploy home to Fort Dix, and its responsibilities are to be taken over by a unit from Missouri, this time a National Guard company. The Peanut Patrol will be headed by another second lieutenant, with the ironic—yet appropriate—name of Kennedy.

Once the endgame comes into sight, the humor in the camp picks up. Relief.

A black lieutenant enters one of our buses, turns back, and yells, "Look! I'm in the front of the bus."

A Spec-4 who must have had duty in a personnel office someplace starts talking about B Company's "DEROS."

A PFC asks, "D-E-R . . . what?"

"Hey, Private, it's D-E-R-O-S, the 'Date Eligible to Return from Overseas Assignment,' you know, man? Down here we're no different from soldiers coming back from a foreign country, you know, overseas."

Another soldier asks about the planes back to McGuire, "Lieutenant, when's the 'Freedom Bird' gonna take us back home?"

With his use of the tag name for the returning flights to Dix, he may have been the first to lay claim to the names of the countless planes that will bring American soldiers home from a real foreign deployment in Vietnam a few years later.

And now Quinlan can get back to the air he likes to breathe.

The day before I leave the campus and the town, I find myself over near the Lyceum, waiting for James to come out of one of his classes. I'm a bit bored and distracted, knowing that we're finally going back home, back north. I glance over at the Circle and the Grove beyond.

I was not in this spot at the height of the confrontation. But I can recall the bizarre scene when Barrett and I came upon this battlefield a few hours later. It was shortly after the two sets of combatants—the marshals and the soldiers on the one side, and the three-thousand-strong mob on the other—finally retired from the field.

The debris from the violent face-off littered the ground. Reminded me of the Minnesota State Fair grounds the day before the cleanup, only more sinister—spent tear gas canisters, broken chunks of concrete, bricks, burned-out and overturned cars, and an abandoned bulldozer that had been used by the mob to attack the marshals. All of this before they were chased off the campus, down University Avenue, toward the square, leaving remnants of the fight. It looked like the stuff that's carried ashore by the force of a high tide, then is left sticking up in the sand once the water washes back out.

I think how out of place that scene was as I look around this beautiful, parklike venue, this Grove and Circle, on this crisp near-December morning. Violent clashes don't often fit their settings. I try to bring it all back. No . . . gone. I can't squeeze any more memory out. So I relax and let my mind go forward.

I see a time, maybe just a few years from now, when Ole Miss students will walk across this beautiful expanse of grass and trees and have a hard time believing that one piece of the school's past that happened here. (Maybe no one will even tell them.) A past when, for one maddening night, this spot was filled with so much racial hatred and violence on a beautiful fall weekend when the university should have been celebrating its football, its homecomings, and its fraternity and sorority traditions.

Just as daily commuters who pass the site of a horrific highway crash the day after the cleanup have no hint of what has happened, so too will passersbys here on the campus have no idea of the violence that occurred that night.

"Give us the nigger!"

This place will once again be the idyllic, picture-perfect college campus. I can see its future as I stand here on this last day before I leave to go back north.

"Finding a solution to this problem is my goal."

Later this afternoon, James comes out of his dormitory building, walks over to my jeep, and hands me an envelope. I say goodbye and good luck and shake his hand, the same soft handshake—guarded and awkward—that it was almost two months earlier.

I open the envelope after I return to the armory and read the one-page, handwritten letter.

Dear Lt. Gallagher,

I know that your assignment over the past few weeks has been unique, if not indeed strange. I have enjoyed your presence and I hope you have not been too unhappy.

The processes of civilization are sometimes hard to understand. Yet, they must go on. In this development, sometimes we find ourselves (some of us) at the apex of a point of friction.

Immediately we are harnessed with a great responsibility. We are all duty bound to carry out this responsibility to the best of our ability. This we will do.

Presently we are faced with a great and grave racial problem in our country. It points deep in many directions. I feel that it is essential that we solve this problem, if America is to hold the place among nations that it deserves. Finding a solution to this problem is my goal.

Best wishes, and lots of luck to you in your mission.

J. H. Meredith[21]

I leave the South with my unit the next day, November 20, 1962. One of the returning New Yorkers captured the moment when he wrote,

Several of the men kissed the earth when we landed in the North. To me the nightmare wasn't over until I saw the magic words "New York" written beside the line in the middle of the Lincoln Tunnel.[22]

10

THE RETURN—1963

"Camp Mud"

In the spring of 1963, I rotate back to Oxford with C Company of the 716th as it replaces an MP company from the 503rd. The mission is the same as it was last fall, to maintain the town patrols, security at Baxter Hall, and, of course, the Peanut Patrol. All to keep the high-profile student and the marshal unharmed. Meredith had talked about not returning for the spring semester unless "there were very definite and positive changes to make my situation more conducive to learning," but he apparently saw change. Sounds like a man conflicted—wants to leave and stay at the same time. Many of the soldiers would have preferred that he had chosen the former option.

We return to a totally different billeting arrangement on this repeat assignment. Late last fall the military in the Oxford area was scattered all over, from inside the armory building to tents in its parking lot and out at the airport. An alert platoon was in the "Hole," an encampment adjacent to Baxter Hall, and a portable shower unit was on a piece of federal land a mile east of the airport.

No one was happy with the situation. The Mississippi National Guard wanted its armory back. The army wanted tighter command and control of its men. Local officials—town and university—wanted the military to have a lower profile. To everyone's relief, the army found a location and brought all the troops together (but for those at the Hole) at a campsite one mile south of the campus, past the married students' housing, on land which the government had purchased.

A unit from the same army engineer battalion that had supported the military effort last fall was called in to build a camp that would be user-friendly for its new occupants. It would be a "fixer-upper" in real-estate-agent-speak, a condition that would shock a Boy Scout's mother, if not her National Scout Jamboree–bound son. But then again, an army first sergeant is not a mother. The army plans it this way, to keep the arriving troops busy, say, on camp "beautification" projects. The orders for the men on the work details are clear and known to army veterans of all generations: "If it moves, salute it, if not, paint it."

On a morning in March 1963, the American flag is raised at reveille over Camp USAFOX (U.S. Army Forces Oxford). At two acres, it's probably the smallest official camp in the U.S. Army. The enlisted men call it Camp Paradise, so christened by the members of the 503rd. Others in the company will soon be calling it "Camp Mud." After a few days of storms drench the campsite, I side with the mudders. For many of the same reasons, others call it "Camp Swampy." The three unofficial camp titles will soon be used interchangeably by the troops. Only in the Pentagon and on the bulletin board outside the orderly tent will the name USAFOX be seen.

The fifty-four-tent outpost could have been a model a few years later for the set of *M*A*S*H*.[1] It has a huge army-issue mess tent (the cooks have come down with us from Dix), an orderly room and shower tent, and one large tent housing the S-2, S-3, and AVN (aviation) sections, as well as the provost marshal. They're all connected by a network of boardwalks and sawdust paths lined on both sides by sandbags painted white. Non-MP battalion members (cooks, clerks, and supply personnel) could spend their whole TDY here in this enclave, not really aware that they're in the backyard of a large public university. The only official recreation for USAFOX soldiers, as was the case last fall, are nightly movies and R&R runs up to Memphis.

There are forms of recreation and entertainment in the camp for which no notices appear on the USAFOX bulletin board. I hear that the camp has a small fluctuation in its daily head count from time to time, due to visits to the site from females. I don't know if the visitors are coeds or townies. (If there's a coed, the dean of women will be sure to say that the poor child must have gotten lost on her way to class.) I don't think these drop-bys are Red Cross canteen ladies or USO volunteers brought in to lift the morale of the troops. Nor do I think that they sign in on the visitor log over in the orderly tent. And in some of the tents I think they're drinking more than Coca-Cola and grape Nehi.

Too bad Frechette's not here with me this time to engage in some junior officer extracurricular activity. Last fall we went on one of the runs up to Memphis and watched the ducks at the Peabody Hotel parade down the red carpet in the lobby and splash into the fountain. In-state, at the invitation of a student, we visited a bootlegger's shed out in a woods not too far from town. (We thought that we were not under the army's alcohol ban if we were off the campus.) For a few dollars passed through a small window off the porch, the spirits provider passed back a bottle of an adult beverage through the same window in return. I couldn't see the person with whom I was doing business, only his arm (a black man's).

We also found a roadside cafe out south of town where the two of us staged championship pinball machine tournaments well into the night. It was on my way back to camp from one of those excursions that I heard the frantic radio voice of the night duty clerk searching for me. He was informing me about the order to report to General Howze immediately (the "Gallagher jabbed a night stick in the youth's ribs" news story).

Outdoor movies for the off-duty troops round out the springtime entertainment delights provided to the troops at Camp Mud (more varied now than they were last October when *Breakfast at Tiffany's* was played more than once). Once the sky blackens over Mississippi, the silver screen set up in the open field comes alive. At that moment the fantasies of a homesick soldier might transport him back to the one drive-in theater in his small town. But the pleasant flashback and mood quickly end when the moviegoer looks to his side in the darkness and sees—not his girlfriend—but a draftee from the Bronx with flatulence.

We might wonder why the army security assignment for Meredith is a continuing one. The marshals are still here. Why then us? There appears to be no trace of the serious violence, or potential for it, which existed last year toward this student. On the surface everyone seems to be getting on with their collegiate lives, including the one black student. But the Kennedy administration can ill afford a setback after all they have gone through to get to this point. They want this one to be in the win column.

And despite the appearances of normalcy, harassment of Meredith remains ongoing, with occasional "insulting language, fireworks, and stamping of feet [over his dormitory room ceiling]."[2] Vandals damaged a car he brought onto the campus. Finally, to dispel any notion that we do not belong here anymore, he received a few death and bomb threats at the beginning of the new semester.

I soon come up to my eighteenth month in-grade as a second lieutenant and I'm promoted. And by military anecdote, if nothing else, I am allowed to continue to be "an officer and a gentleman by an Act of Congress." (I don't think I have ever come across the actual statutory language.) The new camp commander since January, Colonel Hodges, does the honors of pinning the silver bars of a first lieutenant on my collar in a hastily arranged mess tent ceremony, complete with an army photographer. The enlisted men are polite as they wait to resume their lunch until after the colonel shakes my hand. I leave the tent feeling no different than I did when I entered. But I do walk around the camp looking for a second lieutenant to salute me.

The day after I arrive, I renew my reacquaintance with the student Meredith with a handshake. From him it's a thin smile and barely a flicker of recognition, though he remains polite and cordial. I'm simply another uniform. He seems as he did that first day . . . so out of place. Again, not as a result of his color. More like a visiting lecturer down from New York, crossing the campus in that blue business suit. I sense that the students who harassed him last fall simply avoid him now, not out of acceptance but out of resignation.

They just couldn't chase him off the campus, back to an all-black college, the agenda for many of them at the time, except for the ones who wanted worse to happen. He held fast; they blinked.

Then there is the majority here, the students who never hassled Meredith nor protested his admission to Ole Miss, just ignored him, then as now. Their student lives were not affected by his presence, that is, after the tear gas dissipated. To the world he was a story; to them his presence was a distraction on the campus and, to some extent, in the classroom. If he was in your class, you worried that the distraction might compromise the quality of the instruction, like having to sit in class next to the son of the governor or a Miss America finalist. It was these students who looked forward to his graduation almost as much as he did—and for reasons having nothing to do with his color.

We hear that he will be an Ole Miss grad this coming summer. His mission continues toward the degree. And ours continues: simply keep him alive long enough for him to get that degree. Until then, we're here again because of the one fear: the lone gunman.

I pull out my dime-store spiral tablet from last fall.

2 subjects . . . 190 lbs., short sleeve wh shirt/sunglasses/ dimples/dark hair (Anson Sheldon, Jr.)

red head 175 lbs green shirt/glasses

pickup 61 white Ford Miss 22596, maroon 62 Ford 2552

Meredith is still on message. As we leave his dormitory to go across the campus on a fresh spring day, I see the same private person with the same determination that I saw last year. I follow as a dutiful retainer—at the pleasure of my government.

A Campus "Tee Time"

Like the troops, Meredith too has found an outlet for his recreation. He plays golf on a tiny campus nine-hole course. The marshals tell us the night before of a schedule change and his "tee time." The security challenge is obvious as I locate a campus map showing the golf course. The next morning I assign the jeeps at selected points around its boundaries. I do this with particular concern for sight-lines through patches of woods bordering the fairways where any unfamiliar car can pull up, park, and its occupant find cover. The line-of-sight brackets are overlapped by the patrol from the first to the ninth hole. (In the infantry world they're called "fields of fire.")

The word "bizarre" has become all too commonplace in our duties, and it more than fits this morning. Here is one golfer on a small community course with twelve handlers watching him— probably more than any U.S. president might have at the Congressional Country Club outside Washington, D.C. Once I have the jeeps in place I do a commo check, a dry run of the tried-and-true pass on, pick up scheme. Fine, we're covered. We go live.

A short time passes and I sense something's wrong. Too much chatter, not enough code. I cock my ear.

"Magnet 10-15 at the second tee. Selects a 6 iron. Good choice for this short par 3. The gallery goes quiet as he approaches the tee. And now, a practice swing . . ." (all spoken in a PGA-televised microphone whisper).

I quickly thumb the radio switch.

"All Golf units, Peanut Three. Cease nonmilitary transmissions immediately."

Bored troops already. And we just got back here. Golf? What's next? Tennis with that liberal professor?

On Easter Sunday morning, a deuce-and-a-half takes many of the men, dressed in their Sunday best (Class A uniforms), to church services in the town. The bus drops the Catholics off at St. John's on University Avenue. The small church, which seats two hundred, is not prepared to handle the many ethnic Irish, Italian, and Puerto Rican out-of-towners who were raised in big city neighborhood parishes in the Northeast. They try to crowd through the entrance and then turn back out onto the front walkway. I can't recall if the priest said something about the miracle of the Resurrection in his sermon, but I know he doesn't say anything about charity and

fairness toward one's fellow man. Maybe that's too close to upsetting the delicate balance of church and state relations down here.
A parishioner might call the archbishop's office in Jackson to complain. And upsetting something else as well. A second call might
be made to another Jackson number by an informant for the State
Sovereignty Commission.[3]

On our national holidays, army mess sergeants try their best
to feed those soldiers who have not fled the country's army posts
on three-day passes to a little bit of home. The dinner at Camp
USAFOX is a traditional Easter one—ham, scalloped potatoes, and
the expected green beans and rolls. Someone pipes up from one of
the mess tent tables to demand that the special services Spec-4 (the
"movie" guy) give out the time for the Camp Mud Easter egg hunt.

"Soldiers of America"

Midway through the spring, my patrol members come across two
documents that are being distributed on the campus, one meant
directly for the soldiers. It's a one-page, typewritten (possibly by
students), mimeographed letter entitled "SOLDIERS OF AMER-
ICA" and starts out with:

> The Volunteer Citizens of America who face you in Mississippi
> are not your ENEMY.

Seeking a kinship with the soldiers, they say that they are:

> 100% true blue Americans just like you. Most of them are
> Combat Veterans of WWII and Korea. They do not want to
> fight you or any of their other fellow Americans, but they will
> die to preserve and uphold the CONSTITUTION OF THE
> UNITED STATES OF AMERICA, which belongs to both YOU
> and Them. If it is not preserved, AMERICA will die. If you
> attack them, many brave AMERICAN lives will be wasted,

and the COMMUNIST POLITICIANS—CASTRO, KEN-
NEDY & KRUSCHEV [*sic*], Inc., will be the winners. KEN-
NEDY is out to destroy AMERICA, because he is a sick, sick,
COMMUNIST.

* * *

You are under orders to obey the orders of the Commander
in Chief, but your oath also requires that you "DEFEND THE
U.S. AGAINST ALL OF ITS ENEMIES, BOTH FOREIGN
AND DOMESTIC. RED JACK KENNEDY is the most DAN-
GEROUS ENEMY AMERICA has ever had. He has repeatedly
given "AID AND COMFORT TO THE ENEMY," and he has
consistently worked to DESTROY the CONSTITUTION OF
THE UNITED STATES OF AMERICA. If you obey him in
attacking Mississippi, you will DESTROY AMERICA.

* * *

Do not be afraid of Court Martial or disgrace. If you will join
with your fellow Americans here in Mississippi, no force on
earth can conquer us. Together with all other GOOD AMERI-
CANS, we will remove RED JACK KENNEDY and all other
communist PARTY politicians from office, and go on from
there to wipe the HELL-SPAWNED FILTH of COMMUNISM
from the face of the earth.

The exhortation ends by urging the soldiers to:

THINK, AMERICAN SOLDIERS, THIS IS YOUR LAST
CHANCE TO SAVE AMERICA . . . COME AND JOIN US[4]

The plea to surrender reminds me of U.S. propaganda leaflets
that were dropped behind enemy lines in the Korean War, urging
the enemy to give up and join the forces of "democracy and freedom," or words to that effect.

I'm curious. The publisher of this letter (the guy who ran the mim-
eograph machine) missed his maximum marketing target. His timing
is off a bit. Maybe his printing budget was too small to run a larger

edition that could have hit the campus and the streets of Oxford last
fall. That was before 98 percent of his intended readership, the "SOL-
DIERS OF AMERICA," had returned to their home posts. Only a
bunch of MPs (and a few cooks back at the camp) are around now.

But I do tell the NCO in the Peanut Patrol to do a head count
each night for the next few days to make sure that no one has
crossed over to join these "Volunteer Citizens of America."

He thinks I'm serious.

Ole Miss Coloring Book

The second publication that patrol members bring in around the
same time is an eighteen-page booklet entitled *The Ole Miss Coloring Book*. It features comic-book drawings of all the principal players in last fall's integration crisis at the university.

The cover page depicts the skeletal face of a helmeted soldier
above two crossed rifles ("Federal Power" inscribed along the rifle
barrels), with blood dripping from each of the bayonets. Each page
contains caricatures of last fall's participants, with coloring instructions, starting with the soldiers and the campus (color this "red"
and on the next page "bloody"), and then an armed federal marshal
(color him "green" and his trigger "happy").

DOJ lawyers are featured, as is their boss in Washington (Attorney General Robert Kennedy) with the caption "Why didn't he
come?" to Ole Miss, so color him "yellow." And "Bobby's Brother,"
President Kennedy (color him "slightly pink"), makes an appearance in the book as does a "Press" car from New York with a cherry
bomb (color it "lit") taped to the windshield.

According to the author of the book, a "federal court order
determines" that General Walker should be colored "crazy" and the
Bill of Rights should be colored "trampled."

The book goes on. While there were "36,000 troops in Oxford
[last September] there were 5,000 in Berlin—none in 'Cuber.' Color
this typical."[5]

A map of the state of Mississippi is drawn on one page (color it "sovereign but occupied"), as is the face of Governor Ross Barnett (color him "sad, but high principled"). Finally, there is an outline of the head of a man (in black), suggesting a profile of Meredith standing in front of a huge array of soldiers. The description is of the "phenomenon" and, for him, there are no coloring instructions for "it is against the 'law of the land' to color him."

The "Constitution of the United States" is shown on the last page and the publisher of the book urges that it be colored "dead."

But for the flattering sketches of General Walker, Governor Barnett, and (curiously) President Kennedy, the others are portrayed in a less favorable, almost gangster-like style. (*Dick Tracy* thugs come to mind.)

The booklet, copyrighted in 1963, was published in Tallahassee and dedicated to a list of named individuals plus "all the other 'Ole Miss' patriots who stand up to the federal tyranny that occupies their campus," as well as all other "loyal Southerners of both races." Price: 1 to 9 copies = 50 cents and up to 30 cents for more than 50 copies.[6]

Open Letter

On May 3, the student newspaper, *The Mississippian*, publishes an "Open Letter," written by Meredith to his "fellow students," in which he talks about his reasons for attending Ole Miss. It lacks the soaring rhetoric of the letter he gave me in November 1962, but then again its focus this time is the student body and not the world.

In an out-of-body moment, he seems to be distancing himself from himself as he starts out using the third person when mentioning "James Meredith" and the "James Meredith Case." Then, still as though speaking about a court case, he says that he thought it best to weigh in on the matter "since I am so closely connected with the controversy."

Meredith discusses why he chose Ole Miss ("securing greater educational opportunities for myself and my people," etc.). But then he declares that "I have little concern for the phenomenon of inter-gration [*sic*] and desegregation. Neither is my aim."[7]

This is odd. In his November 1962 letter to me, he spoke of the "great and grave racial problem in our country":

> It points deep in many directions. I feel that it is essential that we solve this problem, if America is to hold the place among nations that it deserves. Finding a solution to this problem is my goal.

One can only wonder what he means, if the solution to the "racial problem" is something other than "integration" and "desegregation." If not that, then what is his goal? When he says that the blacks should be given the same opportunities as whites, does he mean that blacks should have equal rights with white people, but need not get close to whites? No need to integrate, no need to desegregate, once rights are in balance. Puzzling and provocative. Impractical and bizarre. He's almost saying, "Let me have the right to walk across the same campus, attend the same classes taught with the same books by the same faculty as the white students, but I'll keep separate from them."

The letters to the editor in response to the Meredith open letter were predictable.

Some praised Meredith ("There are many of us who sympathize. . . .") and some attacked him. For example:

> First let me say—emphatically—that you are no "fellow student" of mine, and as far as phony apologies—forget [word unclear]. After all your contemptuous actions over the past year nothing you could say or do would make me or the people of this state change our attitude toward you. . . .
> The record speaks for itself—you are nothing but an arrogant cocky troublemaker who seeks to advance himself through publicity for worldly gain. Cutting classes and exams, holding press conferences, attending meetings as a pawn and

writing two intimidating national magazine articles about this state, this University and the student body is not, to my way of thinking ". . . securing greater opportunities for myself and my people."

Your race has suffered a great deal [in] this state and throughout the South as a result of your actions whether you realize it or not. The gap between the two races is wider than ever before, and it will take a long time to bridge such a space. If you and your little helpers would leave us alone and let us solve our own problems none of this would have happened.[8]

USAFOX Command Change

In early May a new commander arrives at the camp. Prior to his taking on the new duty, his predecessor had to assure the Pentagon that Colonel William R. Lynch, then stationed in a leadership role at the infantry school at Fort Benning, was "fully indoctrinated and conversant with operations and local people."[9]

The colonel must have undertaken that preparation because, once on the job, he issues a five-page orientation memo to newly assigned soldiers, not unlike a handbook that Ole Miss might give to incoming students over on the campus. They have theirs. Lynch counters with the army's. To the newly arrived USAFOX personnel on his "campus," he writes:

The US Army, this command and you, as members of this command are not in a position to argue nor to judge the merits or principles of the decisions which have been made in regard to the local situation. This is not the most difficult duty you've ever been on but probably most distasteful . . . bound to be, as it may, pit one American against another. Do not be misled though town and campus appear to have been returning to normal ever since events of September and October; we cannot make the assumption that all is as it appears on the surface.

To relax or fail in your duty of constant watchfulness is to invite a return to unsettled conditions.[10]

In mid-May I receive orders for an overseas TDY assignment (Southeast Asia), along with some other members of the battalion at Camp Paradise, and we're transferred back to Dix to await deployment. On my last day with Meredith, I get out of the jeep and go over to him to say goodbye once more. As I do so, I'm thinking that I'm shaking the hand of the most courageous individual I'll ever meet. (Almost fifty years later, I am of the same opinion.) He did the walk. The blacks standing back at that intersection in 1962 after we passed Holly Springs, the blacks who came out of their farmhouse when the helicopter flew over, the black at Faulkner's place . . . none of them walked with Meredith. The civil rights movement in other places involved hundreds of people walking together, banners in front, megaphones, songs, speeches. But he was his own movement. He wanted to walk alone. A bit of an odd character, but maybe one has to be so to do what he did.

His story cuts both ways. Nothing about what this ambitious man from Kosciusko, Mississippi, tried to do was simple. Yet when it's stripped clean to its essence, it was simple and he did it.

After providing some quick on-the-job training, I hand over the baton of the Peanut Patrol to Second Lieutenant Dick Mitchell, a 716th newcomer, born in New Jersey. The next day I leave Mississippi, as a soldier, for the last time.

Summer Registration: A Second Black Student

Meanwhile back at Camp Mud/Paradise/Swampy/USAFOX, the soldiers continue to look toward Meredith's graduation date. But the routine for these short-timers (now it's the 720th MP Battalion on its rotation swing through Oxford) is broken by the news that another black student, Cleve McDowell, is planning to register for the summer session. They are not prepared for a "second"

James Meredith at Ole Miss, nor has Colonel Lynch expected such double duty.

By late May the number of USAFOX memos since last October has grown from Memorandum Number 1 to Number 24. They're all posted on the camp bulletin board, under rainproof plastic, out in front of the orderly tent. They cover most of what the camp commander and, in some cases, the company clerk (think: Radar O'Reilly) consider must-reading for the day in the life of a 716th MP. They run the gamut from mail call hours, to leave and pass policy, to sick call and PX hours, and, of course, to the evening's movie offering. While Colonel Lynch has prepared for his new assignment, he has not anticipated a development that causes him to issue Memorandum Number 25. Entitled "Readiness Posture," with seven annexes, five appendices, and a subtitle—"Contingency Plan for Campus Disorder"—Lynch's plan is to put the camp on full alert over the summer registration period, June 3 through June 6.[11]

Some might wonder why so much fuss simply over the arrival of a second black student on the campus. It becomes clear that the contingency that Colonel Lynch must plan for is the appearance of the governor and what that might stir up—disruption triggered by the support and encouragement of official Mississippi (a rerun of last year's movie). Governor Barnett wants to make a *public* appearance on campus in *public* opposition to the McDowell admission. He has let it be known that he opposes any continued integration of the university.

As it turns out on that day,

During McDowell's actual registration . . . the Peanut Patrol, the marshals, the FBI, and Army Intelligence all had him [McDowell] in sight as planned. There were no crowds at any time. Indeed, there were present only some members of the press and, apparently, a few state officials. There were no state police cars on the campus, although eight were reported in the Oxford vicinity.[12]

The governor did not appear on the campus, and his backup plan, that a state trooper would read a statement to the new transfer student indicating that he, Governor Barnett, wished that McDowell would "not attend the university," also did not occur.[13]

Over the remaining weeks the 716th and the 720th Military Police Battalions play musical chairs by alternating companies in and out of Oxford to see who will eventually be the last unit holding the bag. The dubious "Last Man Standing" award on the Ole Miss stage goes to Company A of the 716th.

In mid-July, as Meredith's graduation date approaches, the incidents of survival humor in the camp increase as they did last fall when our rotation date closed in. In a tongue-in-cheek message to his superior officer at Fort Dix, a 716th lieutenant, on behalf of the company, writes a nine-point request for unit reassignment.

He starts with the comforting message that any superior officer needs to hear, namely:

> As we sit here under a driving thunderstorm (the 6th in as many days), let it be known that our morale is high.
>
> Our request is a simple one: We would like a change of scenery.

As a preface to his nine-point lobbying effort he states:

> Be it known that we, Co "A", 716th MP Bn.[Battalion], having served X days "Bad Time" in the Command post commonly referred to as U.S.A.F.O.X., but better known as "Camp Swampy," do hereby submit [this memo] to make [known] the fact that transfer from USAFOX to the actual 716th Bn., to wit: Ft. Dix, is desired.

Then:

> Prompt action on this matter is urgently needed for the following reasons:

a. So that clothing, equipment & self may be dried out before Jungle Rot sets in.

* * *

c. So that we can enter a latrine peacefully without worrying about having to fight off the . . . Black Widow spider.

d. So that sawdust, gravel, [or] mud [do] not grace our living quarters.

e. So that television may once again be enjoyed without having "Icewater 28" and "Icewater 5" [new radio call signs] commo checking through the [TV] set.

f. So that we will not have to use yellow lights to keep thousands of flying creatures from invading all areas of human habitation.

* * *

Signed:

The Men & Officers
Co "A", 716th MP Bn.
Oxford, Mississippi[14]

On July 24, 1963, the USAFOX command orders that the tents of Company A be struck and that the flag over the camp—under which untold numbers of soldiers had served since that Sunday night last September—be lowered for the last time.

Most likely the company commander orders one of his second lieutenants to make sure that the lights are all turned off before he hops aboard the last outbound bus in the troop convoy on its way up to Millington. There they await the Freedom Birds that will take them home to Dix, thus ending a sad chapter in the history of this country's use of its military.

Shortly after the departure of the last MPs, an engineer unit from Fort McClellan (Alabama) comes over to dismantle the camp, board by board, all to be carted off. It takes twenty deuce-and-a-halfs and six smaller vans to pack up the material and equipment from the site, thus removing from Oxford and the sovereign state of Mississippi all traces of the U.S. military's efforts in the Ole Miss crisis. I doubt that General Grant's troops were as careful in their cleanup when they left this town to return north a century ago. We won't even leave a carbon footprint to be discovered here years later.

The land is released back to the U.S. Forest Service, its former owner, prompting a humorist in the company (of which there are many in the army) to suggest that trees be planted over the whole tract to remove any evidence of the once-occupying army. I wonder if the Forest Service would have allowed the departing army to plant a small sign on the former campsite on the day they left.

It would have been similar to those roadside historical markers that are spread throughout the South, memorializing significant Civil War battles. An updated version of the "Kilroy Was Here" GI graffiti of World War II, this one would be a fitting reminder to passersby who come upon the plaque. It would read:

From September 30, 1962, through July 24, 1963, on this site and elsewhere in the environs of the county of Lafayette, state of Mississippi, members of the armed forces of the United States were billeted who served their country and the U.S. Constitution in support of the racial integration of the nearby public University of Mississippi.

Of course, not long after the last bus carrying members of the 716th would have crossed the Mississippi state line into Tennessee that night, any such plaque would have most likely been vandalized.

11

THE GRADUATION

A Ceremony

On August 18, 1963, 440 seniors from the University of Mississippi gather in their fabled Grove to receive degrees. Among them is a black student, James Howard Meredith, who returns to the campus for the ceremony from the nearby town of Kosciusko. He is awarded a bachelor of arts degree. The ceremony is conducted (under who knows how many watchful eyes) a short distance from the university's Lyceum building where, for him at least, it had all started almost one year earlier. Or, if one delights in coincidences of history, it may have started one hundred years earlier with General Grant's cameo appearance in the town and at the Lyceum.

Epilogue

The 716th Military Police Battalion

In March 1965, the 716th Military Police Battalion, including some who had served at Ole Miss, was deployed to South Vietnam to provide security and law enforcement support there. This was a part of the increasing military role of the United States in Vietnam. Three years later, the 716th enhanced its reputation when its soldiers became the front line of defense of Saigon during the Viet Cong's surprise assault on the city (Tet Offensive). This was the unit's most important contribution to the war effort and, indeed, to the history of the Military Police Corps of the U.S. Army. The battalion's response to the Viet Cong attacks either broke the backs of the multipronged assaults outright or delayed the enemy long enough for regular combat forces to arrive. In the end, not one of the 130 facilities in Saigon for which the battalion was responsible fell into enemy hands. The 716th was later awarded the Presidential Unit Citation for its actions. Through its distinguished performance in Vietnam and other assignments to follow, the 716th went on to become the most decorated Military Police Battalion in the U.S. Army.

The Segregation of the Black Soldiers

A sampling of various after-action or command reports filed in late 1962 by military units at Ole Miss reveal that a number of unit commanders commented on the ordered segregation of their troops:

> The 82nd Airborne Division found that "a serious morale problem" resulted from the fact that the 1st Airborne Battle Group, 503d Infantry Regiment [no relation to the 503rd MPs], had to

leave its Negro personnel at the Airport while the rest of the battle group moved into Oxford.

* * *

The 101st Airborne Division complained that "segregation of Negro troops is highly undesirable. Negro soldiers should perform their normal functions with their units."

* * *

The 2d Infantry Division, which had reported resentment when Negroes were withdrawn from the public eye on 2 October, concluded only that "in operations when racial issues are involved, an early determination should be made concerning the introduction of negro [sic] personnel into the area."

* * *

Of the Oxford units commenting on this question of integration of troops during racial troubles, the only one that took a flatly negative attitude was the 720th Military Police Battalion from Fort Hood, Texas, its commanding officer . . . commenting: "Taking negro [sic] personnel to Oxford was ill advised. Their presence created a great morale problem for the Battalion commander because they could not be used as Military Policemen. It is recommended that in any future operations of this type negro personnel remain at home station."

* * *

The commander of the 716th Military Police Battalion (which did comply with the order to segregate) . . . expressed himself rather strongly [on the subject]: . . . In addition to the morale factor [and communication issues], the unit lost two company commanders, one first sergeant and the communications sergeant [plus several other NCOs].

* * *

[Finally] General Howze thought that "across the board" segregation in the Oxford troubles "had a disruptive effect" on the units involved inasmuch as twenty percent of the strength of the Regular Army was Negro and therefore included company commanders "and other key leaders." He thought the "proper solution" was to give "the field commander all latitude" respecting the matter.[1]

They Served Their Country

I have often wondered whether any of the black soldiers in our battalion who were "stepped back" that night at Millington Naval Air Station (Memphis) stayed in the army. Did they later go off to Vietnam to support and defend the Constitution of the United States against the foreign enemy? I did find out about one, the black captain Linwood Hardmon, who was put in command of the black soldiers from our battalion who were stepped back that Sunday night. He later served with distinction in Vietnam and came back home.

In the words of his widow:

That incident [the step back of the black soldiers at Memphis]
really bothered him over the years. He really worked hard
to get that command and they took it [his company] away
from him. He couldn't go down into Mississippi [that night]
to defend the right from the wrong and yet they sent him to
Vietnam a few years later when the difference between right
and wrong in that war wasn't all that clear.[2]

To those of us in the formation that night, it was a heartbreaking and humiliating scene. It was as if the U.S. Army was telling them "Please step back, you cannot represent your country tonight. Maybe later we'll send you to a war in Southeast Asia." Question: Which military deployment was more of a threat to our country and the Constitution?

No rationale offered for the segregation of the troops ("snipers in the trees," "already incendiary situation," "inflame the rioters," etc.) can overcome the suspicion that political considerations played a role, at least in part, in the decision to take blacks out of the formations. A Democrat was in the White House and both Mississippi senators in Washington, outspoken already in their insistence on the sanctity of states' rights (code: racial separation), were Democrats. Might they have been "inflamed" as well? When an aide to the Ole Miss chancellor complained in the first days after the riots that "Negro troops had been used on patrols" in Oxford, U.S. Senator Stennis said that "he couldn't believe it."[3]

When the black Sergeant Brooks joined the Peanut Patrol after Meredith's complaint that first week, I'm sure the same sentiment was voiced on the campus. And later the next month, Oxford officials complained of the "Army's use of Negro soldiers on a regular water detail in which they drew water from an outlet near the fire station."[4]

James Meredith

In 1989 I met James Meredith in the lobby of an office building in Washington, D. C., where I had my law office. Most of the building housed the offices of a conservative think tank. He was working as a "special assistant" to U.S. Senator Jesse Helms. In a letter he sent to me, the Mississippian from a strong Republican family background said,

> I consider this job in the United States Senate to be the most significant development in my long campaign to make the Black Race full first class citizens.

* * *

The thing that has impressed me most about Senator Jesse Helms over the years has been his total commitment to preserving the traditional family and maintaining high moral standards based on Christian morality. He is constantly criticized for his unbending resistance to the Liberal Agenda, which seeks to destroy these traditional and moral values. He is right, and I admire him for it. That is why I am here.[5]

My Return to Ole Miss

In 2001 an African American professor invited me back to the University of Mississippi to speak to one of his classes in the journalism department about my experience in the James Meredith crisis thirty-nine years earlier. It was my first time back on campus. I picked up a rental car and a road map outside the Memphis airport (this time paying for both). I had a choice of colors with the car and I wanted one as far away as I could get from the OD color of my army days. I drove a bright red compact off the lot and headed for the Mississippi state line. I decided to retrace the convoy route that we took down Highway 78, rather than take the faster interstate. That 1962 trip was during "Operation Rapid Road," as it was officially called by the army. Ours was anything but rapid then; I was sure I would do better this time.

Outside Holly Springs, Mississippi, I took an exit ramp south to Oxford, no longer needing to go through the town. Then it was on to a new Highway 7 down to Ole Miss. It was a straight ribbon of concrete that occasionally came up and over a piece of the old Highway 7 on which we drove down back then. There were no curves around hills this time, no voluntary slow-downs through small hamlets or forced ones from carloads of angry whites. While the ride in 1962 was anything but pleasant, under different circumstances it might have been. In 2001 it was just a straight road of boredom.

As I drove down the new road, I was reminded of a comment made to me by an ex-Mississippian—a white man—a few years earlier. He had a rather novel "take" on racism in his home state. Without a hint of hyperbole in his voice he told me:

> More incidents of racist behavior occurred back in the hollows of the state, back in those pockets where all the towns are surrounded by hills. Not so in the Delta, where you can see everything for miles. You can't get away with stuff where everyone can see what you're doing on the flat ground. But in the hill country not that many people can see you. So you can get away with all that racism stuff.[6]

He might also have meant this kind of hill country, particularly now when the road has been straightened out and "not that many people can see you" back over in those hollows.

Two years after the 716th drove down Highway 7 in 1962, three civil rights activists were pulled off a dark rural stretch of another road in Mississippi and murdered because of what they were doing. They were called "troublemakers" from the North. In an odd way we were so-called activists as well. And troublemakers from the North. I don't know if the Klan was very active in this part of the state in those years, but they would've had their hands (and their sheets) full that night with us northern agitators. Just too many of us to pull over and murder. We had more guns too, that is, those of us who didn't turn in our ammo back at Millington.

I arrived in Oxford and came up onto the campus. My memory of it was blurred by all the physical changes. I expected to see black students walking across the Grove, which I did, but all the post-1962 construction improvements were a surprise.

Other changes were evident as well. The 1960s dress code for coeds had fallen by the way. There was not a dress or a skirt on a single young woman walking on the campus, unless it was worn by a foreign exchange student or a coed on her way to a job interview. If there was any such female apparel nearby, it remained neatly folded in a suitcase back at the women's dorm, placed there by the hands of a caring mother. Slacks, Levi's, and shorts were the norm.

I stopped by the cafeteria and recalled the mid-October 1962 incident when the rock went through the window as the near-riot crowd gathered outside and taunted the one lone African American student as he ate his supper at a table. This time I saw a group of blacks seated together over at one table, not far from that window. No message or significance in that scene. Same-race and same-interest groups often collect together in cafeterias and student unions on campuses all across the country. It may have been a "comfort" choice, but not a virtual "roped-off" section for blacks that morning, nor a symbolic nod to a lingering racial legacy. No, simply a seating option based on free selection. Back at my college it was the "poets' corner" for the serious English majors and, farther over, the jocks' table for the football team.

Here's the real stuff. Not a staged, happy-go-lucky beer commercial with mixed races, but students deciding with whom they might sit (or with whom they might drink a Bud Lite). Let them sit wherever they want to . . . simple real-world choices—self-segregation—made by those who didn't have such choices when I was here the first time. Someone else did the segregating for them then.

And, like Meredith fifty years ago, they might also have deep roots here in Mississippi. They too have a story. They too want to be counted.

And as Robert Khayat said of the black Ole Miss students, shortly after his installation as chancellor, "They now have an ownership stake in Ole Miss."

At the cafeteria, one of the managers came over to me after he found out about my time at Ole Miss years earlier and asked, "Now, Mr. Gallagher, when you came down here in '62 it was really as a cover . . . just a practice run, for Cuba. Right?"

Later in the afternoon I tried to find the house in Oxford with the side driveway that served as the 716th MP Battalion's bizarre access route to the campus that first morning in 1962. It seemed to have disappeared. I also drove south of the campus past what had been the married-student housing to look for the plot of land that once had been the site of the smallest then-active official army post,

USAFOX, the one variously known as Camp Mud, Camp Paradise, or Camp Swampy. But I couldn't find that either. The area appeared to have been part of a southward expansion of the campus some years later. Built over. Vanished. As if it had never existed.

As If It Had Never Happened

As the army camp with all the names soon was "plowed" under, so too did the army smooth over the performance of its soldiers at Ole Miss, almost as if it had never happened. I had heard that medals were withheld and injuries to the deputy marshals went unacknowledged. We were trained to fight our Cold War enemies, real and imagined. But the oath we took as soldiers does say something about our *domestic* enemies as well.

The battle of Ole Miss became a historical footnote, squeezed in between the bookends of two more recognizable mid-twentieth-century events—the Berlin Wall and the Cuban missile crisis—and then pushed off the shelf completely by the big one, Vietnam. Yet there it was—a test of the national government's will power and moral strength to confront racial intolerance, not only from a mob of street thugs, but within one of its very own statehouses. But the federal government did not want to talk about it. It was like a crazy relative up in the attic. Finally, a small town and a large university came forward (and back into the news) to do something about it.

"Open Doors"

In 2002 the University of Mississippi marked the fortieth anniversary of the integration of the school by sponsoring an education initiative that featured a long-term oral history project about the landmark event. It was called "Open Doors" and the goal was to look at both the legacy of the past and the promise of the future. Robert Khayat, the school's chancellor, spoke.

> It is unfortunate, but true, that we cannot undo the misdeeds of the past. We can, however, express our heartfelt regret—as men and women of conscience—that both equal rights and equal opportunity were once long denied to a large segment of our state's population.
>
> Regrets and apologies, no matter how sincere, matter little as compared to the importance of the transformation of this university. Today, Ole Miss is a respected state university, an open, diverse and nurturing community, where people of all races, religions, nationalities, economic groups and political alliances live and work comfortably together.
>
> * * *
>
> Out of the ashes and pain of fear, resistance and intimidation, Ole Miss has risen to champion the values of respect, tolerance and civility.[7]

The observance featured various lectures, historic exhibitions, and other activities. One was a celebration on the town square, attended by former marshals, returning National Guardsman, and regular army soldiers who were called to duty during the September 1962 riot. The military and civilian veterans were recognized by the town and the university in a simple, yet touching, "Keys to the City" ceremony. It turned out to be one of the few times that their service that night—undertaken against their fellow citizens—had been acknowledged.

One clue to the mystery of the long-delayed official recognition surfaced at the time of the 2002 ceremony when William Doyle, writing in the *New York Times*, brought this to light:

> An internal Army memo from May 1963 states: "The focus of additional attention on this [Ole Miss] incident would not be

in the best interest of the US Army or the nation. . . . Decorations should not be awarded for actions involving conflict between US Army units and other Americans."[8]

After the ceremony on the square I sought out James Meredith to give him a copy of his November 1962 letter to me (the original is on file in the school's archival collection). I found myself in a large conference room at the Ole Miss library where he was talking to the press. I was motioned over to the table by a school official and read the letter aloud to James and the assembled press. On my way out, one of his family members came over to me and thanked me for my service. I went a few feet down the hallway and an African American television reporter for a Memphis station also stopped me. He hastily assembled his equipment and interviewed me on the spot about my time with Meredith forty years earlier. At the end of the interview he turned his microphone and his professional face off and, with obvious emotion in his eyes and gratitude in his handshake, said, "I want to thank you in my name, sir, personally, for what you did here forty years ago." I could not help but recognize the moment for what it was, one of those "had-it-not-been-for-him" moments of indebtedness, a debt owed to the courageous black man back at that conference table by the young black television professional standing in front of me.

At the Open Doors ceremony I got the impression that this school, in the deepest of the Deep South states, wanted not only to acknowledge its past, but to showcase—and rightfully so—the racial reconciliation since 1962. Gone from the campus are "My pappy told me," "Hey, nigger lovers," "Our Nigras," and "Good morning, you black bastard!" The university's achievements are (and will continue to be) many, even though some of them receive little notice from its neighbors to the North. These are the same northern neighbors who had little noticed the racial discord in their own 1960s backyards, as Meredith had warned in our dormitory conversation fifty years ago.

Civil Rights Monument 2006

On October 1, 2006, a civil rights monument was dedicated on the Ole Miss campus. The idea for such a testimonial came from a group of students at the University's Center for the Study of Southern Culture, who "decided that the campus needed a symbol reflecting the struggle for equal access that occurred [at Ole Miss]." As in the 2002 Open Doors ceremony, the goal of the event was to focus not only on conflicts of the past but on gains made since those conflicts. The space chosen for the monument was not out in the Grove nor on the grounds of a campus building that might have some symbolic relevance—for example, the law school. The site was located between the school's iconic Lyceum and the J. D. Williams Library. Guests attending the dedication thought that the location was a perfect fit—symbolizing the union of university leadership and scholarship. A main component of the event was the unveiling of a lifelike statue of James Meredith, striding toward a large two-pillared "door," over which the word "Courage" was carved.

Afterword

Parents, School, Church, and Alley

I've been asked over the years whether my attitude on race relations changed as a result of the time I spent in Mississippi. The question assumes a prior attitude about race, which I don't think I had to any measureable degree. I simply wasn't exposed to race as an issue when I was growing up. To fairly answer the question, I will simply say that my attitude toward right and wrong came to me as a kid long before I formed any views on race. And once I did become exposed to racism, I simply saw it as another wrong. But that exposure did not come until my teens.

Growing up in the 1940s and '50s in a corner of Minneapolis, my understanding of racial issues was a bit limited. The city's south side was a working-class neighborhood where, with a few exceptions, all the families were white. The houses were filled with kids with names such as Johnson, Larson, Swenson, and a few non-Scandinavian tokens like Mueller and Murphy. In 1950 the State of Minnesota had a 0.5 percent black population out of a total head count of 2,982,483.[1]

Black families lived in houses up along the railroad tracks. Theirs was a small, tight-knit community, allowed to settle on those few streets at the nod of beneficent mortgage lenders. They were shoehorned into an enclave surrounded by our all-vanilla neighborhood.

I learned to swim in a city lake that few blacks frequented and I played in a park where there were no blacks. I went to an elementary school that had one or two African Americans in its enrollment and to a high school that had five or six, one of whom was our junior class president. He helped our school win the state football championship title the next year.

Thus my exposure to race as a social issue was minimal. If there was bigotry in the city, it was in the shadows in those days. But not everywhere. I did not know that blacks had to sit up in the balconies of the movie houses down on Hennepin Avenue; nor did I know of the grocery store two neighborhoods over that had a sign in its front window that read, "no Indians, no dogs, no niggers." Racism came out into the open in Minneapolis with riots in the late '60s, long after I had left the city.

However, what I did learn growing up were the two opposites of right and wrong. And I learned them from my mentors in those days—parents, school, and church. An additional and unofficial "mentor" was the "classroom" of the alley.

My parents had an influence on my brother and me in subtle (and sometimes not so subtle) ways in shaping our values. But while the lessons might have included how we should treat all of our little friends, some of whom might have differed from us in some ways, those ways never had a racial component.

As I moved on through the grades, the teachers at our elementary school could teach us little if anything about race. Hard to have such a teaching opportunity when we were all white—but for the two Holloway girls from the only black family in the school, one of whom was in my grade.

Without a race angle, the teachers could only discuss issues of right and wrong toward our fellow classmates if there was an in-class incident. Then a teaching moment arose. Maybe a teacher heard about a shoving incident out on the playground, though those opportunities were rare. Only then would the teacher talk about fairness and compassion toward a classmate. And, of course, if we looked around, but for one, they were all white. So, again, no lessons on race there. We had no information on how the blacks were treated in the South. The South? Just some smiling people and a character called Br'er Rabbit.

We had some familiarity with the rights and wrongs of the Ten Commandments. We knew the one against stealing, like the kid who got caught shoplifting at Woolworth's down on Lake Street.

But there were others, like the one about not "covet[ing] your neighbor's wife," that were a bit too advanced for us. I didn't even know what "covet" meant.

We didn't get to the biblical Golden Rule about treating others as you would like them to treat you. Few Catholic kids in my neighborhood in the late '40s and early '50s read the Bible. Summer Bible Camp was for the Lutherans. We were too busy memorizing the Catholic playbook, the brown paperbacked Baltimore Catechism. Relations with others? I don't recall a lot of time spent on how we should treat our fellow human beings.

But we learned a lot of things outside adult supervision and observation. It was when I started going down the alley with other kids my age that we learned more about rights and wrongs. No grown-ups around. Those kids came into the alleys with whatever values they had from their homes.

Wrongs happened in the alleys and in the woods down by the river. You learned of the wrongs up against the garages where the grown-ups couldn't see. Yes, just what that former Mississippian meant when he said that incidents of racist behavior did not occur out on the flat land of the Delta where "everyone can see everyone else." You saw the violence that only young kids can visit on their own kind and your stomach felt it before your head or your heart did. And you knew it was all wrong when one kid got "pantsed" by two bullies and another with an emotional problem got teased by those who supposedly had none. There was no need to recognize a right; those went by with little notice. It was the wrongs that caught you. And you knew it when you saw even the slightest of them.

Then, about five years later, I went down south.

When my best friend in high school and I hitchhiked through the South in 1956, we were two seventeen-year-olds in a strange land, a world not even known to us from the movies we had seen up to that point. Up in Minnesota we had westerns (*She Wore a Yellow Ribbon* and *Red River*), but we knew of no movies called "southerns." Well, there was *Gone with the Wind* and the feel-good *Song of the South* with the happy "Zip-a-Dee-Doo-Dah" jingle. Those movies, along with *Little Black Sambo*, made up my child's view of the South. I thought . . . yes, a happy part of the country. Unless I missed it when I went out to the theater lobby to get a candy bar, I don't recall anyone getting lynched in *Song of the South*. And *Gone with the Wind*? Well, that was one big lawn party with pretty dresses, right? Maybe with a fire at the end.

I felt pretty clear, as only a teenager can, about life's right and wrong stuff. Then I came across the "White Only" and "Colored Only" signs and I had to think about the race thing and how it fit into any personal code of conduct or fairness that I might have had at the time. I knew it was wrong—as surely wrong as some of that stuff down the alleys of my childhood. But we kept quiet. We left the images on the surfaces and felt that it was a way of life down here—wrong, but none of our business.

So it was all new to us. In any event, we kept our seventeen-year-olds' opinions to ourselves when we jumped up into the passenger seat of the rig that picked us up on 78 as we crossed the state line from Georgia into Alabama. And likewise with the white farmer with bib overalls who sat next to us at the counter in a roadside cafe outside Tupelo when we were looking for a hitch up to Memphis. Best to keep those impressions to ourselves and take them home, back north.

Six years later, when an Ole Miss student found out that I was from Minnesota, he said that I could not form a worthy opinion on the issue of race separation because I had no exposure to blacks while growing up. Well, that was the same "you had-to-be-there" rationale that was thrown up by many staunch late-1960s supporters of the war in Vietnam, dismissing the politicians who criticized it because—far from the war—their opinions supposedly could carry little weight. At Ole Miss I heard the same thing from some of the students, the ones who defended the "way of the South" and its age-old social template of race separation. They would say that the northern detractors—far from the "Negro problem"—could hardly appreciate the issue on the ground in the South.

Well, I was exposed to wrongs. Simply because I didn't have racial minorities in my neighborhood when I was growing up didn't mean that I wasn't qualified to have an opinion about wrongs. About harm visited by one person upon another—inflicted by a kid in the alley upon another more vulnerable kid—by a bully and his buddies who "owned" the alley—and the rocks. It just was wrong.

This is not to say that I wouldn't have reached the same conclusion in 1962 had I been aware of the many times blacks had been denied entry to Ole Miss because of their color, or been aware of the Meredith court decisions or what the marshals were going through that night in front of the Lyceum—though those wrongs were committed at a distance from me. However, when the distance disappears and someone throws a brick up into the face of your driver, one of the men in the unit for whom you are responsible—you get to see the wrong "up close and personal" and you forget about all that "Zip-a-Dee-Doo-Dah" stuff.

Notes

1.

1. Paul J. Scheips, *The Role of the Army in the Oxford, Mississippi, Incident, 1962–1963*, Office of the Chief of Military History, Department of the Army, Fort McNair, unpublished monograph 73M, 1965, 2.

2. Ibid., 11.

3. Ibid., 15.

4. Ibid., 17–18.

5. Ibid., 46.

6. *Associated Press v. Walker*, 388 U.S. 130 n. 22 (1967).

7. "The Mississippi Tragedy—Edwin A. Walker: Little Rock and Oxford," *U.S. News & World Report*, October 15, 1962, 42.

8. Russell H. Barrett, *Integration at Ole Miss* (Chicago: Quadrangle Books, 1965), 119.

9. Scheips, *Role of the Army*, 53.

10. David Steinberg (PFC, U.S. Army, 1962), e-mail to author, September 25, 2011.

11. Associated Press, 388 U.S. 130 n. 22 (1967).

12. William Doyle, *An American Insurrection: The Battle of Oxford, Mississippi, 1962* (New York: Doubleday, 2001), 98.

13. Scheips, *Role of the Army*, 50. It is worth noting that even the most casual readers of the newspapers at Drum and at Dix would have come across references to the "Mississippi situation" had those papers been full of such news. The reality is that those papers did not contain that news.

14. Carl Hirsch (2nd Lieutenant, U.S. Army, 1962), e-mails to author, September 21 and 26, 2011.

15. Scheips, *Role of the Army*, 63.

16. Ibid., 64.

17. Ibid., 64–65.

2.

1. Scheips, *Role of the Army*, 67.

2. Ibid., 95.

3. Ibid., 72.

4. Charles Vanderburgh, "A Draftee's Diary from the Mississippi Front: An Unusual Document of Violence, Rebellion, and Today's Peacetime Army, Recorded with Wit and Irony by a Soldier in the Ranks," *Harper's* magazine, February 1964, 37.

5. Al Kuettner, "The Anatomy of a Riot: The Oxford Story," *Minneapolis Sunday Tribune*, October 7, 1962, 1A.

6. See page 4 for decision in case filed May 31, 1961, by James Meredith (*Meredith v. Fair*).

7. John F. Kennedy, "Radio and Television Report to the Nation on the Situation at the University of Mississippi, September 30, 1962," Presidential Audio-Video Archive, John F. Kennedy (JFK) Presidential Library and Museum, Boston, MA. All subsequent JFK quotations herein are from this speech.

8. Sterling Slappey, "I Saw It Happen in Oxford," *U.S. News & World Report*, October 15, 1962, 44.

9. Ibid.

10. Kuettner, "Anatomy of a Riot," 10A.

11. Scheips, *Role of the Army*, 95–96.

12. Slappey, "I Saw It Happen in Oxford," 45.

13. Ibid.

14. Audie Murphy became one the most famous soldiers of World War II and was widely regarded as the most decorated American soldier of the war. As a combat infantryman in the European Theater, he earned the Silver Star (twice in three days), two Bronze Star Medals, three Purple Hearts, the Distinguished Service Cross, and the Medal of Honor. Source: Audie Murphy Research Foundation.

15. Robert Massie, "Mississippi Story," *Saturday Evening Post*, November 10, 1962, 18. This account and others cited throughout the book use the word "student" or "students" in identifying some of the rioters. I would caution the reader not to assume that the reporters were describing Ole Miss students exclusively. While some in the mob that night clearly did not appear to be students at any college or university, there is no assurance that *all* of the others who looked like "students" were enrolled at the University of Mississippi. See Doyle, *American Insurrection*, 261–62, and *Minneapolis Sunday Tribune*, October 7, 1962, 10A.

16. Kuettner, "Anatomy of a Riot," 10A.

17. Federal troops were called into a potentially dangerous racial situation in Little Rock, Arkansas, in 1957–1958. A federal court ordered the integration of Central High School in that city, "enjoining all persons from interfering with the attendance of nine Negro students" at the school. When the nine entered the school, a crowd of a thousand white residents gathered outside and "threatened to storm the school and do physical harm to the students." On the advice of the

police, the students were removed from the school for their own protection. In the coming days, after the situation appeared to be getting out of hand, President Eisenhower ordered the "use of federal troops as required to enforce the court order." A battle group of the 101st Airborne Division (Fort Campbell, Kentucky) was deployed to Little Rock. Two civilians were injured, but further incidents of violence and disorder were averted as the soldiers escorted the students into the school. Ironically, the commander of all the military forces was General Edwin A. Walker, who six years later (in retirement) figured prominently as an inspiration to the rioters at Ole Miss. (See page 26 in text.)

18. Slappey, "I Saw It Happen in Oxford," 45.

19. David Steinberg (PFC, U.S. Army, 1962), e-mail to author, October 9, 2011.

20. Ibid.

21. Doyle, *American Insurrection*, 108. For the reactions of other army units upon receipt of the order, see the epilogue, pages 189–91.

22. Ibid., 230.

3.

1. Massie, "Mississippi Story," 18.

2. "On the Mississippi Campus, the Bitter Siege of Violence," *Life*, October 12, 1962, 35.

3. Massie, "Mississippi Story," 18.

4. Guay Wilson (First Lieutenant, U.S. Army, JAG, 1962), e-mail to author, October 11, 2011.

5. Doyle, *American Insurrection*, 244.

4.

1. Scheips, *Role of the Army*, 42–43.

2. "Mississippi: The Sound and the Fury," *Newsweek*, October 15, 1962, 27.

3. Massie, "Mississipi Story," 19.

4. Vanderburgh, "A Draftee's Diary," 40.

5. Ibid., 38.

6. "Though the Heavens Fall," *Time*, October 12, 1962, 19.

7. "On the Mississippi Campus, the Bitter Siege of Violence," *Life*, October 12, 1962, 39. Doyle found that "[t]he prisoners ranged in age from fourteen to fifty-seven and came from coast to coast, from Georgia to California, with most coming from Mississippi, Tennessee, Alabama, and Louisiana." Furthermore, "[o]f the

prisoners, only twenty-five were students at Ole Miss. And another fifteen were students from Mississippi State at Starkville." *An American Insurrection*, 280–81.

5.

1. "Mississippi: The Sound and the Fury," 23.

2. Many vehicles had gotten into the town before the army cordon and search were put in place. One, a chartered bus with Alabama plates, ended up parked near the town square, lost. The driver swung open the front door when a student came by and asked for directions to the campus. The student stepped up onto the bus and looked down the aisle to see row after row of men in farmer's bib overalls, most of them holding rifles and shotguns between their knees. Mary Robertson, telephone conversation with author, October 28, 2011.

3. In 2002, the university and the townsfolk showed their gratitude when they presented the keys to the city to the National Guard and regular army soldiers for putting down the riot on the campus and stopping the trashing of the downtown. The ceremony took place on the square as part of the "Open Doors" program. (See the epilogue, pages 196–98.)

6.

1. See photo in photo insert.

2. Doyle, *American Insurrection*, 200–201.

3. Scheips, *Role of the Army*, 53.

7.

1. James Symington, conversation with author, December 22, 2011.

2. Thomas Buckley, "Mississippi Students Found Isolated in Culture and Outlook: Range of Social and Political Opinion Is Limited, Survey Shows, and Status and Material Goals Are Dominant Aims," *New York Times*, October 21, 1962.

3. Scheips, *Role of the Army*, 165–66.

4. Ibid., 167.

5. Richard Mitchell (Second Lieutenant, U.S. Army, 716th MP Battalion, 1963), e-mail to author, October 8, 2011.

6. One anecdote is telling. While its authenticity is not certain, its humor is. Apparently, three days into the Ole Miss operation, Joe Dolan, an assistant deputy

attorney general, and his boss, Nicholas Katzenbach, found themselves waiting outside the command tent of the newly assigned commander of all the Oxford forces, Lieutenant General Hamilton Howze. After approximately twenty minutes, they were ushered in to meet the general. As Joe related it to me, he said that the general, unaware of the "rank" of the two civilians, asked of each, "To what rank in the Department of Defense is your position comparable?" Joe answered that he had no idea, but possibly a lieutenant colonel. Katzenbach, not wanting to upstage the general, but in the interest of full disclosure, said, "Undersecretary of the army." In Joe's words, referring to the scene, "Then [General Howze] said, 'Oh, then, perhaps we could meet tomorrow at *your* headquarters.'" Joe Dolan, telephone conversation with author, n.d.

7. Relman Morin, "Federal Government Seeks Acceptance for UM Negro," *Clarion-Ledger*, October 14, 1962.

8. "Mississippi: The Sound and the Fury," 28.

8.

1. Headquarters U.S. Army Forces Oxford, Oxford, Mississippi, Memorandum Number 5, November 18, 1962, "SOP for Special Security Patrol (Peanut Patrol)" (USAFOX).

2. Bill E. Burk, *Memphis Press-Scimitar*, October 9, 1962.

3. USAFOX Memorandum Number 1, November 6, 1962, "Use of Firearms."

4. Regarding the "Yo, Lieutenant" remark after the cafeteria incident—during my two years in the army, I noticed that some enlisted men tried to become too familiar or casual with the younger officers in their units, particularly when the former were two-year college-degree draftees or Berlin crisis "returnees." For them, it was an early version of "pushing the envelope." If the lieutenant did nothing about it (and a nearby NCO ignored it) at the outset, then the habit got worse and the traditional enlisted-to-officer relationship, absolutely essential in the military, would deteriorate. Each lieutenant had to set down his own "marker" early on. Some officers were flexible to a point, not giving up any respect from the rank and file. Some crossed the line, either deliberately or out of ignorance. Others gave not an inch of slack. In such a mix, the attitudes of the enlisted ran from faked respect to earned respect.

5. When he was about to leave Oxford (not long after I had appeared before him), Howze observed, "To guarantee, repeat guarantee, [the] personal safety of Mr. Meredith would require extraordinary measures not now being enforced. For example, it would be possible for a crackpot to secrete himself in a building" that no troops occupied—"and with a rifle shoot Meredith." Scheips, *Role of the Army*, 185 n. 25.

9.

1. The only honor that would really matter to Robert Farley came in 1979 when the building housing the university's law school was renamed Farley Hall.

2. "Flash (Or Should We Say 'Bang'?)," *Rebel Underground*, October 1962.

3. Buckley, "Isolated in Culture and Outlook," 65.

4. Ibid.

5. Carey Rivers, conversation with author, June 6, 2011.

6. Steinberg, e-mail, October 9, 2011.

7. Vanderburgh, "A Draftee's Diary," 43.

8. USAFOX, Memorandum Number 5, November 18, 1962, "SOP for Special Security Patrol (Peanut Patrol)."

9. Carey Rivers, conversation with author, June 6, 2011.

10. Peter Frechette (Second Lieutenant, 716th MP Battalion, 1962), telephone conversation with author, n.d.

11. Mitchell, e-mail, August 8, 2011.

12. To echo what PFC Barrett said ("But this down here is so different"), even our JAG officer came across some of those differences. Despite his remark that, after arriving at Ole Miss, "I played the role of Jack Lemmon in *Mr. Roberts* [the movie *Mister Roberts*], just staying out of everyone's way," he admitted that "I did have two experiences. . . . We went up to Memphis to get an MP out of jail who had been arrested. One of the black girls involved was shocked that our MPs treated her so politely. [In another case] a member of the Ole Miss faculty had his car dented in the excitement and I helped out with his claim against the US Government. Drinking an iced tea at his home, he commented very conservatively, that change often does not take place without agitation. He had no other comment on the racial situation." Guay Wilson, e-mail to author, October 11, 2011.

13. USAFOX, Memorandum Number 5, November 18, 1962, "for Special Security Patrol (Peanut Patrol)."

14. Hirsch, e-mails to author, September 26 and October 27, 2011.

15. Carey Rivers, telephone conversation with author, March 22, 2011.

16. "Ole Miss Vandals Not Yet Arrested: Fear Is Voiced for Safety of Liberal Students," *Commercial Appeal*, November 17, 1962.

17. USAFOX, Memorandum Number 6, November 24, 1962, "Command and Administrative Policies and Procedure."

18. William Faulkner, *Requiem for a Nun* (New York: Random House, 1950), 34–35.

19. "Oxford: A Way of Life Has Ended," *U.S. News & World Report*, October 15, 1962, 60.

20. Vanderburgh, "A Draftee's Diary," 42.

21. James Meredith, personal letter to author, November 19, 1962.

22. Vanderburgh, "A Draftee's Diary," 45.

10.

1. Had the public been aware of the actual size of the camp (see photo in photo insert) and thus the magnitude of the military commitment to protect one man, critics of the Kennedy administration might have howled at the scale of such a taxpayer-funded military mission.

2. Scheips, *Role of the Army*, 211.

3. "The Mississippi State Sovereignty Commission was created by an act of the Mississippi legislature on March 29, 1956. The agency was established in the wake of the May 1954 *Brown v. Board of Education* ruling. Like other states below the Mason-Dixon Line, Mississippi responded to *Brown* with legislation to shore up the walls of racial separation. The act creating the Commission provided the agency with broad powers. The Commission's objective was to 'do and perform any and all acts deemed necessary and proper to protect the sovereignty of the state of Mississippi, and her sister states . . . [from perceived] encroachment thereon by the Federal Government or any branch, department or agency thereof.'" Quoted from the Mississippi Department of Archives and History website: http://mdah.state.ms.us/arrec/digital_archives/sovcom/scagencycasehistory.php.

In *Ever Is a Long Time: A Journey Into Mississippi's Dark Past* (New York: Basic Books, 2005), W. Ralph Eubanks writes: "[Shortly after its creation] the Sovereignty Commission moved from public relations to spying on citizens, trying to uproot anyone or anything that threatened to open up Mississippi's closed society to integration" (71).

4. *"Soldiers of America,"* leaflet, publisher and date unknown.

5. Although the overall number of troops "mobilized" for the Ole Miss crisis totaled thirty thousand (Regular Army and federalized Guard), the number actually committed to the Oxford area reached a maximum of twelve thousand on October 2, of which ninety-three hundred were Regular Army and the remainder were federalized Mississippi Guard. See Paul J. Scheips, *The Role of Federal Military Forces, 1945–1992* (Washington, D. C.: The U.S. Army Center of Military History, 2005), 120–21.

6. D. Ross Thompson, *Ole Miss Coloring Book* (Tallahassee: D. Ross Thompson, publisher, 1963).

7. James Meredith, "Open Letter to Editor," *The Mississippian*, May 3, 1963.

8. Ed Noble, "Letters to the Editor," *The Mississippian*, May 8, 1963.

9. Scheips, *Role of the Army*, 220.

10. USAFOX, [Memorandum], "SUBJECT: Commanding Officer's Orientation for Incoming Military Police," n.d.

11. USAFOX, Memorandum Number 25, June 1, 1963, "Contingency Plan for Campus Disorder."

12. Scheips, *Role of the Army*, 234.

13. Ibid., 233.

14. The Men & Officers (716th MPs), personal letter to Major Charles Trebbe, July 17, 1962.

Epilogue

1. Scheips, *Role of the Army*, 168–70.

2. Telephone conversation between Joyce Hardmon and the author, August 30, 2011.

3. Scheips, *Role of the Army*, 164.

4. Ibid.

5. James Meredith, personal letter to author, October 12, 1989.

6. Conversation with unnamed Mississippian.

7. Robert Khayat, "Open Doors at Ole Miss," University of Mississippi, October 1, 2002.

8. William Doyle, "Forgotten Soldiers of the Integration Fight," *New York Times*, September 28, 2002.

Afterword

1. Campbell Gibson and Kay Jung, *Historical Census Statistics on Population Totals By Race, 1790 to 1990, and By Hispanic Origin, 1970 to 1990, for The United States, Regions, Divisions, and States*, "Table 38. Minnesota—Race and Hispanic Origin: 1850–1990" (Washington, D.C.: U.S. Census Bureau, 2002), http://www.census.gov/population/www/documentation/twps0056/tab38.pdf.

Glossary of Military Terms, Acronyms, Abbreviations, Slang, and Jargon

AFB Air Force Base.

After Action Report (AAR) Document prepared by a unit (usually battalion and above) after participation in a major event (training, exercise, combat), recording the highlights of what took place, often including "lessons learned."

Army Medical Service Corps Noncombat specialty branch of the U.S. Army, consisting of commissioned medical officers and warrant officers whose members perform administrative and operational support duties in all aspects of health care for the military. One medical unit was attached to the 716th the night of September 29, 1962, before it left Fort Dix.

Army Signal Corps Noncombat branch of the U.S. Army that has the mission of providing and managing communications and information systems support for the command.

Article 15 Form of nonjudicial punishment that may be imposed by a commander. It can be compared to a misdemeanor in a civilian context. Examples of an infraction that might result in an Article 15 proceeding on as sensitive a mission as the one at Ole Miss were disorderly conduct, unnecessary harassment of a student, or undue fraternization with any individual during assigned duty.

AVN Aviation. Well after the massive use of air force resources (fixed and rotary) in the buildup to, and during, the Ole Miss crisis, an AVN support (helicopter) unit remained with the USAFOX command until the mission ended in July 1963.

AWOL Absent without leave.

Baseball grenade A riot-control tear gas agent in a baseball-shaped container specially issued for riot control.

Battalion Military unit composed of a headquarters and two or more companies or batteries. It may be part of a regiment and be charged with only tactical functions, or it may be a separate unit and be charged with both administrative and tactical functions. Three MP battalions were deployed to Oxford during the Ole Miss Crisis: 503rd (Fort Bragg, North Carolina), 716th (Fort Dix, New Jersey), and 520th (Fort Hood, Texas).

BG Brigadier general.

Bird Slang for helicopter.

Bird colonel Slang for colonel.

Bivouac Military encampment made with tents or improvised shelters. The 716th was in bivouac both on the hillside encampment near the airport shortly after its arrival in Oxford and also when it moved to the football practice field on the campus. Camp USAFOX normally would not be considered a bivouac.

BOQ Bachelor officers' quarters (buildings housing unmarried or unaccompanied commissioned officers).

Burma-Shave Roadside advertising campaign along U.S. highways during the years 1925 to 1963, consisting of six consecutive small signs, spaced for sequential reading by passing motorists. The last sign was usually the name of the product, a brushless shaving cream.

C-130 U.S. Air Force four-engine turboprop troop and transport aircraft (Hercules). On September 30, 1962, 42 sorties of C-130s transported the entire 716th MP battalion—650 men and 140 vehicles—from McGuire AFB in New Jersey to Millington Naval Air Station, Tennessee, 17 miles north of Memphis.

C rations Meals consisting of canned meat and vegetables, packed in preservatives, along with hard biscuits and accessory items. Before the 716th mess was fully operational on October 1, 1962, battalion members were provided C rations.

C rats Slang for C rations.

Call sign In radio communications, a unique designation assigned to a transmitting station. Call signs at Ole Miss for the 716th variously included "Example 6" (Colonel Brice), "Golf," "Peanut," "Icewater" (Peanut Patrol), and "Magnet" (James Meredith).

Canister grenade A riot-control tear gas agent that provides a continuous discharge of smoke under pressure.

Caribou (CV-2) A specialized cargo aircraft with short takeoff and landing capability. These aircraft transported 716th soldiers in March 1963 on rotation back to Oxford.

CBR Chemical-Biological-Radiological.

CG Commanding general.

Chopper Helicopter.

CID Criminal Investigation Division (Command). Before he assumed command of the 716th MP Battalion, Colonel Brice had taken on a large number of career assignments in CID.

Class A uniform Khaki service or dress uniform for summer wear.

CN Form of tear gas (civilian term: Mace).

CO Commanding officer.

COL Colonel or full colonel.

Combat arms Certain army branches: infantry, armor, artillery, and (combat) engineers. (Expanded in later years.)

Commander-in-Chief President of the United States.

Commo check Communications check on the radio.

Company Military unit of approximately 250 men, usually led by a captain.

Company grade officer Lieutenant or captain.

Conex container Corrugated-steel shipping container.

CP Command post. The control center used by a military unit in deployment; it can be mobile. On the morning that the 716th entered Oxford, the CP was wherever the CO (Colonel Brice) was located.

CS Dominant form of tear gas used because it is considered more effective in crowd dispersal than two of its predecessors, CN gas (Mace) and DM gas.

Dayroom Common area for reading and relaxation in army barracks.

DEFCON Defense readiness condition or alert posture used by the U.S. armed forces. The system contains five graduated levels of readiness which increase in intensity from DEFCON 5 (least intense) to DEFCON 1 (most intense) to match varying military situations. During the Cuban missile crisis in October 1962, while the 716th was on duty at Ole Miss, the U.S. armed forces were ordered to DEFCON 3, that is, an increase in force readiness above that required for normal readiness.

DEROS The date a soldier is eligible to return from overseas.

Deuce-and-a-half Slang for a two-and-a-half-ton military cargo truck.

DOD U.S. Department of Defense.

DOJ U.S. Department of Justice.

Draftee Member of the military involuntarily inducted into service.

EM Enlisted men. Military service members in grades E-1 through E-9 (but sometimes used in a more limited sense to identify those in enlisted grades who are not commissioned officers).

ER Efficiency report. A periodic written evaluation of an officer's performance of duty.

ETA Estimated time of arrival.

Fatigues Standard-issue work uniform.

Field grade officer Major, lieutenant colonel, or colonel.

FM Field manual.

.45 45-caliber semiautomatic pistol. Standard sidearm equipment for MP enlisted men and all officers.

Gung-ho Slang for a military person who is very (perhaps overly) enthusiastic.

HQ Headquarters.

"Humor in Uniform" Popular section in the magazine *Reader's Digest*, featuring readers' submissions of humorous anecdotes about life in the military.

JAG Judge Advocate General. The legal arm/corps of the U.S. Army. First Lieutenant Guay P. Wilson was the JAG officer attached to the 716th on its deployment to Oxford in September 1962.

Jeep One-quarter-ton truck.

Jump Wings Army Parachutist Badge awarded to those who have completed the U.S. Army Basic Airborne Course, usually at Fort Benning, Georgia.

Klan Short for Ku Klux Klan. Extremist organization opposed to the Civil Rights Movement.

Lifer Slang for a career military person, more often enlisted men who "re-up" (reenlist). Used as a derogatory term by those with an antimilitary outlook.

Light colonel Slang for lieutenant colonel.

Loadmaster Air force enlisted member of the flight crew responsible for the loading of all in-transit cargo and troops.

LOH Light (weight) observation helicopter.

LTC Lieutenant colonel (Colonel Brice).

LTG Lieutenant general (General Howze).

M-1 .30-caliber semiautomatic rifle.

Magnet Radio call sign for James Meredith.

MAJ Major (Major Beach).

MATS Military Air Transport Service.

Mess Army dining hall or tent for soldiers.

Mess truck A mobile kitchen truck.

MG Major general.

Morning Report Daily document produced by every unit of the army that details personnel status on that day.

MP Military police.

NCO Noncommissioned officer.

NCOIC Noncommissioned officer-in-charge.

Noncom Slang for noncommissioned officer.

OCS Officer Candidate School.

OD Officer of the Day. Also, olive drab, the basic U.S. Army color. Army vehicles, field clothing, web gear, ammo cans, and so on were in the OD color for many years.

OIC Officer-in-charge. The author was the first OIC of the Peanut Patrol in October 1962.

Orderly room (or tent) Administrative office of a unit of the U.S. Army.

"Peculiar institution" Common euphemism for slavery in the United States.

PFC Private first class.

Platoon A military unit (three squads) composed of approximately forty personnel (usually led by a second lieutenant).

Plebe A first-year cadet at a military academy.

POL Petroleum, oil, and lubricants.

Poncho liner Thin blanket of nylon tied to a rubberized poncho. Also used as a blanket.

Port arms Position specified in the manual of arms in which a rifle is held diagonally in front of the body with the muzzle pointing upward to the left.
PX U.S. Post Exchange.

RA Regular Army.

Recon Reconnaissance.

Roger "I have received all of the last transmission" (spoken in radio communication).

ROTC Reserve Officer Training Corps. A college-based, officer-commissioning program. Provides the majority of the army's officer corps, the remainder coming from West Point, the Officer Candidate School (OCS), and direct commissions.

R & R Rest and recreation off post for servicemen and servicewomen. For soldiers stationed at Ole Miss, Memphis was the only choice.

S-2 Staff officer for intelligence.

S-3 Staff officer for operations.

Scuttlebutt Slang for rumor.

Seaman Sailor.

Sergeant major Highest enlisted (NCO) rank in a unit (usually battalion or above). It refers both to a military rank and a specific administrative position. The sergeant major acts as the senior enlisted advisor to the commanding officer.

Short-timer Slang for a soldier with few days remaining in his or her service.

SOP Standard operating procedure. A set of instructions covering those features of operations which lend themselves to a definite or standardized procedure without loss of effectiveness. The procedure is applicable unless ordered otherwise.

SP Shore patrolman. U.S. Navy security personnel performing duties not unlike those of U.S. Army military police.

Spec-4 (or Sp4) Specialist 4th Class.

Squad Military unit, usually consisting of twelve personnel.

Stand-down Release from alert status.

Steel pot Helmet.

STRAC Strategic Army Command. Also slang for army personnel who adhere to strict military behavior and dress.

Straight-legs Slang for nonairborne military personnel.

TAC Tactical Air Command. The air force unit that ferried the 716th MP Battalion from McGuire AFB to Millington Naval Air Station on September 30, 1962.

TDY Temporary duty.

Ten (10) series In radio communications, a set of numbers running from 1 to 20 which describe an action or instruction, all preceded by the number 10. Military police used the 10-series in 1962 at Ole Miss (for example: "10-14" precedes a designated location).

TO&E Table of organization and equipment; document which prescribes the organic structure and authorized equipment of military units.

TOP A battalion sergeant major or a company first sergeant (more commonly) is unofficially but often referred to as "top" or "top sergeant" due to his seniority and position at the top of the unit's enlisted ranks.

USAFOX U.S. Army Forces Oxford.

USAF U.S. Air Force.

USN U.S. Navy.

Warrant officer Military officer subordinate to commissioned officer and superior to enlisted personnel. The army has five warrant officer ranks whose members are skilled specialty officers.

Wedge formation V-shaped formation used by MP personnel in crowd control.

West Point United States Military Academy at West Point, New York.

XVIII Airborne Corps Large military command unit in the U.S. Army, designed for rapid deployment anywhere in the world. Referred to as "America's Contingency Corps," it is headquartered at Fort Bragg, North Carolina. In the early days of the Ole Miss crisis, Lieutenant General Hamilton J. Howze III, Commanding General of the XVIII Airborne Corps, was in command of all military forces deployed to Oxford.

Zippo Butane cigarette lighter popular with military personnel.

Index

101st Airborne Division, 24, 26, 60, 78, 85, 107, 124, 146, 190, 209

2nd Battle Group, 23rd Infantry Regiment [2nd Infantry Division]. See Task Force Bravo

503rd MP Battalion, 22, 24, 34, 40, 43, 47, 58, 62, 68, 74, 170–71, 189

716th Military Police Battalion, 5, 9–12, 14, 16, 18, 27, 39, 45, 48, 59–61, 67–68, 78–79, 85, 94, 98, 100, 109, 118, 127, 143, 166, 170, 182–87, 189–90, 194–95

720th Military Police Battalion, 78, 182, 184, 190

82nd Airborne Division, 24, 189

Abrams, (Major General) Creighton W., 6, 26, 28, 96

Adams, (Spec-4) John, 14–15, 17, 19, 91, 94–95, 97, 111, 113, 118–19, 124, 161, 165

B Company, 11, 65, 78, 166

Barnett, Ross, 7, 9, 166, 179, 183–84

Barrett, (Private First Class) Ronald, 34–35, 38–39, 44, 49, 52, 54, 56, 58, 61, 64, 75, 82–83, 86, 88, 90–91, 144, 151, 160, 165, 167

Barrett, Russell H., 138

bathrooms. See segregated facilities

battle of Ole Miss, 196

Beach, (Major), 60–61, 63, 83, 85

beauty pageants, 147, 149

Berlin Wall, 6, 12, 163, 196

Billingslea, (General) Charles, 26, 31, 58, 69–70, 98, 119

black college students. See college students

black soldiers. See soldiers

Bounds, Mr. (cafeteria manager), 110–12

Brice, (Lieutenant Colonel) Emmett T., 8–9, 28, 31–34, 45, 57, 60, 66, 85, 92–93, 98, 124, 129

Brooks, (Sergeant), 109, 192

Buckley, Thomas, 139

C Company, 4–5, 7–8, 11, 13, 25, 32, 170

Camp Drum, New York, 3–11, 158

Camp "Mud." See Camp USAFOX

Camp "Paradise." See Camp USAFOX

Camp "Swampy." See Camp USAFOX

Camp USAFOX (US Army Forces Oxford), 170–72, 176, 181–82, 184–85, 196

Charles, Ray, 84

citizen soldiers. See soldiers

civil rights disturbance, 57

Civil Rights Division in the Justice Department, 93

Civil Rights Monument. See Meredith, James; University of Mississippi

civil rights movement, 99, 112, 127, 165, 182, 194

Civil War, xxv, 186

class. See middle class; upper class; working class

coeds. *See* college students
college students: black, 194–95;
        female, 100, 107, 140, 145, 149,
        172, 194; white, xxiii–xxiv, 76,
        83, 102–3, 109–10, 112–13, 119,
        122–23, 128, 137, 139, 141, 143,
        148, 157, 165, 168, 174, 204, 208
Colored Only signs, 86, 106, 204
communism, 138, 163, 177
Confederate flags, 50, 77, 84
Crawford, Broderick, 121
"crazed gunman" profile, 114
Crow, (Lieutenant) Bobby, 42–43
Cuban missile crisis, 116, 146, 196

De La Beckwith, Byron, 114
Deep South, 35, 50, 75, 198
Department of Justice. *See* Justice
        Department
desegregation, 180
Diaz, (Corporal), 79–80
dining facilities. *See* segregated
        facilities
Doar, John, 91, 93, 110–12, 122
drinking fountains. *See* segregated
        facilities
Dukes, Jimmie, 107

Elliot, Richard, 69
equal rights, 145, 180, 197
Executive Order No. 11053, 19

Falkner, (Captain) Murray C.
        "Chooky," 42
Farley, Robert J., 138
Farrell, (Lieutenant) Vince, 116
Faulkner, William, 42, 81, 87–88, 160,
        182
Federal Bureau of Investigation (FBI),
        70, 76, 115, 183
federal court orders, 19, 178, 208

federal government, 3, 50, 124, 196, 213
federal laws, 163
Federal Marshals. *See* U.S. Marshals
federal troops, 8, 26, 77, 92, 208
federal tyranny, 179
female college students. *See* college
        students
Ford, J. W., 28
Fort Bragg, North Carolina, 5, 16, 22,
        24, 26, 34, 40, 47, 68, 129, 132
Fort Campbell, Kentucky, 24, 209
Fort Dix, New Jersey, 3–5, 9, 14, 35, 45,
        57, 67, 71, 83, 91, 158, 166, 184, 187
fraternities, 94, 121, 138–39, 141, 146–
        47, 166, 168
Frechette, (Second Lieutenant) Peter,
        xxiii, 11, 65, 75, 97, 146, 172
Freedom Rides, 143

Gallagher, Henry T.: 1956 trip to
        the South, 36, 50, 86, 106, 143,
        203; attitude about race, 201–5;
        childhood and race relations, 127,
        201–5; nightstick news story, 128–
        29, 131, 133–35, 172; relationship
        with James Meredith, 98, 123, 169,
        192; returning to University of
        Mississippi in 2001, 193, 197–98;
        telephone call to mother, 88–89
Garrett, Harley F., 138
Geitz, (Sergeant), 70–72, 75
General Sherman's March. *See*
        Sherman, (General) William
        Tecumseh
Grant, (General) Ulysses S., 77, 186–87
Guihard, Paul, 74–75, 85
Gunter, Ray, 75–76

Hardmon, (Captain) Linwood, 45–47,
        191
hecklers, 111, 137, 139, 142, 151

Hester, L. C., 127

Hodges, (Colonel), 173

Holly Springs, Mississippi. *See* Mississippi

hotels. *See* segregated facilities

Howze, (General) Hamilton J., III, 108, 129–31, 172, 191, 211

humor, army, 17, 97–98, 119, 145, 166, 184–86

injuries, 47, 62, 75–76, 151, 196

J. E. Neilson's Department Store, 85–86, 161

JAG (Judge Advocate General's Corps), 57, 212

Jarrell, (Seaman), 34, 37–39, 44, 49–50, 52, 53, 60, 65

John Birch Society, 7

Justice Department, 91, 93, 100, 123–25, 133, 136, 165–66

Katzenbach, Nicholas, 91, 93–94, 98, 108, 110, 131–32, 211

Kennedy, John F., 16, 29–30, 39, 44, 63, 93, 104, 138, 146, 163, 176–79

Kennedy, Robert, 6, 44, 93, 104, 163, 178

"Kennedy coon keepers" (also "Kennedy Koon Keepers"), 111, 138

Khayat, Robert, 195

KKK. *See* Ku Klux Klan

Klan. *See* Ku Klux Klan

Kosciusko, Mississippi. *See* Mississippi

Ku Klux Klan, 114, 194

Lafayette County, Mississippi. *See* Mississippi

Little Rock, Arkansas, 26, 43, 47, 57, 93, 208–9

lone gunman, 114, 174

loyalties of local law enforcement uncertain, 70–71, 83, 104

loyalty (regional), xxiv–xxv, 101, 143

Lynch, (Colonel) William R., 181, 183

maps, 33–34, 36–38, 40, 49, 51, 60–61, 86, 94–95, 121, 132–33, 144, 175, 193

marshals. *See* U.S. Marshals

McDowell, Cleve, 182–84

McShane, James P., 98, 100

Memphis, Tennessee, xxiv, 3, 6, 16, 26, 30–31, 36–37, 54, 60, 73, 85, 87, 106, 118, 128, 135, 153, 159, 171–72, 191, 193, 198, 204

Memphis Press-Scimitar, 31, 128, 133–34

Meredith, James: bomb threats, 97, 173; Civil Rights Monument, 199; courage, 182, 198–99; death threats, 155, 173; denial of university admission, 4, 205; dining arrangements, 110–12, 128; golf, 175; graduation, 174, 187; first day of classes, 100; Jesse Helms, 192–93; personality and demeanor, 142, 153, 157; reasons for attending University of Mississippi, 179–80; relationship with Henry T. Gallagher, 98, 123, 169, 192; residence, 29, 154–55; security detail, 85, 88, 95, 97–98, 103–4, 113, 116, 121–23, 133, 162; use of the press and public relations, 109, 156; view of midwestern racial issues, 156; view of northern racial issues, 144, 156; view of southern white students, 102–3, 139; university registration, 25, 78, 82–83

middle class, 82, 139–41, 148

Minneapolis, Minnesota, 7, 14, 18, 54, 75, 88, 125, 142, 144, 154, 201–2

Minnesota, xxiii, xxv, 6, 8, 36, 50, 58, 68, 75, 82, 86, 106, 114, 132, 142, 144, 149, 156, 167, 201, 203–4

Mississippi: Holly Springs, 50, 52–54, 65, 182, 193; Kosciusko, 98, 155, 182, 187; Lafayette County, 81, 160, 186; Oxford, xxiii, 6–7, 14, 25–26, 28, 31–32, 34, 37–38, 40, 42, 47, 50–53, 57–61, 67–70, 72, 75, 77–78, 80, 82, 85–88, 92, 99, 107, 109, 113–14, 116, 118–19, 124, 129, 132, 139–40, 145, 147, 158–62, 164, 166–67, 170–71, 175, 178, 182–83, 185–87, 190–95, 197–98; Tupelo, 87, 106, 204

Mississippi Highway Patrol, 49, 57, 69–72, 80, 83, 104, 125

Mississippi National Guard. See National Guard

Mississippi State Police, 7, 69, 183

Mississippi State Sovereignty Commission. See State Sovereignty Commission

Mitchell, (Second Lieutenant) Dick, 182

Mize, Sidney C., 5

mob, 31–32, 41, 47, 63–64, 70, 78, 80, 84, 86, 89, 104, 139, 141, 160, 165, 167, 208

movies, xxv, 26, 31, 61, 63, 66, 71, 76, 87, 90, 93, 117, 131, 133, 145, 159, 171–72, 176, 183, 202–3

Mullins, (Radio Operator), 90

Murphy, Audie, 41, 208

National Association for the Advancement of Colored People (NAACP), 138

National Guard, 24–25, 29, 31, 42, 58, 62, 76, 80, 92, 99, 104, 106, 159, 166, 170, 197, 210

Naval Air Station at Millington, Tennessee, 6, 21, 23, 31, 47–48, 59, 159, 185, 191, 194

"Nigra," 104–6, 147, 163, 198

northern racial issues, 45–46, 101–2, 105, 144, 152–53, 156, 164–65, 198, 202

OD. See Officer of the Day; olive drab

Officer of the Day, 27, 32

Ole Miss. See University of Mississippi

Ole Miss Coloring Book, The, 178

olive drab, 35, 61, 103, 193

O'Neill, (Corporal), 124

"Operation Rapid Road," 193

Oxford, Mississippi. See Mississippi

Oxford National Guard. See National Guard

"Pappy." See parental influence on southern culture

parental influence on southern culture, 101–3, 105, 125, 139, 165–66, 198

"Peanut Patrol," 115–16, 120, 129, 146, 166, 170, 178, 182–83, 192

"peculiar institution," 143

Presley, Elvis, 87

race separation, xxv, 101–2, 105–6, 140, 142, 161, 166, 192, 204

racial hatred, 81, 100–101, 141, 143, 168

racial integration, 7, 26, 110, 113, 178, 180, 183, 186, 190, 196

racial relations of soldiers. See soldiers

racism, 102, 140–41, 194, 201–2

Ray, James Earl, 114

"Rebel Underground," 137–38

rednecks, 81, 162

rioting, 32, 34, 40, 43–44, 47–48, 50, 55, 57–58, 68–70, 75–76, 83, 88–89, 92, 104, 124, 128, 131, 140, 143, 153, 160–61, 163, 165–66, 179, 192, 195, 197, 202, 208–9

Rowan Oak, 87

rules of engagement, 127

segregated facilities, 110–12, 155, 161–62

segregation, 26, 109, 114, 142, 195

segregation of black and white soldiers. *See* soldiers

segregationists, 26, 114, 142

self-segregation, 161, 195

sense of place, xxiii

Sherman, (General) William Tecumseh, 67, 73–74

Silver, James W., 138

sit-ins, 143

snipers, 44, 47, 53, 107–8, 115, 118, 192

soldiers: black, 46–47, 67, 108–10, 144, 152, 191; boredom, 32, 139, 145, 150–51, 157, 159, 193; citizen, 11–12; morale, 25, 47, 153, 157, 159, 172, 184, 189–90; racial relations, 45–46, 106, 109, 143, 152; segregation of black and white, 47, 109, 189–92; "step-back," 46, 67, 107, 153, 189–92; white, 46, 144, 152

sororities, 107, 138, 140, 147, 166, 168

southern culture compared to northern culture, xxiv, 102, 105–6

southern hospitality, 105–6

southern "way of life," xxiii–xxv, 82, 102, 106, 143, 156, 164, 204

State Sovereignty Commission, 176, 213

states' rights, 163, 192

Steinberg, (Private) David, 4, 7, 9

"step-back." *See* soldiers

STRAC (Strategic Army Command), 5, 8–9, 13–16, 19, 21, 23

Symington, Jim, 163

Task Force Alpha, 68

Task Force Bravo, 68

tear gas, 23, 28, 30–32, 62–63, 67, 70, 83, 87, 92, 124, 126, 167, 174

Top, (Sergeant Major), 96

Troop E, 42

Tupelo, Mississippi. *See* Mississippi

University of Mississippi, xxiii–xxiv, 4, 25, 27, 29, 50, 60, 77, 152, 187, 192–93, 197–98; Baxter Hall, 97, 107–8, 111–12, 119, 124, 126, 155, 170; Civil Rights Monument, 199; faculty, 138–39, 180, 212; Faculty House, 85, 91–92, 98; football team, 50, 105, 140–42, 144, 147, 158, 166, 168; Fulton Chapel, 149; The Grove, 92, 167, 187, 189, 194, 199; J. D. Williams Library, 198–99; Lyceum, 30–31, 41, 43, 50, 53, 62–63, 69–70, 75–76, 78, 81, 92–93, 167, 187, 199, 205; military presence, 42, 54, 58–59, 128, 184, 186, 192; "Open Doors," 196, 198–99, 210; racial integration, 100, 102, 106, 110, 113, 157, 186; racial reconciliation, 198

upper class, 140

Upper South, 35, 50

U.S. Fifth Circuit Court of Appeals, 4

U.S. Marshals, 29, 31–32, 41, 43–44, 53, 58, 62–63, 75–76, 78, 81, 90, 93, 97–98, 100, 104, 110–11, 115, 118–21, 123–26, 136, 155, 167, 170–71, 173–74, 178, 183, 196–97, 205

USAFOX. *See* Camp USAFOX

Vance, Cyrus R., 6, 31
Vietnam War, 11, 36, 45, 67, 167, 189,
    191, 196, 204

Walker, Edwin A., 7–8, 13–14, 26, 78,
    80–81, 160, 178–79
"way of life." *See* Southern "way of life"
Wheeler, (General) Earle, 95
white college students. *See* college
    students
White Only signs, 86, 106, 111, 155, 204
women college students. *See* college
    students
working class, 141, 148, 201
wounds, 65, 76, 78